The Lombards

The Peoples of Europe

General Editors
James Campbell and Barry Cunliffe

This series is about the European tribes and people from their origins in prehistory to the present day. Drawing upon a wide range of archaeological and historical evidence, each volume presents a fresh and absorbing account of a group's culture, society and usually turbulent history.

Already published

The Mongols
David Morgan

The Basques
Roger Collins

The Franks
Edward James

The Bretons
*Patrick Galliou and
Michael Jones*

The Illyrians
John Wilkes

The Gypsies
Angus Fraser

The Early Germans
Malcolm Todd

The English
Geoffrey Elton

The Lombards
Neil Christie

In preparation

The Picts
Charles Thomas

The Armenians
Elizabeth Redgate

The Celts
David Dumville

The Normans
Marjorie Chibnall

The Huns
E. A. Thompson

The Spanish
Roger Collins

The Sicilians
David Abulafia

The Goths
Peter Heather

The First English
Sonia Chadwick Hawkes

The Irish
*Francis John Byrne and
Michael Herity*

The Etruscans
*Graeme Barker and
Thomas Rasmussen*

The Norsemen
John Haywood

The Russians
Robin Milner-Gulland

The Romans
Timothy Cornell

The Portuguese
Kenneth Maxwell

The Lombards

The Ancient Longobards

Neil Christie

BLACKWELL
Oxford UK & Cambridge USA

Copyright © Neil Christie 1995

The right of Neil Christie to be identified as
author of this work has been asserted in accordance with the
Copyright, Designs and Patents Act 1988.

First published 1995
First published in USA 1995

Blackwell Publishers, the publishing imprint of
Basil Blackwell Ltd
108 Cowley Road
Oxford OX4 1JF, UK

Basil Blackwell Inc.
238 Main Street
Cambridge, Massachusetts 02142, USA

British Library Cataloguing in Publication Data

A CIP catalogue record for this book is available from the British Library.

Library of Congress Cataloging-in-Publication Data has been applied for

ISBN 0–631–18238–1

Typeset in 12 on 13 ½ pt Sabon
by Pure Tech Corporation, Pondicherry, India
Printed in Great Britain by Hartnolls Limited, Bodmin, Cornwall

This book is printed on acid-free paper.

Contents

List of Plates

List of Figures

Preface

This book offers the first study in English of the history and archaeology of the Longobards (Lombards). This west Germanic tribe, long on the fringes of the Roman Empire, played no real part in the dissection of the western Roman provinces in the fourth and fifth centuries AD but emerged as a powerful protagonist in the course of the sixth century. Pushing across the Danube to occupy Hungary in the 520s the Longobards subsequently invaded Italy, the former Roman heartland, in 568. Here they successfully countered the Byzantines and established a Kingdom that endured for more than two centuries before its demise at the hands of Charlemagne. Even after that date the splinter province of Benevento, elevating itself into a principality, maintained the Longobard name in a precarious existence in the south of Italy into the eleventh century.

Unlike the Franks in France, the Longobards did not capture all of the former Roman province and accordingly only a part of modern Italy derives its name from this people: Lombardy or Lombardia. This north-central region of Italy had formed the focal point for the Longobard Kingdom in Italy, with the capital based at Pavia, to the south of Milan, and it is clear that it retained a strong Longobard population even beyond the Carolingian conquest. The Carolingians initially called all of northern Italy 'Langobardia', following the practice of the Byzantines; but by the end of the ninth century the name seems already restricted to the modern province. Byzantine gains in the south-east of Italy in the tenth century had seen the annexation of part of the Longobard Principality of Benevento and the creation of the theme or military district of Langobardia – but despite a healthy enough Longobard population, politico-military power struggles eventually saw the replacement of this name with that of the old Roman designation 'Apulia'.

Our prime documentary source for the study of Longobard history is the later eighth-century monk Paul the Deacon, who wrote an unfinished *Historia Langobardorum*. The only English translation of this important text is that by William Foulke, published in 1907, but with inaccuracies in both translation and interpretation; in contrast various modern Italian editions of Paul the Deacon's *Historia* exist, ranging from the finely illustrated volume edited by Roberto Casanelli (1985) to the cartoon picture-book version prepared by Alessandro D'Osualdo (1989) (see pl. 12). Like the Germanic tribes of the Visigoths and Burgundians, the Longobards also promulgated a law code, composed in Latin and comprising laws passed between 643 and 755: this provides fascinating insights into the minds and social relationships of the Longobards and also allows for an examination of the Longobard impact on and assimilation of Italian culture.

Such texts, backed up by other residual linguistic traces (personal names, church graffiti, loan-words and place-names), yield clues as to the Longobard mother tongue, identifiable as 'high' western Germanic, comparable to that spoken by the Alemanni tribe, and not too far removed from the 'low' western Germanic tongue of peoples such as the Angles, Saxons and Franks. The occurrence of loan-words in Italian dialects and the distribution of place-names of Longobard derivation further help point to likely prime areas of Germanic settlement. In Lombardy, for example, over 230

Longobard place-names have been identified; interestingly, however, Longobard material artefacts or burials have been located at just *c*.90 sites, and of these only a small handful actually have place-names of Longobard origin. This must not be viewed as a sign of a lack of correlation between the two types of sites but rather a lack of systematic archaeological study – new finds, whether from excavation, field survey or merely from agricultural or building work, are constantly adding to our picture.

The Longobards have for long received a bad press, with too much credence being given to the words of the sixth-century popes of Rome who saw nothing but unchecked blood-lust and destruction in the long-bearded invaders – an 'unspeakable race', in the eyes of Pope Pelagius II. But set in a proper historical and social context the Longobards were not so far removed from the rest of the population of western and Mediterranean Europe. Indeed in the eighth century the Longobards were in many ways more advanced artistically and architecturally and more economically buoyant than their Byzantine neighbours in Italy. Yet warfare was endemic to the early Middle Ages and the few chronicles that do survive for the period understandably focus on the bloody conflicts within the peninsula. At the same time, however, literacy was making a comeback in eighth-century Italy and the evidence of charters and laws, dealing with land sales, property disputes, wills and so forth, duly reveal the more mundane human side of Italian society.

Structurally, little of the Longobard era survives intact: their foundation of churches and monasteries formed just the initial phase of a long sequence of building and decorative activity. Intricate interlace decorated choir screens, lecterns or altar panels are nonetheless a feature of many churches with or without obvious Longobard origins. Only quite recently have the first secure traces emerged of Longobard urban settlement activity; rural sites, by contrast, remain almost wholly obscure and are visible merely as place-names or through burial finds. Indeed it is still very much the case that the Longobards can mainly be traced through museum collections of buckles, brooches and weaponry, obtained from furnished graves in cemeteries dotted throughout Hungary and Italy. The majority of these cemeteries, in Italy at least, were excavated unsystematically in the nineteenth or earlier twentieth century and often it is hard to relate finds to specific graves. As with all Germanic or 'barbarian' peoples, archaeological study has for too long tended to concentrate on the decoration and distribution of their artefacts, drawing from this research arguable theories regarding social structures and evolution. Settlement archaeology finally allows us to insert such data into a more coherent and complex analytical framework.

It is surprising how little attention the Longobards have received outside Italy, although there has been a burgeoning of interest in Germany and Britain since the 1980s as witnessed in the publication of Wilfrid Menghin's *Die Langobarden* in 1985, and Chris Wickham's *Early Medieval Italy* in 1981. A series of exhibitions in Marburg-Hamburg, in Vienna and, lately, in Cividale-Passariano, each backed up by excellent illustrative catalogues, have brought further light to bear on the tribe. In Italy there have been a small number of syntheses concerning Longobard history, some with a strongly archaeological slant, notably Alessandra Melucco Vaccaro's *I Longobardi in Italia* (1982). However, most studies fail to give adequate coverage to the pre-Italian phase of Longobard evolution, and more significantly, all lack any real consideration of Longobard settlement archaeology – though, admittedly, this gap was due primarily to a lack of relevant archaeological data. But a spate of recent systematic urban excavations, concentrated in northern Italy, now allows for an extremely illuminating discussion of the survival of, and the Longobard impact on, antique urban and rural settlement patterns. This book therefore attempts to offer a more balanced study of the Longobards, by combining various historical and archaeological sources, in order to present as detailed a picture as possible of Longobard society in its evolution from a martial barbarian tribe to a complex urbanized State, with equal emphasis on its people, settlements, material culture, religion and art. But any statements offered here must be taken as provisional: new excavations, field surveys, anthropological analyses, as well as artefactural, architectural or environmental study are constantly adding to the limited current data and promise to transform our concepts of early medieval Europe still further.

Finally, a note on names. Throughout this book I have used the name 'Longobards', as opposed to 'Lombards', which has long been the term preferred by English-speaking scholars. In Italy, the term 'Longobardi' is used, being closer to the original German name for the tribe and avoiding possible confusion with modern day Lombardy and its inhabitants; German scholars use the more accurate 'Langobarden'. For the Middle Ages, architectural historians refer to the Lombard style, relating to a church architecture developed within Lombardy, but this has nothing directly to do with the ancient Germanic tribe; likewise medieval writers like Dante refer to 'Lombardi' in the sense of the region's inhabitants, who, by the fourteenth century, were a mixture of races, though admittedly with some Longobard roots. It makes far more sense, I feel, to talk about 232 Longobard – as opposed to Lombard – place-names in Lombardy. My apologies if offence is taken!

Acknowledgements

It is of course essential to acknowledge fully the assistance of the various museums, superintendencies, publishers and individuals who have provided photographs and other illustrations. I have done my best to supplement these by contributing pictures of sites rather than artefacts. This book seems, to me at least, to have taken decades: it has its roots in a PhD thesis undertaken at the University of Newcastle upon Tyne and has utilized research carried out whilst a scholar at the British School at Rome and as the Sir James Knott Fellow at Newcastle in 1987–9, but has benefited most directly from a British Academy Post-Doctoral Fellowship at the Institute of Archaeology, University of Oxford, between 1989 and 1992. The staff at each institution are warmly thanked for their hospitality. The British Academy, T. W. Greene Fund (Craven Committee, Oxford) and Ilchester Fund (Taylor Institution, Oxford) have awarded me grants at various times to allow for invaluable fieldwork in Austria, Hungary and Italy, which has also provided me with material for other publications. Various individuals have helped me overcome hurdles, bear criticism and other assorted problems. These include – amongst others too numerous to mention – Graeme Barker, Tom Brown, Barry Cunliffe, Hazel Dodge, Kevin Greene, Attila Kiss, Simon Loseby, Lidia Paroli, Alan Rushworth, Bryan Ward-Perkins and Chris Wickham. Furthermore, I should thank the patient staff at Blackwell Publishers, notably Gillian Bromley, Jan Chamier, Alison Dickens and Ginny Stroud-Lewis, and the copy-editor, Stephanie Maury. Last but not least, of course, I would be suitably crucified if I failed to note the brave suffering of my wife, Jane, plus noisy children, who coped admirably with my incessant tea-drinking and with the background noise of Turkish folk music.

Chronological Table

AD 1–100	Earliest references to Longobards by Roman authors
166–8	Longobard involvement in Marcomannic Wars against Rome
410	Visigoths occupy Rome
453–5	Death of Attila; dissolution of Hunnic Empire
476	Odoacer overthrows the last Western Roman Emperor in Italy
488–9	Longobards occupy Rugiland
489	Ostrogoths under King Theoderic invade Italy
493–526	Theoderic head of the Ostrogothic Kingdom of Italy
507–10	Longobard defeat of Heruls
526/7	Longobards cross Danube to occupy part of Pannonia
535	Byzantine invasion of Italy led by Belisarius; start of the Gothic War
540	Belisarius occupies Ravenna
546/7	Emperor Justinian cedes portions of Pannonia and Noricum to the Longobards
548–67	Longobard conflicts with the Gepids

Lists of Rulers: Kings, Emperors, Dukes, Exarchs and Popes

Longobard Kings pre-568

Agelmund	(?*c*.380– 410)
Lamissio	(?*c*.420)
Lethu	(?*c*.420– 60)
Hildeoc	(?*c*.470)
Godehoc	(?*c*.480)
Claffo	(?*c*.500)
Tato	(?–*c*.510)
Waccho	(*c*.510– 40)
Waltari	(*c*.540– 47)
Audoin	(547– 60)

Longobard Kings in Italy

Alboin	(560–72)
Clef	(572–4)
Authari	(584–90)
Agilulf	(590–616)
Adaloald	(616–26)
Arioald	(626–36)
Rothari	(636–52)
Rodoald	(652–3)
Aripert I	(653–61)
Perctarit	(661–2, 672–88)
Godepert	(661–2)
Grimoald	(662–71)
Garibald	(671–2)
Cunicpert	(679–700)
Alahis	(*c*.688–9)
Raginpert	(700–1)
Aripert II	(701–12)
Ansprand	(712)
Liutprand	(712–44)
Hildeprand	(735–44)
Ratchis	(744–9, 756–7)
Aistulf	(749–56)
Desiderius	(757–74)
Adelchis	(759–74)

Longobard Dukes

Cividale		Benevento		Spoleto	
Gisulf I	(569–c.81)	Zotto	(c.570–90)	Faroald I	(c.576–91)
Grasulf I	(581–90)	Arechis I	(c.590–640)	Ariulf	(c.591–600)
Gisulf II	(590–610)	Aio	(c.640–1)	Theudelapius	(c.600–53)
Cacco, Taso	(c.610–25)	Rodoald	(c.641–6)	Thransa-	
Grasulf II	(c.625–53)	Grimoald I	(c.646–71)	mundus I	(c.663–700)
Ago	(c.653–62)	Romuald I	(662–87)	Faroald II	(c.700)
Lupus	(c.662–3)	Grimoald II	(687–9)	Wachilapo	(c.705)
Wechtari	(663–71)	Gisulf I	(c.689–706)	Thransa-	
Landari	(663–71)	Romuald II	(c.706–31)	mundus II	(710–44)
Rodoald	(671–c.700)	Audelahis	(731–2)	Hilderic	(739)
Ansfrit		Gregorius	(732–40)	Agiprand	(744–?)
Ado		Godescalcus	(c.740–2)		
Ferdulf		Gisulf II	(c.742–51)		
Corvulus		Liutprand	(751–8)		
Pemmo	(720–37)	Arichis II	(758–87)		
Ratchis	(737–44)				
Aistulf	(744–9)				
Anselmus, Petrus	(749–56)				
Hruod- gaudus	(775–6)				

Longobard Princes

Benevento (to 980)		Salerno (to 900)	
Arichis II	(774–87)	Siconulf	(839–49)
Grimold III	(788–806)	Waifer	(861–80)
Grimoald IV	(806–17)	Waimar I	(880–901)
Sico	(817–32)		
Sicard	(832–39)		
Radelchis I	(839–52)		
Radelgar	(851–3)		
Adelchis	(853–78)		
Gaideris	(878–81)		
Radelchis II	(881–4)		
Aio	(884–90)		
Ursus	(890–1)		
Peter, bishop of Benevento, regent	(897)		
Radelchis II, restored	(897–900)		
Atenulf I	(900–10)		
Landulf I	(910–43)		
Landulf II	(943–61)		
Pandulf I	(943–81)		

Byzantine Emperors

Justinian I	(527–65)
Justin II	(565–78)
Tiberius I	(578–82)
Maurice	(582–602)
Phocas	(602–10)
Heraclius	(610–41)
Constantine III	(641)
Heraclio	(641)
Constans II	(641–68)
Constantine IV	(668–85)
Justinian II	(685–95, 705–11)
Leontius	(695–8)
Tiberius II	(698–705)
Philippicus	(711–13)
Anastasius II	(713–15)
Theodosius III	(715–17)
Leo III	(717–41)
Constantine V	(741–75)
Leo IV	(775–80)
Constantine VI	(780–97)
Irene	(797–802)

Exarchs (incomplete)

Narses	(551–68)
Longinus	(c.568–72)
Baduarius	(c.575–7)
Decius	(c.584)
Smaragdus	(585–9)
Romanus	(589–96)
Callinicus	(596–9)
Smaragdus	(602–8)
John	(608–16)
Eleutherius	(616–19)
Gregory?	(619–25)
Isaac	(625–43)
Theodore Calliopa	(643–5)
Plato	(c.645)
Olympius	(c.649–52)
Theodore Calliopa	(653–66)
Gregory	(666–?)
Theodore	(c.678–87)
John Platyn	(687–c.95)
Theophilactus	(701–5)
John Rizokopus	(709–10)
Eutychius	(710–13)
Paul	(c.723–6)
Eutychius	(727–51?)

Popes (from 556 to 816)

Pelagius I	(556–61)
John III	(561–74)
Benedict I	(575–9)
Pelagius II	(579–90)
Gregory I	(590–604)
Sabinian	(604–6)
Boniface III	(607)
Boniface IV	(608–15)
Deodatus	(615–18)
Boniface V	(619–25)
Honorius I	(625–38)
Severinus	(640)
John IV	(640–2)
Theodore I	(642–9)
Martin I	(649–55)
Eugenius I	(655–7)
Vitalian	(657–72)
Deodatus II	(672–6)
Donnus	(676–8)
Agatho	(678–81)
Leo II	(682–3)
Benedict II	(684–5)
John V	(685–6)
Conon	(686–7)
Paschal I	(687–92)
Sergius I	(687–701)
John VI	(701–5)
John VII	(705–7)
Sisinnius	(708)
Constantine I	(708–15)
Gregory II	(715–31)
Gregory III	(731–41)
Zacchary	(741–52)
Stephan I	(752)
Stephan II	(752–7)
Paul I	(757–67)
Stephan III	(768–72)
Hadrian I	(772–95)
Leo III	(795–816)

1

Longobard Origins

From Scandinavia to the Elbe

The origins of the Longobards, as set out in Longobard texts of seventh- and eighth-century date composed in northern Italy, are a mish-mash of legendary figures, heroes, gods and concocted tradition, served up with occasional hints of fact. The Longobards sought their homeland far to the north-west, in Scoringia or Scandinavia, the fabled birthplace of so many of the major Germanic nations. Since this was the view held by Graeco-Roman authors, we cannot exclude the possibility that the Longobard tradition had somehow been coloured by this opinion by the time it was first recorded in writing. Nevertheless, the tradition may contain a grain of truth. Support may lie in the fact that the Longobards' first historically attested home was the region of the lower course of the River Elbe, in modern Lower Saxony, south of Schleswig-Holstein, thus close to Denmark and the Scandinavian mainland (fig. 1).

Our earliest sources are the Roman authors Velleius Paterculus, Strabo and Tacitus.[1] Strabo links the Langobardi or Longobards to the larger Suevic realm running from the Rhine to the Elbe, and tells us that the Hermondori and Langobardi lived over the Elbe:

[1] Velleius, II. 106; Strabo, VII. 1.3.291; Tacitus, 40. In the mid-second century Claudius Ptolemy (II.11.9 and 17) affirms their continued presence along the lower Elbe, setting them between the *Chauci* and *Suevi*.

Figure 1 Romans and Germans in the first century AD
(after Todd 1987).

... and at the present time these latter, at least, have, to the
last man, been driven in flight out of their country into the
land on the far side of the river. It is a common characteristic of all the peoples in this part of the world that they
migrate with ease, because of the meagreness of their liveli-
hood and because they do not till the soil or even store up
food, but live in small huts that are merely temporary structures; and they live for the most part off their flocks, as the
nomads do, so that ... they load their household belongings

on their wagons and with their beasts turn whithersoever they think best.

Strabo refers to campaigns under Augustus and Tiberius that had pushed the Germans back beyond the Rhine and Elbe, if only temporarily. Each of our sources makes clear the large numbers of tribal units scattered across the region, in part incorporated in or allied to larger tribal groupings such as the Suevi. Many of these tribes subsequently disappear from history: the survival of the Longobards both as a name and as a people attests to their relative consistency of numbers over time and to a fierce streak of independence. Indeed, Tacitus says that they were: 'illustrious by lack of number: set in the midst of numberless and powerful tribes, they are delivered not by submissiveness, but by peril and pitched battle . . .'.

In fact, the Longobards had, according to their own traditions, once been called by the name 'Winnili'. The name change is attributed to the result of a victory over the Vandals in Scoringia,[2] before they had been acknowledged by the Romans. Given that the Vandals appear to have occupied the lower reaches of the River Oder to the east by the first century AD this victory may have prevented any further westward movement by the tribe who had sought to impose payment of tribute upon the Winnili. Subsequently the Longobards ('Long Beards') moved into the region of Mauringia, perhaps identifiable with Mohringen and the River Maurine in Lower Saxony, and thus possibly their recorded seat near the River Elbe.[3]

According to Paul the Deacon, our main Longobard historian, but who was not writing until the late eighth century, Scoringia was a small island; since a number of Danish islands, such as Lolland and Zealand, links

[2] Paul *HL*, I. 7–10.
[3] Confirmation of this equation comes in the seventh-century anonymous Geographer of Ravenna (*Anon. Rav.*, I.11), who records: 'Patria Albis [= Elbe] Maurungani certissime antiquitus dicebantur'.

Germany with Scandinavia, any could reasonably be claimed as the Longobard base. Anthropologists in fact have pointed out the similarity in bone type between later Longobard skeletons and those of the Roman-period population on Swedish Gothland, and, whilst no great weight should be put on such data, this may support the tribe's broadly Scandinavian origin.[4]

The chronology of these preliminary migratory movements cannot be closely determined. More concrete data may, however, be available for the Longobard settlement of the lower Elbe, although here, too, corroboration of details is lacking. The major problem lies in attempting to define a tribe through a distinctive material culture, that is on the basis of a fixed grouping of such archaeological evidence as pottery and metal-work types, burial customs and house plans. A distinctive material culture would require that tribes be coherent units with at least some independent stylistic and social traits. The reality is different: our historical sources indicate a great fluidity of tribal structure and confederacies in the late German Iron Age and during the early centuries of the Roman Empire; whilst numerous tribes are named, many broader tribal frameworks are outlined, such as that of the Suevi, who are credited with control over much of the western Rhine–Elbe territory in the first century AD. The Longobards are shown as one small portion of the Suevic confederacy, though this may have entailed no more than nominal allegiance or tribute payment. Appurtenance to a larger unit suggests the likelihood of cultural interchange, which would blur, at least for certain periods, any presumed distinctive traits between allied tribes.[5] This was indeed the case at a later date, in the fifth century, when Thuringian metal-work and pottery ex-

---

[4] I. Kiszely, *The Anthropology of the Lombards*, British Archaeological Reports, Internat. Ser. no. 61, 2 vols (Oxford, 1979), 9–12.

[5] W. Menghin, *Die Langobarden. Archäologie und Geschichte* (Stuttgart, 1985), 19; M. Todd, *The Northern Barbarians, 100 BC – AD 300* (London,

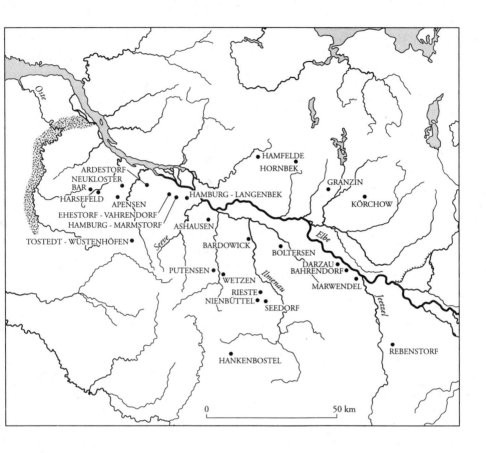

Figure 2 The lower Elbe and the distribution of presumed Longobard urnfields (Kiszely 1979, fig. 2, after Wegewitz 1972).

tended along the whole Elbe basin, from the river's mouth as far as Bohemia and Moravia, well beyond

1975), 19–21, 55, likewise stresses the near impossibility of identifying one tribe from another through 'culture-provinces'.

the area known to have been under direct Thuringian control.

Nonetheless, a fairly distinct Longobard culture has been reconstructed by German archaeologists and historians in Lower Saxony. In particular, Wegewitz has discerned a compact grouping of urn-cemeteries centred on the district of Bardengau, whose name is thought to derive directly from its early occupants, the Longobards.[6] This region, with its focus at the early medieval town of *Bardenwic* (modern Bardowiek), extends from the River Oste in the west, near the mouth of the Elbe, to the Jeetzel in the east (incorporating the districts of Heilanga, Moswidi and Drevani). A concentration of cemeteries lies south of the Elbe, particularly around modern Hamburg, but sites also extend north towards Lübecker Bay (fig. 2). Excavations, largely dating back to the later nineteenth and earlier twentieth centuries, revealed a series of extensive cremation-cemeteries, in some cases containing up to 8,000 urns. Many of these date back to the sixth century BC, and they run, apparently without any major break in continuity, into the second and third centuries AD. This implies a fairly stable associated settlement pattern, although as yet very few domestic sites have been archaeologically sampled. Some of the cemeteries cease to be used in the third century BC, which suggests an emigration of the population; and yet others originate only in the third century or in the first century BC (e.g. the site of Putensen, with 988 burials extending into the third century AD). Wegewitz identifies a reduction in finds during the first half of the first century BC followed by the appearance, from *c.*30 BC, of weapon graves, containing especially lances, swords and shields.[7] These, he argues, represent a

[6] W. Wegewitz, 'Stand der Langobardenforschung in Gebiet der Niederelbe', in A. Tagliaferri (ed.), *Problemi della civiltà e dell'economia longobarda. Scritti in memoria di G. P. Bognetti* (Milan, 1964), 19–54.

[7] W. Wegewitz, *Rund um den Kiekeberg. Vorgeschichte einer Landschaft an der Niederlbe*, viii of Hammaburg, Vor- und Frühgeschichte aus dem niederelbischen Raum (Neumunster, 1988), 76–127.

new people, perhaps indeed the Longobards. The cemeteries of this new people, peculiarly, are of two principal types, named after particular urnfields: 'Rieste' cemeteries, featuring weapon graves and Roman metal tablewares and given over solely to male burials; and 'Darzau' cemeteries, composed of female tombs containing domestic or dress items. How firm this division was is not really clear: both types contain a large number of unaccompanied urn-burials, which may be of children or slaves whose sex, however, is largely undetermined. No close anthropological study has been made of the unburnt bones from these largely unscientific excavations. The weapon graves indicate a very martial society in which the use of the lance as a throwing and thrusting weapon is paramount. At the site of Putensen the weapon repertoire included 211 lances and 32 spears compared with just 9 swords, 5 axes and 64 shield fittings; at Ehestorf-Vahrendorf the figures were 35 lances, 6 spears, 35 shield bosses and no swords (pls 1 and 2). In both cases the finds cover three generations. While these finds point largely to infantry warfare, a small number of spurs is also present (e.g. 18 from Putensen, 12 from Harsefeld), which signifies a use of cavalry, at least amongst the nobility. This fact may be significant, in that much later the Longobards are attested as being skilled horsemen – a trait otherwise rare amongst the western Germans.

The phase identified by Wegewitz also coincides with the main period of importation of Roman goods, in the form of bronze basins or buckets, other metal-work and glass-ware, into these Germanic zones, which led to increased social stratification amongst the German populations, as reflected in the grave goods. Rome's proximity in both the military and the cultural sphere thus introduced new dislocating factors into early German society – trade and patronage.[8] In a 'market zone'

---

[8] B. Cunliffe, *Greeks, Romans and Barbarians. Spheres of Interaction* (London, 1988), 171–92.

Plate 1 *Iron shield boss and ritually bent spearhead from Cremation B236 at Putensen. (Hamburger Museum für Archäologie – Helms Museum.)*

Plate 2 Iron boss with projecting point and 'mushroom' rivets for attachment to a wooden shield from Cremation B283 at Putensen. (Hamburger Museum für Archäologie – Helms Museum.)

extending from the Rhine to the River Weser the circulation of gold and silver Roman coin implies intense trading activity; beyond the Weser a range of Roman metal tablewares occurs such as dolphin-handled *situlae, paterae* with handles ending in rings or swan-heads and plain bronze buckets and flagons, with a notable concentration of these in the Danish islands, signifying that people were capitalizing on the southward flow of prized Scandinavian commodities such as amber and furs. Germanic noblemen controlled the flow and distribution of such imports and exports and, accordingly, increased their wealth and standing; they could redistribute wealth to obtain followers and retinues, over whom they maintained power by the regular control of the trade mechanisms.

Elite or princely burials reflect the uppermost levels of these adapting Germanic societies, with a blatant display of exotica and imports in their grave assemblages and with the adoption of inhumation as the burial rite. The Bardengau features four such rich graves: two inhumations (Marwendel) and two cremations (Apensen and Putensen). Interestingly, of these only the first century AD burial at Putensen contained weapons; the others, probably of second-century date, reflect the relative peacefulness of that period on either side of the Rhine. Such princely burials (Lübsow graves of *Furstengräber*) terminate abruptly with the beginnings of Germanic upheaval in western–central Europe, represented by the Marcomannic invasions and the German campaigns of the Roman emperor Marcus Aurelius (164–80). The wars totally upset the fragile balance that had been created: suddenly the markets were removed; the tribal elites lost their sources of wealth and stability; retinues sought alternative sources of wealth and new overlords; and tribal conflict put land and resources at a premium. Demand for land, population increase, or a basic desire for the booty offered by tribes or Romans to the south prompted certain northern or eastern European tribes to migrate. In the best documented instance, the Marcomanni and Quadi are recorded as the prime participants in the overspill into Roman territory across the Danube in the 160s–170s AD.[9] Interestingly, some Longobards – presumably splinter groups of warrior bands dispatched by, or with, leading nobles – are attested as fellow plunderers in these events.

The knock-on effects of the wars were considerable, with many areas of Germanic Europe witnessing a break or disruption in their settlement patterns, as reflected in cemeterial data. The Bardengau is no exception to this, with the later second and early third century marking a possible thinning-out of population and the cessation of many of the long-lived urn-cemeteries. Accordingly, a large-scale migration of population is envisaged, al-

---

[9] H. Böhme, 'Archäologische Zeugnisse zur Geschichte der Markomannenkriege, 166–180 n.Chr.', *Jahrbuch der Römisch-Germanischen Zentralmuseums Mainz*, xxii (1975), 153–217. Cassius Dio, 71.3.1, claims that 6,000 Longobards and *Obii* crossed the Danube, but were soon driven back.

though it should be noted that there has been too little settlement archaeology to prove this. It is conceivable that this uprooting followed on from the battles against the Vandals and the otherwise unknown Assipitti tribe, both of whom may have been amongst those northern tribes responsible for the second-century turmoil. The Longobard traditions claim victories, but it is possible that these external pressures prompted the tribe to tag along with the general chain of Germanic movement. We can doubt a total evacuation of the lower Elbe: if the Bardengau's name does derive from the Longobards, the tribe would probably have had to occupy the territory for longer in order for the name change to be fixed into the documentary record; alternatively, the Bardengau may have retained a reduced Longobard settlement after the migration of the bulk of the tribe. From the third century the area came under the general sway of the Saxons, who were attested already in the Holstein region by the second century AD: the survival of a fairly independent Longobard folk may be indicated in the subsequent close relations between the two tribes, with Saxons accompanying Longobards to Italy and some Longobards amongst the contingents of Saxons that invaded England in the fifth century.

Urn-cemeteries of the third–fifth centuries do exist in the Bardengau, notably that on the Sandberg in Vahrendorf, not far from the Longobard cemetery of Ehestorf-Vahrendorf. This contained at least 40 burials, whose associated finds suggest no major break with the earlier material culture; however, both males and females are now being buried in the same cemeteries, marking a significant change from the preceding Rieste–Darzau division. From the fourth century, individual inhumations occur within the urn-cemeteries, and there is an occasional tendency for burial beneath tumuli or small mounds – possibly a Saxon characteristic. Only from the seventh century do inhumations wholly replace cremations, leading to a high number of row-grave inhumation-cemeteries. Certainly by the time of Charlemagne's campaigns against the Saxons in the 790s we find no reference to Longobards as a separate tribal entity, so we can assume that they had long since been absorbed by the Saxons.[10]

Nonetheless, we must remain cautious in these arguments. Excavations outside the Bardengau zone remain somewhat patchy and do not, as yet, clearly help to distinguish a Longobard territory from those of neighbouring tribes. Many of the cultural traits identified by Wegewitz, such as the use of weapon graves, of separate male and female cemeteries and of distinctive metalwork, can now be shown to extend across a much broader territory, running from the Weser to the Vistula.[11] The probability is that the Bardengau belongs culturally to the wider grouping of the Suevi and, later on, the Saxons and stands out merely because of its better archaeological documentation. A further indication of this is the absence of finds to document the movement along the Elbe of a particular tribe into Middle Germany and thence Bohemia. Longobard material in Bohemia, while 'Elbe-Germanic' in character, lacks elements that directly tie the tribe in with its presumed ancestors in Lower Saxony.

We can say little, therefore, about the Longobards themselves in these formative centuries, although we should not doubt that they conform roughly to what we know of Germanic society and settlement in general, based on our limited historical sources and on excavated data. In terms of society, tribes were based around a series of strong kin groups; cutting across these blood ties the warrior aristocracies formed the backbone to the armies, who stood subordinate to chiefs, themselves

[10] Wegewitz, *Rund um den Kiekeberg*, 135–78.
[11] Todd, *Northern Barbarians*, 64–72.

elected for specific campaigns by the councils of elders and the general warrior assembly. In the case of the Longobards, Paul the Deacon records the choice of two chiefs (*duces*), Ibor and Aio, elected to lead the tribe from Scandinavia in search of new lands – impossibly, Paul has these generals retire only with the election of the first Longobard king, Agelmund, some four centuries later![12]

In place of the large, nucleated *oppida* (hill-forts) of Celtic Gaul or Britain, the Germans lived predominantly in small, scattered and undefended farmsteads, villages or hamlets housing a number of kindred family units and sited reasonably close to their cemeteries. On the basis of excavated sites in Holland and northern Germany, these settlements are greatly varied in layout, but display some planning, often around a central, focal space. Many centres show a notable degree of continuity. This is, of course, corroborated by the durable cremation cemeteries of northern Europe. House plans are fairly standard, with two main varieties recognized: the hall, or aisled, house, mainly used as private dwellings (and shared with the livestock) but also, in a larger format, for public assembly; and the sunken-featured structure, with at least one area of the building cut down into the soil, and generally serving as a workshop or storage area. Almost nothing is known about the presumed Longobard settlement zone of the Bardengau: stray ceramic finds and distinctive deep-set stone ovens give some support to a scattered, open system, but houses are otherwise unknown.[13] Cultivation of land was organized or at least partitioned by the community and each person turned their hand to farming or stock-rearing; while mixed farming was common, stock-rearing (in particular

[12] Paul *HL*, I.3 and 14; *Origo*, 1, refers to a *principatum*. M. Todd, *The Barbarians. Goths, Franks and Vandals* (London, 1972), 24–33, offers a concise discussion of early Germanic society.

[13] Wegewitz, *Rund um den Kiekeberg*, 128–34, 148, notes the presence of *Grubenhäuser* in the region between the first and tenth centuries AD.

cattle) was often the most dominant element of the economy. Pottery would consist of simple, handmade, home-produced items, with occasional imported Roman wares to show status.

From the Elbe to Bohemia

Details of the Longobards' subsequent progression south-eastwards from Lower Saxony towards the Middle Danube are vague at best. Paul the Deacon baldly states that his people moved from Mauringia to Golanda, Anthaib, Banthaib and thence to Vurgundaib, staying in each region 'for some time' or 'for a few years'; he places in this period the election of the first Longobard king, Agelmund.[14] The date of the creation of this institution, 'in the manner of other tribes', is uncertain, but may belong to the early fifth century. The whereabouts of these various stopoff points cannot be closely determined, although Banthaib can, in all probability, be viewed as: Bajina aib = Boiohaemium = modern Bohemia. Logically, the migration will have progressed slowly along the course of the Elbe. Golanda may refer to Gothic held lands, perhaps vacated by Goths as they moved eastwards towards the Black Sea; Vurgundaib suggests former Burgundian lands, perhaps between the middle Elbe and the Oder, given that the Burgundian tribe may have first emerged further east, between the Oder and Vistula, and migrated south-westwards in the third century, towards the Black Forest. Anthaib remains elusive (fig. 3).

Our first chronological guide comes with the record of a conflict with the Bulgars (i.e. Huns), during the reign of king Agelmund. Paul the Deacon describes a

[14] Paul *HL*, I.13–14. *Origo*, 2, having omitted Mauringia lists the territories as 'Golaidam . . . Anthaib et Bainaib seu et Burgundaib'.

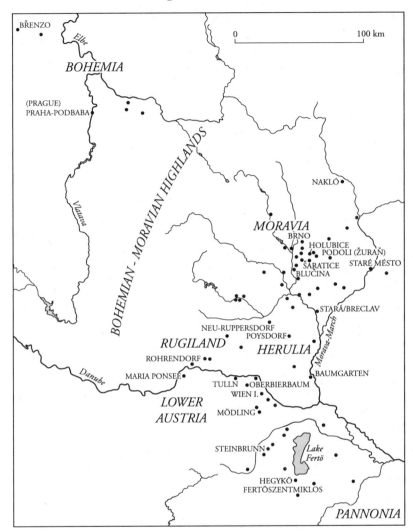

BŘENZO

0   100 km

BOHEMIA

(PRAGUE)
PRAHA-PODBABA

NAKLÓ

BOHEMIAN - MORAVIAN HIGHLANDS

Elbe

Vltava

MORAVIA
BRNO
HOLUBICE
PODOLI (ŽURAŇ)
ŠARATICE   STARÉ MÉSTO
BLUČINA

STARÁ/BRECLAV

NEU-RUPPERSDORF
POYSDORF
RUGILAND   *HERULIA*
ROHRENDORF

Danube   MARIA PONSEÉ   BAUMGARTEN
TULLN   OBERBIERBAUM
WIEN I.
LOWER
AUSTRIA   MÖDLING

Morava-March

STEINBRUNN   *Lake*
Fertö

HEGYKÖ
FERTÖSZENTMIKLOS

PANNONIA

Figure 3   Presumed Longobard find-spots in Moravia,
Bohemia and Lower Austria (after Kiszely 1979,
figs 8 and 11).

Hunnic assault on a Longobard settlement, resulting in
the death of Agelmund and the capture of his daughter,
and a subsequent reprisal under the new king Lamissio,
who achieved a notable victory, carrying off much

plunder and thereby 'making the Longobards even more feared in war' (*HL*, I. 16–17). We can only guess at the scale of these events: they may have been little more than raids; at the same time the Longobard victory may have been enough to limit or deflect Hunnic supremacy in the Elbe zone. The principal push westward of the Huns from the Carpathian basin happened during the reign of Attila in the 440s; although Huns had been employed previously by the Romans against the Burgundians on the middle Rhine. While the northern extent of Attila's empire cannot be securely established, it is likely that many of the tribes beyond the Elbe owed only nominal allegiance to the Huns. Yet the cultural and material influence of these nomads, and the wealth generated by their assaults on Roman soil, was considerable and is reflected in a number of very rich female graves and male weapon tombs in a wide band around the Danube, radiating out from the Carpathians.[15] Bohemia was included in this exhibition of accumulated wealth.

Profound political and territorial changes followed the rapid dissolution of the Hunnic Empire after 455, as manifested in the emergence of various new and smaller Germanic kingdoms. Along the middle Elbe the Thuringians established a sizeable kingdom, which endured until the 520s; along the middle Danube the Rugians and the Heruls occupied their own independent lands. Between these zones a new Germanic presence is attested in Bohemia that shows both close cultural affinities with Thuringia and wider links with the Alamanni and the Franks to the west. Their cemeteries feature organized row-graves of W–E orientation containing inhumations. Male graves are furnished with weapons and occasionally are accompanied by horse burials; females are dressed in items of Merovingian style, namely pairs of

[15] Summarized in Menghin, *Die Langobarden*, 42–6.

brooches worn on the shoulders and below the waist; bird's-head, pincer- and S-brooches are prominent and indicate a Thuringian milieu, while occasional Scandinavian items point to more northerly contacts along the Elbe. There are also instances of decorative skull deformation amongst females, suggesting residual Hunnic traits. In addition, some graves, often cut to a depth of over 2 m, feature corner or end posts, indicating the employment of internal chambers, biers or roofs. Significantly, on the basis of the recurrence of these grave-types and finds, from *c.*500 we can trace the subsequent movement of this Bohemian population, to Lower Austria and Moravia, areas documented as Longobard in our written sources. In effect we have a fairly clear indication that the Longobards controlled and settled Bohemia in the second half of the fifth century AD.[16] However, it remains difficult to trace the progress of the tribe backwards in time and space.

The Longobards' adoption of inhumation in orderly row-graves is part of a broader trend that swept across much of central and western barbarian Europe from the fourth century. Earlier instances of inhumations in coffins or burial-chambers, which emerge with the series of first- and second-century AD princely graves north of the Elbe, are assumed to be adoptions of Roman burial rites.[17] These persist into the third century in Jutland, the Elbe-Saale basin and Slovakia, but with the subsequent decline in the quantities of Roman imports we can see a decrease of wealth and associated élite inhumations. In the fourth and fifth centuries, however, when barbarians were in ever closer physical contact with the Empire, whether through invasions, through service in the Roman ranks as mercenaries or federates, or through settlement on

---

[16] See J. Zeman, 'Böhmen im 5. und 6. Jahrhundert', in W. Menghin, T. Springer, & E. Wamers (eds), *Germanen, Hunnen und Awaren. Schätze der Völkerwanderungszeit* (Nurnberg, 1987), 515–27.
[17] Cunliffe, *Greeks, Romans and Barbarians*, 185–6.

Roman soil, and when the Romans themselves had adopted Christianity and had wholly switched to the rite of inhumation, the flow of ideas may have intensified and further encouraged the transition to inhumation cemeteries. This did not signify a Christianizing of the Germans: they continued to bury their dead with prized possessions, weapons, jewellery and full dress; and orientation varied from W–E to N–S. In south-east Europe, by contrast, the missionary activities of the Arians effected the conversion of the Goths in the fourth century, and while females were still buried with grave-goods, males were unaccompanied. Other tribes adopted a mixture of rites, for example the Saxons, who practised largely inhumation in areas under Frankish influence, but cremation further afield; others, in areas largely unaffected by Roman imports, retained cremations, for example the Angles, even once settled in England. Gothic influence on the Hunnic confederacy may have had a part in the regularization of the Germanic inhumation rite, prompting the nobility of the allied tribes to adopt a W–E orientation. In time this permeated down to all ranks of tribal society, and by the end of the fifth century a series of sizeable W–E row-grave cemeteries is visible across much of the Rhine-Elbe-middle Danube zones – the so-called *östliche-Merowingischen Reihengräberkreis.*[18]

The Longobards in Bohemia in the second half of the fifth century were part of this 'culture'. However, their cemeteries here are not extensive, numbering rarely more than thirty graves, which attests to a limited stay ('for some years', says Paul the Deacon). On the basis of the metal-work styles, the Longobard presence endured for no more than a generation, perhaps between *c.*470 and *c.*520. A few cemeteries such as Prague-Podbaba extend into the mid-sixth century, and occasional mid-sixth-century elements do appear elsewhere, but on too small

[18] J. Werner, 'Zur Entstehung der Reihengräberzivilisation', *Archaeologica Geographica*, I (1950) 23 ff; Menghin, *Die Langobarden*, 46–9.

a scale to suggest continued Longobard settlement; more probably they relate to a Longobardicized native population, which maintained contacts with the Longobards after *c.520*. A ninth-century source, the *Codex Gothani*, adds to our limited picture by recording the extant remains of the palace of King Waccho (*c.510–40*). Even if the concept of a royal palace is hard to believe, an association with the king is nonetheless significant and may help prove a fairly durable occupation. The termination of the Longobard presence in Bohemia may even coincide with the attested occupation of northern Pannonia in 526/7. If this is correct, we can visualize a concentration of Longobards on the Danube and March (Morava) rivers from 526; their resources may have been insufficient to allow them to continue with the occupation of Bohemia, leading to their quitting of the area (see fig. 3). Alternatively, the shift may have been forced, owing to the arrival of Slavs from the north and northeast, who certainly held the region by the 540s. One site is of interest in this discussion: Březno, near Louny, to the north-west of Prague. This settlement dates from the late fifth century and features partially sunken rectangular timber houses, supported by six main uprights. During the first half of the sixth century there was an early, pacific arrival of Slavs who settled alongside the existing native Germanic village in similar houses, though these tended to be of squarish plan, with internal, corner-set stone ovens and external storage pits. A merging of the different cultures is shown by the mixing of pottery and dwelling types. The early Slavic presence is attested in Bohemia and Moravia by material of Prague type, recognized most clearly in the handmade pottery, often used as cremation urns. Such finds occur also in southern Moravia, where they overlap slightly with the Longobard occupation, suggesting some form of Slavo-Germanic coexistence. However, the Germanic population at Březno may well have been Longobard. In this case the move from Bohemia may not have been forced; instead the area may have been given up to the (allied?) Slavs with whom contacts continued to be cultivated in Moravia.[19]

From Bohemia to Pannonia

History, tradition and archaeology combine fruitfully only with the occupation by the Longobards of the vacant kingdom of Rugiland in the late fifth century AD. This kingdom, identifiable with lands north of the middle Danube between the Wald- and Weinviertel in north-east Lower Austria, had fallen into the hands of the Rugian tribe in the confused years following the collapse of the Hunnic Empire in 455. Bordered to the west by Suevi and to the east by Heruls, the Rugi had strengthened their position through treaty with the Roman emperor Majorian (457–61) and through tribute paid by the frontier towns of Noricum Ripense – a situation vividly depicted in the near contemporary *Life of St Severin* (composed *c*.510), which records a fairly stable *modus vivendi* between Rugi and Noricans, with the latter paying yearly tribute and trading Roman goods across the Danube in return for protection from Heruls, Thuringians, Alamanni, bandits and others.[20] The Byzantine policy of playing one barbarian tribe off against another caused the annihilation of the Rugi in 487–8, when the emperor Zeno urged them into conflict with Odoacer, the barbarian mercenary commander who had deposed the last Western Roman emperor in 476 and who was then master of Italy and, nominally at least, of the de-

---

[19] See I. Pleinerova, 'Germanische und slawische Komponenten in der altslawischen Siedlung Březno bei Louny', *Germania*, xliii (1965), 121 ff; Z. Váňa, *The World of the Ancient Slavs* (London, 1983), 32–6.

[20] *Vita Sev.* 1, 9 and 31. The topography and settlement data are discussed in J. Haberl & C. Hawkes, 'The last of Roman Noricum: St. Severin on the Danube', in C. & S. Hawkes (eds), *Greeks, Celts and Romans* (London, 1973), 97–156; cf. Menghin, *Die Langobarden*, 23–9.

caying provinces of Noricum and Raetia. The Rugian
king was captured and beheaded in Italy in 487; in 488
the disorganized Rugi caved in against Odoacer's campaign force; surviving Rugi either were incorporated into
Odoacer's ranks or fled eastwards to join the Ostrogoths; unknown numbers of Romanized native Noricans
were encouraged to migrate to the security of Italy.[21]

Archaeology has proved that Noricum Ripense was not
totally deserted after these events: life stuttered on in
a number of the late Roman towns and fortresses,
although the level of activity and material culture was
low. Less is known about the Rugian tribe itself: Rugiland, like much of the middle Danube territory, merely
offers fifth-century material of broadly Germanic character, combined with native late-Roman/Byzantine influences, residual native tribal elements and eastern-Germanic
and Hunnic traits. As in Bohemia, a series of spectacular-
ly furnished female graves and well-equipped warrior
graves relate to the period of Attila's Empire, but these
need not of course belong to Rugian nobility. The Rugi
were merely one of the Hunnic allied tribes who successfully outlived the Confederacy and who were able to
carve out their own compact kingdom in the ensuing
power vacuum, but without any long-lasting effects on
the landscape.

In contrast, the arrival of the Longobards in 489 allows
a first clear recognition of a people settling in this zone.
A number of sizeable cemeteries have been identified that
exhibit usage well into the sixth century, contemporary
with sites south of the Danube and further east along the
River March on the Austrian–Slovakian border (see figs
3 and 4). According to the *Origo* (4) and to Paul the
Deacon (*HL*, I. 19), the Longobard king Godehoc led his
people into Rugiland and stayed there for many years. In
the early 500s King Tato occupied the land immediately

---

[21] *Vita Sev.* 42 and 44; year 487, *Auctarii Havniensis Extrema*, ed. T.
Mommsen, MGH, *Auctores Antiquissimi*, ix (Berlin, 1892), pp. 337–9.

south of the Danube known as the Feld, probably to be equated with the Tullner Feld, extending perhaps between Tulln and the old Roman fort of *Vindobona* (Vienna).[22]

These movements – unlikely to have been prompted by the Byzantines, even if the latter knew of them – did not endear the Longobards to their eastern neighbours, the Heruls. As a result, there was armed conflict within three years, culminating in a battle on the Feld, probably *c.*508. This confrontation, provoked by a Longobard failure either to pay tribute or to recognize Herulian supremacy, or perhaps by a blood feud, resulted in a decisive Longobard victory and the scattering of the Heruls. More importantly, the Longobards now replaced the Heruls as the dominant power along the middle Danube and thereby deprived the Ostrogoths, then residing in Italy, of an ally. This brought the Longobards fully to the attention of the Byzantine court, which keenly observed them as potential tools in forthcoming diplomatic power manoeuvrings.[23] In the meantime the Longobards, their numbers swelled by surviving Heruls and also by the remnants of the Rugian tribe, occupied Herulia, the region extending along the lower March north of its confluence with the Danube, into the territory of modern Moravia. A series of row-grave cemeteries has been identified within these territories, giving a fairly clear idea of the extent of Longobard settlement between *c.*490 and *c.*530 (see fig. 3). However, most of the sites in question have suffered from extensive and systematic robbing in antiquity, most within a generation or so of their abandonment. This is apparent from the fact that graves were individually robbed, indicating that their positions were visible on the ground; bodies were occasionally unceremoniously bundled into a corner of the

[22] Paul *HL*, I. 20; *Origo*, 4.
[23] As attested by Procopius, the sixth-century Byzantine historian (BG II. 14).

grave when the processes of decomposition were still incomplete; where decomposition had occurred, the looters had wrenched brooches and earrings off the bodies, thus destroying the upper portions of the skeletons; and in such instances skulls are notably absent from the graves. Occasionally fragments of early Slavic pot occur in the fill of these graves, implying that the burials were robbed by these newcomers, whose settlement in the region may begin as early as the first half of the sixth century.[24] Fortunately, the grave-robbers were not interested in the ceramic vessels that generally accompanied the deceased, and the survival of these offers at least a rough chronological guide for the duration of the cemeteries.

Two concentrations of cemeteries occur in Rugiland, commencing in the late fifth century. A northern group, represented by a set of scattered, destroyed and often individual burials, lies in the Znaim district of Slovakia; to the south, closer to the Danube, cemeteries of between 10 and 40 tombs have been identified around Krems and Hollabrunn in Lower Austria.[25] Despite extensive robbing, we can gain a reasonable picture of the range of grave-goods. Weapon graves are the most distinctive, with adult males buried with a complement of weaponry, dependent upon status: lance and shield, long sword, arrows and, occasionally, spurs. Personal ornaments include brooches, buckles, knife and belt pouches with flint, whetstones, tweezers and combs. Various dress and other personal items occur in female tombs, notably pairs of brooches worn on the chest and hanging from the waist, earrings, necklaces, rings and pouches; a possession probably indicating high status consists of weaving

[24] See H. Adler, 'Zur Ausplunderung langobardische Gräberfelder in Österreich', *Mitteilungen der anthropologischen Gesellschaft, Wien*, c (1970), 138–47.

[25] H. Friesinger & H. Adler, *Die Zeit der Völkerwanderung in Niederösterreich* (Vienna, 1979), 36 ff; Menghin, *Die Langobarden*, 52–7.

equipment, including weaving sword and spindle-whorls.

The material as a whole fits into the broader Meroving-ian, middle-German context of the later fifth and sixth centuries. In particular, the pottery (pl. 3), which origin-ally contained food or drink as sustenance for the jour-ney to the next world, in form and in decoration offers us clear typological links not only with Bohemia and middle Germany (notably with cemeteries like Schönebeck and Wormlitz), but also, more importantly, with the middle Elbe and lower Mulde and thus with possible previous 'stations' of the Longobards on their migratory route. The Rugiland pottery occurs as beaker-like vessels, ribbed and bi-conical bowls, either plain or decorated with in-cised lines or wedges (*Keilstich*) – all without local ante-cedents. A noticeable addition to the Longobard ceramic range appears to coincide with the occupation of the Feld in the north-east sector of the former Roman province of Noricum Ripense. Here we find the adoption of wide-mouthed, wheel-thrown pots with burnished decoration (*Eingeglattmustern*), which represent the efforts of a sus-tained local pottery tradition. The maintenance of this 'industry' may have relied on earlier trading demands by Rugians and Heruls. Such wares also occur in Longobard cemeteries further east, in Pannonia Superior, and north of the Danube in Herulia and show a relative production boom under Longobard patronage.

The Feld, whose physical extent remains uncertain, but whose eastern border may have been formed by the Wienerwald (Cetius Mons), was the Longobards' first taste of settlement upon former Roman soil. It is difficult to discern whether this entailed a physical occupation of old Roman frontier forts such as *Faviana*, *Commagena* and *Vindobona*, most of which are recorded in the *Vita Severini* and have produced archaeological proof of ac-tivity in the fifth century. For example, the detailed excava-tions at *Carnuntum* (Deutschaltenburg), further east identified post-Roman, fifth-century dry- and clay-

Plate 3 Longobard handmade pot with grooved decoration from Breclav. (Brno Museum, Czech Republic.)

bonded civilian structures, burials, burnished ware and other stray finds, while ninth-and tenth-century documents attest the survival of the defences in Hungarian times. Although specific Longobard finds are lacking from within these forts, the laying of cemeteries in close proximity to them must be significant.[26]

The longevity of Longobard settlement in the Feld is demonstrated at the cemetery of Oberbierbaum near Maria Ponsee, where between 1965 and 1972 a total of 95 graves were excavated, forming part of a larger cemetery of up to 120 burials.[27] Not all the graves relate to Longobard immigrants: a number belong to the Romanized native population, suggesting thereby a

[26] G. Alföldy, *Noricum* (London and Boston, 1974), 213–26; M. Kandler, 'Archäologische Beobachtungen zur Baugeschichte des Legionslager Carnuntum am Ausgang der Antike', in H. Wolfram & F. Daim (eds), *Die Völker an der mittleren und unteren Donau im 5. und 6. Jahrhundert* (Vienna, 1980), 83–92.
[27] H. Adler, 'Maria Ponsee', *Fundberichte aus Österreich*, ix (1966–1970), 26–30, 147–8, 211–12; xi (1972), 120–1.

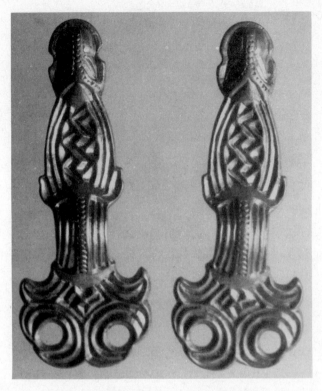

*Plate 4 Claw bow-brooches from Holubice, Grave 95.
(Brno Museum, Czech Republic.)*

pacific merging of cultures and the reuse of an existing necropolis. Robbing was extensive, but enough survived to indicate three main grave-groupings: a north group, exhibiting close Thuringian and middle German ties, similar to burials known in Rugiland; a south group with little Germanic material of middle Elbe character but offering burnished pottery of late Roman tradition; and a poorly furnished, probably native, west group. In addition, the cemetery contained three horse burials: one of the horses (Grave 9) was buried with its noble owner, whose possessions included a set of weaponry; the other two were buried with a hunting dog (Graves 52 and 72,

*Plate 5 The grave-goods from the Smith's Tomb at Brno.
(Brno Museum, Czech Republic.)*

the former set close to another well-equipped warrior's
tomb, 53). Similar horse burials are known at Aspersdorf
and Unterrohrendorf in Rugiland, and reflect a pagan
Germanic ritual of horse sacrifice to accompany the deceased owner, a custom particularly evident amongst the
more nomadic Slavs and Avars.[28] A further feature of
many graves is the stepping-in of sides and the provision
of post-holes at either end of the grave or at its corners
to support a wooden tomb structure; the frequent traces
of planking relate to such funerary 'houses'. At Erpers-
dorf, post-holes occurred in only two of the 23 excavated
graves, although others showed traces of coffins or
planked sides. Coffins also occur in Rugiland, but the

[28] Váňa, *Ancient Slavs*, 57, 60–2.

provision of a bier or funerary 'house' is absent here; its presence in Herulia may suggest it as a possible source. Certainly such structures recur in Longobard tombs in Pannonia in the course of the sixth century.

The years subsequent to the Herul defeat by King Tato saw Longobard expansion into Herulia, the area of the north-east Wienviertel and south-east Moravia, focused on the River March. Like the Rugi, the Heruls are, archaeologically speaking, largely anonymous, and the full extent of their kingdom is therefore vague at best. The limited, controlled excavation that has taken place in the region is problematic, leaving us to derive data chiefly from destroyed burials or stray finds; a few larger cemeterial units do exist but extensive robbing of these for their ornamental metal-work hinders close chronological analysis (pls 4 and 5). A Longobard presence seems to emerge only in the early sixth century, again with a likely fusion with the natives (e.g. at Smolin, Saratice). One of the better published sites, Poysdorf, with just nine graves, included burials of two warriors, a lady with three gold bracteate brooches and a goldsmith, all of whom suggest a high status grouping. As with graves in the Feld, post-holes and planking reveal the presence of at least two tomb 'houses'.[29] Of exceptional importance, but as yet still unpublished, is the extensive cemetery at Holubice (Holovice), containing over 100 graves and signifying a notable occupancy in this zone. Indeed, late pottery and brooch types here and at Borotice and Lužice may show that the Longobards remained in Herulia until the mid-sixth century.

In 1962 Joachim Werner argued that the enigmatic tumulus of Žuraň near Podoli in northern Herulia, from

---

[29] J. Tejral, 'Probleme der Völkerwanderungszeit nördlich der mittleren Donau', in Mengin, Springer & Wamers (eds), *Germanen, Hunnen und Awaren*, 351–60; J-W. Neugebauer, 'Ein Nachtrag zum Langobardenfriedhof von Poysdorf in Neiderösterreich', *Fundberichte aus Österreich*, xv (1976), 133–9.

whose height in 1805 Napoleon watched over the battle of Austerlitz, contained a royal Longobard burial, perhaps that of King Godehoc. Werner calculated that this was the focus of Longobard power in the early sixth century previous to the annexation of Pannonia after 526/7. But more recent studies suggest a Herulian monument, comparable to contemporary burial tumuli in Sweden, and deriving from trade contacts between Herulia and the Baltic. Excavation in 1853 and 1949 at the Žuraň tumulus revealed two burial chambers of *c*.3 × 5m, both badly robbed: one chamber held the fragmentary remains of a man and horse, the other a female, with five further horse burials close by. The tumulus itself was an artificial stone mound of *c*.40 m diameter, girded by a 2 m thick dry-stone wall. A similar mound 50 m in diameter has recently been identified at Schmalzberg near Neudorf, overlying a small first/second-century AD cemetery; subsequently it was robbed out and later covered by a ninth-century Slavic settlement.[30] The robbing may have happened in the sixth century; certainly at Žuraň one chamber contained sherds of an early Slavic pot of this date. Thus the royalty of the Longobards may need to be sought elsewhere, perhaps in the wealthy burials excavated at Hauskirchen and Maria Ponsee.

The ancestors of these royals had brought the Longobards far from their homeland. By the time of their arrival on the fringes of the decayed Roman Empire, the events of their long migratory trek had probably already become legend. While their continued links with Thuringians and Saxons suggest that they had not wholly forgotten their roots along the River Elbe, their eyes had

---

[30] J. Werner, *Die Langobarden in Pannonien. Beiträge zur Kenntnis der langobardischen Bodenfunde vor 568*, Abhandlunger der Bayerische Akademie der Wissenschaften, new ser., 55 (Munich, 1962), 106–8; Menghin, *Die Langobarden*, 61–4. C. & J-W. Neugebauer, 'KG Neudorf (MG Neudorf bei Staat, VB Mistelbach)', *Fundberichte aus Österreich*, xxiv–xxv (1985–6), 331–3.

undoubtedly now turned southwards and inevitably they were drawn across the Danube into the fabled realms of the old Roman world, where Byzantium, the partial heir to the Empire, offered sufficient promise of wealth. The transformation of the Longobard tribe from a small but ferocious sub-group of the Suevi to a powerful, perhaps multinational, kingdom on the Danube was in turn to lend itself to Byzantium's own aims.

2

The Longobards in Pannonia

In the mid-520s AD the Longobards moved into the
northern territory of the former Roman province of Pannonia (modern north-west Hungary). Despite the ravages
of the fifth century, which had seen the collapse of
Roman rule in the province (*c*.425), the establishment of
the Hunnic power base in the Carpathians and across the
Hungarian plains (427–55), the emergence of new, smaller, Germanic kingdoms (of the Quadi, the Suevi, the
Ostrogoths and the Gepids) after 455, the expansion of
the Ostrogoths (456–73), and despite the protectorate of
Odoacer, King of Italy (476–88), and subsequently that
of Theoderic from Ostrogothic Italy (489–526), the Romanized native population, and many of the old Roman
structures, from villas to forts to fortified cities, had
largely survived – albeit at a reduced level – economically, physically and politically. As their predecessors
had done, the Longobards appear to have maintained
this framework and utilized it to their own benefit. During the next 40 years the Longobards were brought into
diplomatic, and occasionally armed, contact with the
sizeable powers of the Franks, Ostrogoths, Gepids and,
most importantly, the Byzantine Empire. They also encountered the growing might of both Slavs and Avars,
whose movements from north and north-east were forc-
ing and forming the final stages of barbarian/nomadic
settlement in Europe. To have emerged from these pressures not just unscathed but invigorated boded well for
the subsequent and final phase of Longobard migration.

The Sequence of Longobard Settlement in Pannonia

The Longobard annexation of Herulia in 505–8 might already have given them a toe-hold on north-west Pannonia. Not long after, in fact, Paul the Deacon records a victory over the Suevi, who had controlled a territory between the Heruls and Danube, in the north, and the Ostrogoths and Lake Balaton, to the south, since 456. The Longobard victory came in the long reign of Waccho (*c.*510–40), who had overthrown Tato and defeated Tato's son Hildechis to seize the crown. We could assume a period of consolidation before any expansionist moves, yet Paul the Deacon suggests that the conquest was fairly prompt and easy.[1] Waccho then further bolstered his and his tribe's position through strategic marriage alliances: his first wife was a Thuringian princess, subsequently dropped in favour of his second wife, daughter of the Gepid king, who bore him two daughters, who in time were married off to Frankish kings, while his third spouse was daughter of the subjugated Herul king. These ties secured both external contacts and borders and, in the case of the third marriage, aided in the integration of the surviving Herul population.

The Suevi, by contrast, appear politically defunct. The date and extent of their conquest by the Longobards are disputed. Both Paul (*HL*, II. 7) and the *Origo* (5) later speak of a 42-year Longobard occupation of Pannonia before the march on Italy, thus putting their entry to *c.*526. The timing appears significant: 526 saw the death of the Ostrogothic king Theoderic and the start of major internal troubles for his Italian kingdom. Since 493 Theoderic had, through skilful diplomacy, marriage ties and selective military intervention, extended his kingdom's political boundaries and achieved far-flung alliances with

[1] Paul *HL*, 1. 21; *Origo*, 4.

his western, Germanic neighbours. Even before 526, however, these gains were being worn away, primarily by the Franks, who, like the Byzantines, capitalized on Gothic instability afterwards.[2] Our chief documentary source for the period, Cassiodorus, certainly includes southern Pannonia (Savia and Sirmiensis) in the Ostrogothic sphere of control; nominal authority may have extended further north, beyond the River Save, but there is nothing to prove this. Beyond lay the allied Suevic kingdom, extending north and south of the Danube, perhaps as far south as Lake Balaton, and apparently including Budapest. It is possible that the Goths did not count Suevia as part of Pannonia, which would restrict the designation to the southern regions. Two possibilities exist: one is that the Longobards, under Waccho, delayed attacking Suevia until 526 and then pushed down towards the river Drau and threatened Gothic Pannonia, where many Suevi had fled. Alternatively, Suevia fell before this, and our sources' references to Longobards in Pannonia from 526 relates only to a subsequent expansion up to the Drau line. Support for the latter hypothesis emerges not just from such archaeological data as early cemeteries in north Pannonia, plausibly predating 526, but also from the documented marriage alliance between Waccho and the Gepids in the 510s, suggesting neighbourly contact along the Danube. Without knowing more of the extent of Suevia, both possibilities must remain open. However, the burial of a metal-work hoard in the amphitheatre at *Aquincum* (Budapest), datable to 500–25, may conceivably link in with a Longobard assault in the 520s.[3]

---

[2] For the Goths, see H. Wolfram, *History of the Goths* (Berkeley, CA, and London 1988); for their archaeology see V. Bierbrauer, *Die ostgotischen Grab- und Schatzfunde in Italien*, Biblioteca Studi Medievali, vii (Spoleto, 1975).

[3] I. Bóna, 'Ungarns Völker im 5. und 6. Jahrhundert. Eine historish-archäologische Zusammen schau', in Menghin, Springer & Wamers (eds), *Germanen, Hunnen und Awaren*, 121, 124–6.

It is difficult to determine the density and extent of early Longobard settlement in northern Pannonia. Most probably they held onto the regions of Rugiland, Herulia and Feld well into the sixth century, though this may have somewhat stretched their resources. Hence we find Waccho seeking alliances and attempting to integrate both Herul and Suevic survivors into his forces. In the case of the Suevi we have some archaeological testimony, both in the continued development of their metal-work types in Longobard burials, and in the form of distinct cemeteries located near Sopron (*Scarbantia*) in north-west Pannonia. Named after the site of Hegykö, these cemeteries contain such a striking amalgam of Romanized native, Suevic, Herul and other Germanic traits as to suggest that the new rulers deliberately settled these older populations here, and also that the merging of these cultures was successful. 'Ethnic cleansing' appears not to have been a Longobard tactic.

Progress across the Danube brought the Longobards into the field of view of Byzantium. From the early 530s Byzantium, under the emperor Justinian (527–65), embarked upon an attempted reconquest of the former Roman West. Italy was a prime goal in this venture, for which secure land communications were required from west to east across the Balkans. Byzantium could ill afford diversions and accordingly sought various allies amongst neighbouring barbarians requesting them to protect, or at least not hinder, the land route. Justinian included amongst his 'Christian' allies the Longobards, and King Waccho duly stood by this alliance in 539 when Vitigis, the Ostrogothic king, sought his assistance. Clearly the financial rewards of the alliance with Justinian promised to be better than those proffered by Vitigis.[4]

[4] Proc. *BG*, II. 22.

Waccho's successor, Walthari, the last of the Lething dynasty, ruled for seven years (*c*.540–7). He was replaced by Audoin of the Gausus clan, who, according to our Longobard sources, 'shortly after, led the Longobards into Pannonia'.[5] This must mean the remaining portions of old Pannonia, the Gothic held zones. Proof of this comes in a Byzantine source, the Greek historian Procopius, who, in his account of the bitter wars for supremacy in Italy between Ostrogoths and Byzantines, supplements our otherwise sparse documentation. He is certainly informative as regards the events of 546/7: in order to counter the growing threat of the Gepids who were raiding imperial lands and holding the city of *Sirmium*, 'the emperor Justinian had bestowed upon the Longobards the city of Noricum and the strongholds of Pannonia, as well as many other towns and a very great amount of money. It was because of this that the Longobards departed from their ancestral homes and settled on the south side of the River Ister (Danube), not far from the Gepids.'[6] Byzantium here was involved in a dangerous game, playing off one barbarian tribe against another: Longobards, Gepids and Heruls were all in conflict, yet were all – even at the same time – allies to Justinian. Physically, however, Byzantium was not strong enough to occupy these territories herself, and she lacked manpower even for her armies; accordingly Longobards, Heruls, Slavs and Huns all fought as federates in the East Roman ranks and were given nominally imperial lands on which to settle. Yet Byzantium had wealth enough to pay these allies enormous quantities of tribute ('contributions') in gold and silver in order to maintain her security.[7] The Longobards readily exploited

[5] Paul *HL*, I. 21–2; *Origo*, 4–5.

[6] Proc. *BG*, III. 33, noting that the Longobards celebrated by raiding *Dalmatia* and *Illyricum* and dragging off captives!

[7] A. Kiss, 'Die Goldfunde des Karpatenbeckens vom 5–10. Jahrhundert', *Acta archaeologica academiae scientarum Hungaricae*, xxxviii (1986), 105–45.

this bountiful opportunity. It meant, however, confrontation with the Gepids, their former allies, which developed into war on a number of occasions in 547–52 and 565–7, with variable support offered by the Byzantines. A notable victory on the Asfeld, to the west of *Sirmium*, in 552, could have secured the conquest of the Gepid kingdom, but Justinian, distracted by events in Italy and probably scared of the consequences of an enlarged Longobard realm along the Danube, forced a peace treaty upon the two sides, which endured into the 560s and to Justinian's death.[8]

As part of the alliance treaty of 552 the Longobards had dispatched 2,500 warriors plus 3,000 armed retainers to join Narses, the Byzantine commander-in-chief in Italy, to aid his efforts to bring the bloody war with the Ostrogoths to a conclusion. Other allied forces included 3,000 Heruls, numerous Huns and 400 Gepids.[9] Narses met the Ostrogoths under their king Totila in pitched battle at *Taginae/Tadinum* (present Gualdo Tadino) in central Italy; not trusting in his barbarian auxiliaries, he had them dismount and fight with lances in the centre of the battle line, thus exposing them as bait to the Gothic charge. His tactics were successful since the Goths were routed, their king killed. Although it did not mean the end of the war, the tide had decisively turned in the Byzantines' favour. But the Longobard recruits were not to be included in the final campaigns:

First of all he [Narses] was eager to be rid of the outrageous behaviour of the Longobards under his command, for in addition to the general lawlessness of their conduct, they kept setting fire to whatever buildings they chanced upon and

[8] See I. Bóna, *The Dawn of the Dark Ages: The Gepids and the Lombards in the Carpathian Basin* (Budapest, 1976), 18–19, 26–7, for a historical summary. For the initial conflict of 547, Proc. *BG*, III. 34, gives eloquent, if fictitious, speeches to both Longobard and Gepid envoys at the Byzantine court. Conflicts with the Gepids: Proc. *BG*, IV. 18 and 25; Paul *HL*, I. 23–4.

[9] Proc. *BG*, IV. 26.

violating by force the women who had taken refuge in the sanctuaries. He accordingly propitiated them by a large gift of money and so released them to go to their homes, command- ing Valerian and Damianus, his nephew, with their commands to escort them on the march as far as the Roman boundary, so that they might harm no one on the return journey. (Proc. *BG*, IV. 30–3).

Yet Longobards continued to serve in the Byzantine ranks in Italy and in the east and were even present at Justinian's court in Constantinople. They had received a scolding after *Taginae*, but Byzantium could ill afford to lose their armed support. Paul the Deacon certainly saw no problems, saying how the 'victorious Longobard mercenaries had headed home laden with many gifts' and how that 'for all the time that the Longobards held Pannonia they were allied to the Roman State' (*HL*, II.1). But the most important factor relating to this episode was that the Longobards had had a taste of Italy and seen something of its lands, towns and fortresses, as well as of the character of Byzantine warfare. This knowledge put them in very good stead for later events.

Bones, Brooches and Beads

The archaeology of Longobard Pannonia consists almost entirely of cemeteries, individual tombs and stray finds deriving from tombs. We know far more about how the Longobards died than about how and where they lived. In contrast with Lower Austria, far fewer cemeteries have been robbed, allowing for specialized and extensive studies not just on the metal-work but also on the bones themselves, with the latter providing insights into diet, disease and blood groups. Over 30 cemeteries, plus vari- ous individual graves, are so far known; over half of these has been discovered and excavated since 1960. Although many have been fully excavated, few have

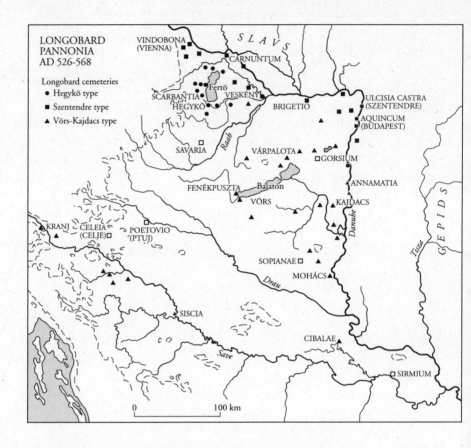

Figure 4 Longobard cemeteries and finds in Pannonia.

received any detailed publication, which creates problems for an overall interpretation. Hungarian archaeologists have, however, synthesized many of the data and
offer notable conclusions; in particular, Istvan Bóna
argues for three distinct cemetery types in Longobard
Pannonia, representing different ethnic components or
chronological phases (fig. 4).[10]

[10] Bóna, *Dawn of the Dark Ages.*

The first type, as noted, is named after Hegykö a site lying east of Sopron, and represents a combination of native and other Germanic peoples, gathered in the area of Lake Fertö. Longobard elements also occur in graves of this type, showing that these necropoleis did not belong to 'refugee-camps': indeed, some of the Suevic-Herulian metal-work types, notably the large bow-brooches, with rectangular head-plates with spiral decoration and stone-inlay trapezoidal end-plates, recur in Italy and show that some of this population and their craftsmen accompanied the Longobards in 568.

In the same general area, extending from the neighbourhood of Vienna to beyond Budapest, but exhibiting a fairly close correlation with the setting of former Roman military establishments (*castra, castella* and *burgi*) along the Danube, are cemeteries of Szentendre type. Many of these are large cemeteries (*c*.80–100 graves), indicative of use throughout the Longobard Pannonian phase. Finds show significant connections with the material culture identified as Longobard in Lower Austria and Bohemia, primarily in terms of pottery, but also in the grave ritual, with deep-cut graves often enclosing tree-trunk coffins or post-built mortuary houses. Nevertheless, new Pannonian traits are also evident: for example, old, Thuringian-style handmade wares are being replaced by vessels of late-antique tradition, namely globular pots, beakers, flasks and jugs featuring distinctive burnished decoration, wavy lines or stamped ornament. It is clear that such vessels were exported north of the Danube into Moravia, verifying the continued Longobard presence here. Of particular interest is the production of stamped wares in Pannonia, which continued into the early years of occupation in Italy (pl. 6). The origin of the ornamentation is problematic, however, and cannot easily be explained away as Roman or native Pannonian; nor is it likely to be Gepid, since it first appears in Gepid lands east of

*Plate 6 Typical stamped Pannonian Longobard pottery
vessel. Szentendre Grave 56. (Hungarian National Museum,
Budapest.)*

the Danube in the same era and presumably denotes
trade with the Longobards. Possibly, it is of Saxon
origin, given that stamped ornament of the same form
and variety is prevalent on Saxon cremation urns in
England in the sixth century and occurs earlier in the
Elbe zone and in Lower Saxony: we know in fact that
Saxons accompanied the Longobard tribe to Italy in
great numbers as allies, and their presence in Pannonia
may be attested in occasional groups of cremation graves
(e.g. at Kajdacs). Stamped ornament persists only for a
short while in Italy; perhaps coincidentally, the Saxons

returned home towards the North Sea only a few years after 568.[11]

The third cemetery type belongs to the secondary phase of Longobard settlement, beginning *c.*546/7, when the tribe were given lands in southern Pannonia by Justinian. To provide sufficient settlers for the new territory the lands north of the Danube were largely given up; but, even so, the Longobards were hard pushed to control these new areas, as may be reflected in the meagre spread of cemeteries of Vörs-Kajdacs type (formerly known as Várpalota type) south of the Drau river – although this may owe rather to the failure of local archaeologists to identify relevant sites. There is, however, a concentration around the fertile Lake Balaton and along the Danube between Budapest and Osijek (fig. 4), which consists of fairly short-term cemeteries, abandoned around AD 568. Finds show little or nothing that harks back to the Transdanubian phase but much that finds comparison with materials taken to Italy.

Overall, the necropoleis reveal organized planning with plots of 80–120 × 80 m, which implies related settlement groupings of *c.*80–100 persons. In some cases it is possible to discern family burial plots, though at other sites more rigid, communal settings occur. In the northern region the cemeteries were full – it is claimed – by 568; in the south, sometimes only patchy burial is visible (e.g. just seven graves at Kadarta). In the Hegykö group, however, burial may have begun before the Longobard arrival.

Bone analysis allows for some anthropological interpretation: it is a commonly held view that the Longobards were tall and fair-haired, conforming to the

---

[11] Longobard stamped wares: Werner, *Die Langobarden in Pannonien*, 54–60. Compare the stamp types on Anglo-Saxon pottery: C. Hills and K. Penn, *The Anglo-Saxon Cemetery at Spong Hill, North Elmham, Part II*, East Anglian Archaeology, Report no. 11 (Dereham, 1981), 7–22. Saxons in Italy: Paul *HL*, II. 6; III. 5–7.

German model. According to Kiszely, 'the Lombard men were very masculine: they were strong, tall, their bones were robust, the adhesional surfaces were rough. The women were much more gracile, gracefully shaped and, as for the form of the long bones, they did not engage in hard physical work. The degree of robustness differs greatly between men and women of the Nordic-Cro-Magnonid type.'[12] They were not a pure stock: bones of varied type suggest intermarriage with pre-Longobard Germanic groups and with Romanized natives. There is no proof that the Longobards practised intentional skull deformation in the manner of the Huns and of German tribes like the Goths and Thuringians. Most cemeteries lack burials of infants younger than two to three years, and we are ignorant of how the numerous stillborn and very young infants were buried. The average lifespan, however, was *c*.30–5 years, although there were many individuals who lived beyond 50 years. Iconographic representations of the Longobards are lacking for Pannonia, but we can extrapolate broadly from Italian sculptural evidence, seal rings, decorated gold-sheet crosses and shield plaques (see pls 8, 22 and 28). These images, almost exclusively male, show men with characteristic beards and moustaches, shaggy hair parted centrally or cut with a fringe, dressed in long-sleeved tunics extending to the middle of the thigh and belted at the waist, and with trousers or leggings underneath. In military scenes men have helmets and tunic length lamellar armour, and wear plain trousers. Paul the Deacon (*HL*, IV.22) fortunately records the now-lost frescos that once adorned the royal palace at Monza near Milan, commissioned *c*.600 by Queen Theodelinda:

[12] Kiszely, *Anthropology of the Lombards*, 161–7, 172–210. Bóna, *Dawn of the Dark Ages*, 35, states: 'Their women were also tall (about 1.70 m) on average . . . and were perhaps rather heavy. In contrast to the males, who had longer faces with prominent features including a firm chin and aquiline nose, the facial – that is cranial – features of the females were plain and unremarkable.'

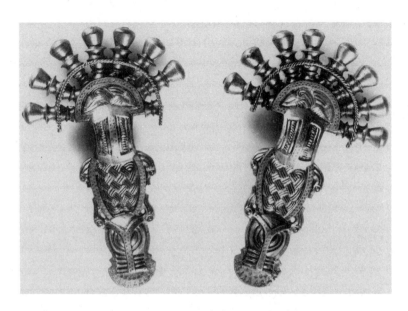

Plate 7 Bow-brooches from the rich female grave, 56, at Szentendre. (Hungarian National Museum, Budapest.)

These pictures clearly show how in those times the Longobards wore their hair and how they dressed and what ornaments they carried. They exposed their forehead and shaved all the way round to the neck, while their hair, combed down on either side of the head to the level of the mouth, was parted at the centre. Their clothing was roomy, mainly made of linen, like the Anglo-Saxons wear, decorated with broad bands woven in various colours. Their boots were open at the big toe, held in place by interwoven leather thongs. Later on they began to use thigh boots, over which they put woollen greaves when out riding, in Roman fashion.

Pannonian grave-finds tell us much about Longobard dress at all social levels, with quality and quantity the main status pointers. Girls and women appear to have worn long-sleeved single-piece linen undergarments extending down to the knees and fastened at the neck by a brooch of disc or S form; a thicker outer garment hung down to the shins and was fastened by a similar brooch at chest level; an additional pair of brooches, often chunky bow-brooches, closed this garment near the groin (pl. 7). A belt ran around the waist, and from this hung two or more cords that held ornamental trinkets, a knife, a comb and a pouch, often containing spinning equipment (spindle whorls, needles, scissors). The belt straps may have been borrowed from native or Byzantine fashion and are a sign of influences that would develop. Stockings were tied at the knees and shoes fastened with straps or buckles. While finger rings, armlets and earrings were uncommon – except amongst Romanized native womenfolk and females buried in Hegykö type cemeteries – beaded necklaces are a frequent find, along with hairpins.

For men the emphasis was on weaponry, with a more limited display of dress accessories: belt buckles, associated belt ornaments (pl. 8) and the contents of the pouch (whetstone, flint, knife, comb and tweezers) are all we have to help us reconstruct a, most likely, smock-type upper garment tied at the waist, partly covering trousers below. Only rarely do brooches attest to the use of a

Plate 8 A belt-piece from Grave 34 at Szentendre featuring crude depictions of two male faces. (Hungarian National Museum, Budapest.)

cloak. Short and long swords, lances and shields may occur over or in the warrior's grave, depending on status; bows and arrows are attested only in poorer graves, suggesting that this was the weaponry granted to the half-free in Longobard society. Armour and helmets were luxury items, possessed only by the elite: as yet, however, none have been recovered in Pannonian tombs.

These weapons were largely viewed as functional, and so few were decorated to any high degree. Elaborate decoration was restricted to the buckles and brooches, the analysis of which usually provides our only chronological guide. The fifth century had seen a universal migration-period art style develop, representing a fusion of late Roman, Hunnic and Gothic forms and motifs, particularly in the combining of animal elements with Mediterranean meander and spiral patterns, and in the inlaying of metal-work with almandines or coloured glass paste. The art was so diffuse that distinctive ethnic traits are hard to define. However, probably from the 530s, the Longobards came to formulate their own art style, strongly influenced by a new northern-European ornament type known as Zoomorphic (or Animal) Style I, originating around the close of the fifth century.[13] Longobard Pannonian brooches consist of semicircular head-plates crowned by knobs or protuberances resembling animals heads, ovoidal foot-plates shaped like animal heads and body ornament depicting ribbon-like contorted animals with beaks and long claws, often set in an heraldic scheme with two animals back-to-back (see pl. 7). On some examples, designs similar to the stamps used on pottery form subsidiary decoration. Fine, and probably late, examples of Animal Style I brooches occur at Szentendre (e.g. Graves 29 and 56) and Kajdacs. These

---

[13] H. Roth, *Die Ornamentik der Langobarden in Italien. Eine Untersuchung zur Stilentwicklung anhand der Grabfunde*, Antiquitas, 3rd ser., xv (Munich, 1973); A. Melucco Vaccaro, *I Longobardi in Italia. Materiali e problemi*, (Milan, 1982), 42–52.

were high status items, produced chiefly in gilded silver. While there are some likely instances of imports from north Germany and Scandinavia (e.g. Hegykö Grave 18), the discovery of a smith's tomb at Poysdorf in Lower Austria (Grave 6), containing tools such as tongs, hammers, a file and lead models of a bow- and S-brooch, is proof that the Longobard nobility could commission new pieces on the spot.[14]

The male aristocracy stand out chiefly through the range of weaponry placed in their tombs: rich nobles' graves contain short and long sword, lance and iron-bossed shield, plus knife and belt-fittings, with additional features such as gold ornament, horse-fittings or indeed accompanying horse or hound burial. The tumulus grave at Veszkény with gilded silver trappings for two horses probably belonged to a duke, head of one of the numerous clans or *farae* that made up Longobard society (pl. 9). A lower rank is shown by graves with shield and lance, lance and sword, or shield and sword, or one item only. The lowest army level was made up of half-free archers.

Many scholars have tied these material divisions in with what is known of Longobard society from seventh- and eighth-century Italian law codes, despite the obvious time-lag involved.[15] Hence we may identify the following hierarchy: dukes (heads of *farae*), nobility, *arimanni/barones* (free warriors), *faramanni* (young or poorer freemen), *aldiones* (half-free) and *skalks/servi* (servants or slaves, not permitted to bear arms). Hungarian anthropologists have sought to bolster these divisions by analysis of blood and bone type at the Szentendre cemetery, arguing that the nobility was entirely composed of tall, well-nourished, blood group A Nordic-Cro-Magnonids (i.e. 'true' Germans) and that the *aldiones*

[14] Menghin, *Die Langobarden*, 68–70.
[15] For example Bóna, *Dawn of the Dark Ages*, 73–82.

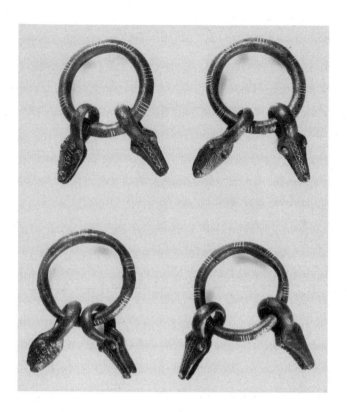

*Plate 9 An indication of the value of the horse to the
Longobard nobility in Pannonia: four silver-inlaid harness
pieces from the princely grave at Veszkény. (Hungarian
National Museum, Budapest.)*

were a German-Roman mixture, as were the women of
these two categories, while the servants were 'southern
or local types', that is peasant indigenes or Romans. At
Szentendre such native serfs were buried at the fringes of
the cemetery. The accuracy of such controversial data
needs to be reassessed, for the image sounds too convinc-
ing; unfortunately Italy has had little comparable osteolog-
ical study, but where studies have been made few sites

show such proportions of pure Longobard stock as those claimed for Pannonia.[16]

Town and Country: Natives and Longobards

As said, despite the mass of graves, we know virtually nothing about where and how the Longobards lived, what crops they cultivated and how they defended their lands. The evidence from Březno in Bohemia and from sixth-century Gepid village sites beyond the Danube might point to the use of semi-sunken buildings, but so far no Longobard examples have come to light. However, the Longobards now occupied lands formerly held by the Romans and provided with towns, fortresses and villas, largely built of stone. Since, for the most part, they were still standing and inhabitable, these 'alien' dwellings were probably adopted by the newcomers, both because it was convenient and to ensure control over the conquered Romanized population. Certainly Justinian's donation of 547 specifically refers to the castles and towns of the provinces, and it would have been fitting for the Longobards to inhabit these in order to show themselves as civilized allies, capable of maintaining the settlement network. The Gepids, for their part, had long held the city of *Sirmium* as well as towns like *Bassianae* against the Byzantines and the Goths.

However, proof of this situation is hard to find. It is true that many Longobard cemeteries, particularly those of Szentendre and Vörs type, occur pointedly close to such Pannonian *castra* and *castella* as *Brigetio* (Szöny), *Aquincum* and *Cibalae* (Vinkovci) (fig. 4), but very few finds have been recovered from within these centres to indicate any permanent or substantial Longobard presence. What finds do occur, generally stamped pottery

[16] Kiszely, *Anthropology of the Lombards*, 170–2, 182–201, 230.

Plate 10 Scarbantia *(Sopron): the late-Roman circuit walls.*

or brooches, might have been accidentally dropped by the Longobards whilst plundering the ruinous towns; alternatively, they might have been goods traded with the native inhabitants. All too frequently these are stray finds without context, and we cannot always be certain of their provenance. Nonetheless, their distribution is striking, extending from *Cibalae* in the south through *Annamatia* (Baracs) to *Brigetio* and *Carnuntum* in the north, and is suggestive of a notable settlement bias towards the Danube. Of significance are the results of the 1979–82 excavations at Roman *Scarbantia* (Sopron) in north-west Hungary close to Lake Fertö (pl. 10): here, over and around the forum, which was no longer maintained after *c*.350, excavators found much fourth-century domestic activity, followed by the erection of five or more modest houses in the fifth–sixth century, built of rubble or timber over stone footings, or inserted into late Roman structures. A Longobard S-brooch, decorated with red glass inlay, was recovered in the presumed destruction/collapse level of one timber-built house, whose floor also contained a (most likely) fifth-century tile with an incised picture of a man praying with arms raised.[17] The location of the brooch need not mean that its owner helped destroy the house; it could have been lost by a Longobard living close by, some time after the event. Most importantly, the Sopron excavations reveal the survival of an urban community well beyond the collapse of Roman rule in Danubian Pannonia in the late fourth century. Various other sites, such as *Carnuntum* and *Savaria*, offer a similar scenario of townspeople clinging on, building crude or insubstantial houses over or within earlier edifices and burying their dead within the town defences – thus matching the pattern noted for Noricum Ripense to the west.[18]

A further instructive case is that of *Valcum* (Keszthely-Fenékpuszta), located on the south-west corner of Lake Balaton (fig. 5). Here, periodical excavations since 1883 have largely reconstructed the outline of the fort defences $(377 \times 358$ m), featuring walls 2.5 m thick, 12 large projecting round towers of 15 m diameter ranged along each flank, and inset north and south gates. Internally, houses, a palace structure, an early Christian church (Basilica 2) and a late Roman granary (*horreum*) have been examined. The site is equated not with a military fortress but with a fortified agricultural settlement, forming a focus for local farming communities or for imperial estates; five similar late-Roman establishments are known – including Környe and *Tricciana* (Sagvar) – possibly positioned to form a defensive line rearwards of the

---

[17] J. Gömöri, 'Grabungen auf dem Forum von Scarbantia, 1979–82', *Acta archaeologica academiae scientiarum Hungaricae*, xxxviii (1986), 347, 350–5, 364–5.

[18] See the gazetteer in K. Póczy, 'Pannonian Cities', in A. Lengyel & G. Radan (eds), *The Archaeology of Roman Pannonia*, (Lexington, KY, and Budapest, 1980), 245–6, 254–69.

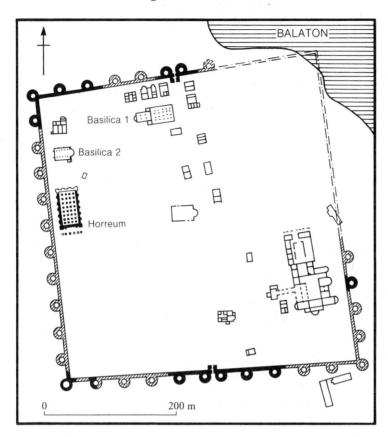

Figure 5 The late antique and early medieval fortress town of Keszthely-Fenékpuszta.

Danubian forts. A major fire in the mid-fifth century, which destroyed houses, towers and large grain deposits, seems to have led to a temporary evacuation. *Valcum*'s revival has been linked to the Gothic king Thiudimer establishing his base near Lake Balaton in the 460s, and to this Gothic phase (terminating in 473) may belong a small cemetery plot 200 m distant. An extensive cemetery of *c.*500 graves outside the south gate offers hints of continuous activity from the fourth into the ninth century, but the poor recording of finds from here prevents an accurate assessment of the material. Within the walls, 31 graves flanking the granary and 16 graves near the church can be assigned to the sixth and seventh centuries. Finds from these well-furnished tombs exhibit late-Roman, native, Byzantine, Longobard, pan-Germanic and Avar characteristics, which both support and confuse the various hypotheses: some scholars argue for a Byzantine federate garrison combining natives and Germans, installed after 540, but presumably under nominal Longobard control from 547 given the presence of the Longobard cemetery of this date in Vörs, to the south-east. However, specific Longobard artifacts are few, and so other authors prefer to view the granary burials as post-568 and linked to an Avar occupation, though primarily composed of a mixed native and German population. Specific Avar elements support an Avar presence, but perhaps not until around 600. Alternatively, it can be argued that the native populace, of various ethnic components, continued to inhabit *Valcum*, maintaining churches and walls, and nominally respected whoever ruled the zone. Christian symbols on rings and brooches and basic dress styles appear to bolster this view. Any possible domination by the Avars terminated in *c*.630 with the site's destruction, perhaps by siege. Where the survivors went is unclear, but the revival of Fenékpuszta in the ninth century and the emergence of the so-called Keszthely culture suggests that the old population lived on regardless.[19]

This example shows how wary we should be of viewing stray Longobard finds as a sign of a fixed Longobard presence. Trade, gift exchange and accidental loss are all possible explanations. The Longobards, like most of the Germanic migratory hordes, were not numerous, per-

[19] L. Barkóczi, 'A 6th Century Cemetery from Keszthely-Fenékpuszta', *Acta archaeologica academiae scientiarum Hungaricae*, xx (1968); R. Müller, 'Die spätrömische Festung Valcum am Plattensee', in Menghin, Springer & Wamers (eds), *Germanen, Hunnen und Awaren*, 270–4.

haps amounting to 70,000–100,000 persons: too few to scatter widely across Pannonia, as reflected in the relative concentration of sites near the Danube. Furthermore, they may have depended upon the native farmers to continue cultivating the land and provide the Longobards with their surpluses. In return, the newcomers respected the natives and their religion and in time combined with them: intermarriage provided new stock to the immigrants and soon new troops. But as the case of *Valcum* shows, when the time came for the Longobards to move into Italy, probably only a small portion of the native population migrated with them – the rest remained where they were, trusting in their lands.

In the countryside there is an occasional correlation between Longobard cemetery and Roman villa to support the theory of a working partnership (e.g. at Gyönk, Kadarta), and some fortified late-Roman villas do appear to have persisted even beyond Longobard rule.[20] With no associated villages so far uncovered, we rely on burial data to inform us about Longobard rural and economic activities. High cholesterol levels point to a meat, milk and cereal diet, suggesting a preponderance of stock-rearing, as is borne out also by the food placed in graves: usually mutton, goat meat or chicken, or, less often, joints of cow and pig. Furthermore, the pastures of Pannonia were ideal for cattle, sheep and horse breeding, so we can assume that most Longobards concerned themselves with animal husbandry. The cereals may have been mainly provided by native farmers. Much of this discussion, however, remains speculative, since far too little evidence is yet available for assessing native 'survival' and, therefore, agricultural output. That hunting was popular amongst the élite is borne out by instances of horse and hound burials (as at Kajdacs, Vörs and

[20] E. Thomas, 'Villa Settlements', in Lengyel & Radan (eds), *Archaeology of Roman Pannonia*, 312–20.

Szentendre). If the Longobards considered agriculture the job of serfs, then it is not surprising that tools such as picks, shovels or buckets were not used as grave goods; only by settlement excavation could we hope to recover such objects. Metal-workers are known from graves at Brno (see pl. 5) and Poysdorf, which predate the move to Pannonia, but craftsmen like these obviously will have continued to attend the nobility. In the villages smiths will have produced such everyday goods as knives, shears and scythes, but nothing is known of these workshops, nor of the kilns that produced the characteristic stamped pottery. The contribution of the Romanized populace to these small 'industries' is likewise obscure.

And how was the new Longobard kingdom defended? It is impossible to discern whether the occupation of Pannonia prompted any significant change in the Longobard mode of warfare, particularly in terms of the use of fixed defensive structures. The concept of forts and watchtowers was alien to the Longobards, and, of course, such structures were useless unless centrally organized. Germanic warfare was highly mobile and had been countered by Rome in the late Empire by the construction of walls around cities rearward of the frontier (*limes*) (see pl. 10), with many towns, presumably, either provided with standing garrisons or in touch with the field army; though, as Roman power waned in certain frontier zones, many towns were forced to fend for themselves. It is unlikely that there was any coherent provincial defence when the Longobards occupied the Pannonian zones; the hoard at *Aquincum* is the only defensive response to the invaders we have, and, in the absence of any secure archaeological data, we can only speculate whether the Longobards had used siege tactics. Their assault on *Sirmium* in 567 did not reveal an obvious skill in this area.

The proximity of Longobard cemeteries to certain Roman defensive stations, particularly along the Danubian *limes* and along major highways, must be significant and should imply some physical Longobard presence in the forts. These centres had remained settled and thus could not be ignored; Justinian's donation of 'towns and fortresses' implies as much. We have nothing to show if the Longobards took shelter alongside the natives within the fortifications when hostilities threatened, but this was certainly a tactic they adopted in northern Italy when confronted by Frankish and Avar incursions; not all the Longobards were powerful, six-foot tall warriors, and their old folk, children and women, some of whom were Longobardicized natives, will have been more than content to hide behind solid circuit walls. And indeed, there was a threat to counter: the Gepids. The concentration of find-spots in eastern Pannonia, ranged along the Danube, matches a concentration of Gepid sites along the parallel course of the Tisza river. As yet there are few known Gepid finds in the land between the two rivers and no sites of a fortified nature; consequently the area is viewed as a 'no man's land' separating the Longobards from the Gepids.

Pagans and Christians

A feature of many of the urban and fortified centres is the presence of late-Roman churches maintained into the sixth century; there is also a discrete scattering of Christian accessories, such as church plate, reliquaries, box altars and lamps (pl. 11). These must relate almost wholly to the Christian, Romanized indigenous population and attest to an active, city-based Church organization.[21] The finds also imply that the ruling barbarian

---

[21] E. Thomas, 'Die Romanität Pannoniens im 5. und 6. Jahrhundert', in Menghin, Springer & Wamers (eds), *Germanen, Hunnen und Awaren*. For Christianity in *Pannonia*: A. Mócsy, *Pannonia and Upper Moesia* (London and Boston, 1974), 325–36, 351–3. A bishop Vigilius is attested at Sopron

*Plate 11 Felsödörgicse: pulpit panel, probably dating to the
sixth century, from a lost church. (Hungarian National
Museum, Budapest.)*

tribes were tolerant of native religion. Although the majority of tribe members retained their pagan beliefs, many

until 568; otherwise little is known of the other Pannonian bishoprics after
*c.*400.

people from the leading classes adopted Arianism, an heretical strain of Christianity. In the late fourth and in the fifth centuries Visigoths, Ostrogoths, Vandals and Burgundians all adhered to the Arian creed. Arianism also spread to the Germans along the Danube from the mid-fifth century, affecting the Heruls, Suevi and Rugi, and by the early sixth century the Gepid nobility had also converted. According to a ninth-century source, the Longobards were partially converted when they occupied Rugiland in 489; certainly by the time of their migration to Italy a sizeable proportion of the tribe must have been Arian. However, even before then Justinian had counted the Longobards amongst his 'Christian allies', and it seems likely that some leading Longobards converted strategically to Catholicism, in order to secure the alliance with Byzantium. King Alboin (560–72) married the Catholic Clodosuintha, daughter of the Frankish monarch Chlotar I, but could not be persuaded from his Arian faith nor to forbid Arian missionary activities among his people.[22] For the Gepids we hear only of an Arian bishop of *Sirmium*, where the bishopric may have, originally, been an Ostrogothic institution.

Overall it could be argued that the Longobards were religiously indifferent, and that to some degree their nobility employed Christianity as a diplomatic tool. Certainly, such cemeterial finds as funerary meals, runic inscriptions on brooches, zoomorphic ornaments and associated horse and dog burials demonstrate a predominantly pagan character for the bulk of the tribal population. Only in Hegykö type cemeteries can we observe some Christian influences, such as the paucity of vessels within graves and the occasional presence of engraved crosses on the tongues of buckles, but here we are dealing

---

[22] Bóna, *Dawn of the Dark Ages*, 83–92. The conquest of Rugiland, Herulia and Suevic Pannonia and the occupation of Gothic Pannonia led to the incorporation by the Longobards of many Arian Germans – again no 'ethnic cleansing' was performed here.

with Arian Germans and Catholic indigenes. Finds at *Valcum* likewise offer occasional Christian traces, which need have no direct relationship with Longobards. As we will see shortly, in Italy too paganism remained evident, and only from the early seventh century does Christianity take on a more prominent role.

Gepids, Byzantines and Avars, AD 565–568

King Alboin's profession of the Arian faith and his marriage to Clodosuintha cannot have endeared him to the Byzantine court. As it was, the Byzantines had hardly given the Longobards their full backing as allies: they had prevented the Longobards from overrunning the Gepids in 552 and had dissipated their forces by recruiting Longobards as federate troops for Italy and Persia. In 554 Justinian's generals had finally defeated the Ostrogoths in Italy, and by 561 they controlled all of the peninsula as far as the Alps. In effect, the Byzantines and the Longobards became neighbours, so it was in the Empire's interests to keep the Longobards subdued. The Longobards also must have felt threatened; their one known response was the Frankish marriage alliance.

Justinian's death in November 565 spelt danger to the delicate balance on the middle Danube. His successor, Justin II, quickly made a series of miscalculations, which weakened his Empire's position and played into Alboin's hands. The most important participants in these events were the Avars, a new stock of ferocious nomadic horsemen from Central Asia, who followed the destructive example of the Huns and who were pushed westwards by the even more ferocious Turks. In 558 the Avars had fought for Justinian against the Savirs and Utigurs along the north coast of the Black Sea; in 562 Justinian had renewed the alliance with the Avars and granted them an annual gold subsidy, regarding them as a powerful tool for future manoeuvrings. Justin II, however, curtailed these payments on his accession and likewise terminated the truce with the Persians;[23] his motives may have been financial, since the subsidies were a huge drain on the imperial coffers, but from a politico-military viewpoint his reasoning was to prove disastrous.

In 566 Alboin renewed hostilities with the Gepids, who were now ruled by Cunimund, a bitter personal enemy of the Longobard king. While Cunimund was fighting elsewhere against the Slavs, the Longobards attacked Gepid-held *Sirmium*. Cunimund sought and received Justin's support in return for the promise of surrendering the city to the Byzantines; the Longobards, defeated, fell back, though Cunimund retained *Sirmium*. Clodosuintha had since died, depriving the Longobards of Frankish support. With the Byzantines ranged against them, Alboin obtained the assistance of the Avars on the lower Danube. The Avars were eager to establish a more secure footing along the Danube: they demanded the Gepid lands, a tenth of the Longobards' total livestock and half of any booty recovered from the forthcoming conflict. Alboin agreed, and in 567, in a short campaign, his forces pushed across the Danube and the Tisza into the Gepid heartland, overwhelmed the enemy army and killed Cunimund himself (pl. 12). The Avars had been slow in moving down towards *Sirmium* from Transylvania; although too late to participate in the Gepid rout, they were on hand to expand into Gepidia and to loom over *Sirmium*, now in Byzantine hands.[24] The Longobards had achieved a complete victory and had headed

---

[23] Menander, 8.
[24] Menander, 12.1–2; Paul *HL*, I. 27, added that Alboin had Cunimund's head severed from his body and the skull made into a drinking cup; that he then forced the Gepid king's daughter Rosemunda into marriage; and that she suffered the ordeals but later took her revenge. Menander, 12.3–8 and 27.1–3 described the subsequent Avar siege and capture of *Sirmium*. Cf. F. Wozniak, 'Byzantine diplomacy and the Lombardic-Gepid wars', *Balkan Studies*, xx (1979), 139–58.

home with a mass of booty and prisoners. They had drastically altered the balance of power along the Danube by replacing the relatively weak Gepids with the energetic Avar war machine, which was aided to the north and east by various Slav groups and such subject tribes as the Kutrigurs. Avars and Slavs focused their enmity on Byzantium, with raids (not always in concert) into Dalmatia, Thrace and Greece, while there is some evidence also for continued resistance in Gepidia until *c.571*. The Byzantines for their part failed to counter Avar inroads effectively, thereby dragging out the conflict in the Balkans and around *Sirmium*; from 571 the renewed war with Persia reduced the forces available in Europe, providing the Avars with ample room for manoeuvre.[25]

Many scholars view the rapid build-up of Avar power as a primary cause for the Longobards' decision to migrate into Italy and they consider Alboin's alliance with the Avar *khagan* (king) as a major political blunder. However, the Avars needed much time to settle and they cannot have regretted having as allies the Longobards, who had already proved their worth in battle. Nor did the Slavs constitute an immediate threat: as noted previously, there had been a peaceful overlap between the two tribes in the areas of Bohemia and Moravia and there is nothing in our sources to show that relations had subsequently deteriorated. More pertinent was the evident weakness of Byzantine Italy, apparent to the Longobards from having served in the imperial ranks since the 550s. Only recently had Italy been fully wrested from the Ostrogoths and Franks; since then, it had suffered plague, religious disputes against Byzantium and even rebellions by federate troops in the Alpine districts, while the peninsula's famous, but aged, governor-general Narses had been pushed into retirement by Justin II,

---

[25] Menander, 12.5, 15 and 21.

Plate 12 The Gepids and the Longobards clash. (From A. D'Osualdo's Arrivano i Longobardi, *Udine, 1989.)*

leaving something of a power vacuum. Buoyed by his success against the Gepids, Alboin may have been tempted to seek greater glory in the fertile lands of Italy. But there are odd hints in the sources that this was something other than an invasion: our seventh- and eighth-century texts link the name of Narses to the migration, claiming that the nonagenarian patrician invited the enemy in, as a result of a personal vendetta with Justin II and his wife Sophia. Paul the Deacon provides a dramatic account of the episode:

Having conquered and destroyed . . . the Gothic nation and vanquished those other enemies . . . Narses, who had accumulated a wealth of gold, silver and every other treasure, aroused the jealousy of the Romans, for whom he had long laboured against the enemy; but these Romans opposed him and complained to the emperor Justinian [i.e. Justin] and his wife

Sophia: 'We Romans were better off as subjects to the Goths
than we have been under the Greeks [Byzantines] ever since
that eunuch Narses began governing us and forced us into
servitude, whilst our most holy emperor was ignorant of these
events. Either liberate us from his grasp, or we most surely will
hand the city of Rome and ourselves over to the barbarians'.
But hearing this, Narses curtly replied: 'If I have done the
Romans wrong, let me suffer evil for it'. And the emperor was
so enraged that he immediately dispatched Longinus to Italy
as prefect to replace Narses. Discovering this, Narses was
horrified and, fearing above all the anger of the empress, did
not dare to return to Constantinople. For in fact it is said that
the empress had told him that as he was a eunuch he would
end up in the women's quarters helping the girls there to
disentangle the yarn. To which Narses replied: 'And I will
order her such a cloth that the empress will not be able to
remove it from her back for as long as she lives'. Overcome by
hatred and fear Narses retired to Naples and then sent ambassadors to the Longobards, inviting them to quit the barren
fields of Pannonia to come and conquer bountiful Italy. And
he sent with this message baskets of fruit and other Italian
produce so as to tempt them along. The Longobards happily
leapt at the chance they had been waiting for, thinking of all
the advantages which the future now promised. That night in
Italy, terrible portents were visible, namely lines of fire in the
sky, shimmerings of the blood which later came to be scattered.[26]

Even if this story seems far-fetched, we cannot exclude
the possibility that Narses did invite the Longobards,
perhaps, not out of spite, but as an official action of
federate settlement, sanctioned by the imperial auth-
orities in Constantinople and designed to repopulate and
strengthen northern Italy, which had been devastated by
the Gothic Wars. The Longobards had already been

---

[26] *HL*, II. 5 elaborating on *Lib. Pont., vita Iohannes*, I. 157. Also noted
briefly in *Origo*, 5; and by Spanish (Isidore of Seville, *Chronica Maiora*,
402), Frankish (Fredegar, III. 65) and British (Bede, *Chronica Maiora*, 523)
historians.

granted *Pannonia* and part of *Noricum* and had proved themselves adequate allies. A planned Longobard entry into Italy could explain many facts: the failure of contemporaries to record it as an invasion; the lack of opposition to their arrival; their rapid, seemingly bloodless occupation of towns in *Venetia*; and the absence of references to the flight of refugees. As we will see, if this was the case, the invitation was a serious and fatal miscalculation on the Byzantines' part. Whatever the cause, the effect was that Italy was submerged once more in bitter warfare.

The March

Paul the Deacon relates how King Alboin called upon his allies the Saxons to join the Longobards in occupying the Italian plains; over 20,000 Saxons with their women and children duly accompanied the Longobard throng. The migration began two days after Easter in AD 568 and proceeded south-eastwards towards the Julian Alps. The route taken is uncertain, although it may be assumed that an advance military force secured the passes and cleared the path into Italy, probably by marching along the direct Ptuj–Celje–Ljubljana–Cividale route (see figs 4 and 7). There is no mention nor archaeological evidence of resistance, not even in sites in the old Roman barrier defences of the *Claustra Alpium Iuliarum*. The bulk of the migrating people required much time to reach the border. They are unlikely to have crossed the Alpine ridges in wintertime, and they either arrived in autumn 568 or delayed crossing until spring 569.[27] Various estimates have been made of the numbers involved, ranging from 80,000 to 200,000 adult males, and thus up to

---

[27] Paul *HL*, II. 6–8; Greg. *HF* IV. 41. On the march and its probable route: C. G. Mor, 'La marcia di re Alboino', in Tagliaferri (ed.), *Problemi*, 179–97.

*c.*400,000 all told – calculations based on Paul the Deacon's figure of 20,000 Saxon warriors, which itself was probably guesswork. A figure of *c.*150,000 persons may be more realistic, providing a fighting core of *c.*60–80,000 men. This figure exceeds that of 100,000 suggested for the Ostrogoths who so successfully held Italy after invading in 489. The patterns of Longobard and Ostrogothic settlement distribution are very similar, with a strong (archaeological and documentary) concentration of population in the north. Paul the Deacon (*HL*, II.26) stresses another important factor, namely that, like the Ostrogoths, the Longobard host incorporated various other tribal groupings: 'Indeed Alboin led with him to Italy a multitude of peoples from different tribes, conquered by himself or by other of the Longobard kings. Hence today we still call many villages by the name of their earliest inhabitants, such as the Gepids, Bulgars, Sarmatians, Pannonians, Suevi, Noricans, and so on.'

Did this migration entail a total evacuation of Pannonia by both Longobards and natives? Because we rely on cemetery data and lack the benefit of associated coin, epigraphic or settlement finds, we must be very cautious in this discussion. Some authors certainly prefer to see a total uprooting, formalized in the burning of the old homes, as described by one near-contemporary source.[28] In support of this opinion are the obviously brief usage of cemeteries of Vörs-Kajdacs type and the near total absence of Italo-Longobard period manufactures. But the prospect of migration and a search for new homes cannot have appealed to everyone in Longobard Pannonia, and a number at least will have been loath to leave their homes and farms, perhaps having married local women, and having enjoyed stability for a generation or more. The Avar threat, if even considered a threat, was not imminent, whilst Italy was largely an alien world, which

[28] Marius Av. II. 24, *anno* 569.

they knew would not fall into their hands without a fight. A total migration would imply that the monarch and his retinue exerted a powerful authority; but the attested rivalry between *farae* (clans) in itself might argue against unanimity in the decision to transfer.

As in Moravia, where a series of finds testifies to continued Longobard activity or trade at a few sites perhaps after 546/7, so in Pannonia there is a scattering of individual finds which hint at but do not prove a limited persistence of Longobards after 568. Material at Veskény and Moszentjános, for example, belongs to the mid-sixth century or later and could plausibly post-date 568. Furthermore, there are instances of Longobard tombs found within and below Avar cemeteries, as at Jutas, Gyönk, Rácalmás and Várpalota, but evidence to prove a direct transition is ephemeral.[29] Some of the earliest known Avar finds in Hungary derive from the lands west of the Danube, and find-spots in north-east Pannonia show some correlation with Longobard sites and, in a few cases, with earlier Roman fortifications. The best studied of these is Környe, featuring 152 graves, including twenty horse burials. Characteristic finds were the composite bows with bone reinforcements, triple-winged arrowheads, lanceheads, horse equipment (including stirrups, first attested in Europe under the Avars), belt fittings and jewellery (bright necklaces with eye-beads, earrings), datable to the second half of the sixth century and the first half of the seventh. In addition, Germanic dress items such as hairpins and inlaid belt pieces, as well as three swords and a shield, were recovered, which point directly to a German settlement in the area. Interestingly, anthropological analysis showed no positive Mongoloid component: these were people who dressed and

---

[29] Werner, *Die Langobarden in Pannonien*, 23–48, 120–1; Bóna, 'Ungarns Völker im 5. und 6. Jahrhundert', in Menghin, Springer & Wamers (eds), *Germanen, Hunnen und Awaren*, 126.

fought in Avar style but were a conglomerate of ethnic types.[30]

We can, however, pinpoint a series of strategic settlements in the Alpine foothills of north-west Yugoslavia that demonstrates Germanic activity beyond 568 and perhaps as late as *c*.600. While it is tempting to see in these a Longobard outer defence zone buffering the Italian territories and controlling access along the River Save,[31] interpretation of the data is problematic and a Longobard presence is difficult to ascertain. Nominally, Justinian's donation gave the Longobards control over towns like *Poetovio* (Ptuj) and *Celeia* (Celje) and forts like Velike Malence (successor to *Neviodunum*) and *Carnium* (Kranj), but, as we have seen, there is precious little material that can definitely be considered Longobard outside the Danubian sectors of Pannonia. What excavations at the cemeteries of Kranj, Rifnik and Bled-Pristava have actually shown are the late-Roman origins of defended hill-top sites, with a presence of Goths and natives into the late sixth century; but they proffer only occasional hints of Longobard contact: for instance, Rifnik yielded a coin of the Longobard king Clef (572–4) as well as stamped pottery, while Velike Malence offers a single stamped pot.[32] It may, in fact, be the case that Longobard control over these fortified sites began only in 568, though there is little to show the installation of garrison units at these or at any of the former *Claustra* bases. It is more logical, therefore, to argue that Friuli,

[30] Á. Salamon & J. Erdélyi, *Das völkerwanderungszeitliche Gräberfeld von Környe* Studia Archoeologica, v (Budapest, 1971).

[31] Werner, *Die Langobarden in Pannonien*, 121–30; Kiszely, *Anthropology of the Lombards*, 21, 129–37.

[32] On these sites see the contributions of L. Bolta, I. Pirkovic, M. Slabne and Z. Vinski in *Arheološki Vestnik, Acta Archaeologica*, xxi–xxii (1970–1); cf. T. Ulbert, 'Zur Siedlungskontinuität im sudöstlichen Alpenraum, vom 2. bis 6. Jahrhundert n. Chr.', *Von der Spätantike zum frühen Mittelalter. Vorträge und Forschungen*, xxv, ed. J. Werner & E. Ewig (Munich, 1979), 141–57.

just beyond the Julian Alps, was where the Longobards concentrated their defensive forces.

That fairly peaceful conditions prevailed to the east is shown by continuity on sites like Kranj and Rifnik. However, by *c.*600 at the latest such communities had ceased to exist owing to the territorial expansion of both Slavs and Avars. At their departure in 568, the Longobards had concluded a perpetual treaty with their allies the Avars whereby they handed over Pannonia, apparently on the condition that, if they were to return, the Avars would peacefully make way for them.[33] Whilst we must doubt the authenticity of such a unique agreement, nonetheless we lack any immediate signs of hostile behaviour by the Avars against the Longobards. The absence of precise contemporary records for the zone makes the period 568–600 especially confused and obscure, particularly regarding the expansion of the Slavs southwards from Moravia, the sequence of Avar occupation in Pannonia and the nature of Slavo-Avar movements from the 580s. What can be gleaned is that the bishoprics, and thus towns, of *Poetovio* and *Celeia* were defunct by *c.*587 and *Emona* (Ljubljana) very soon after; by 591 the Slavs had penetrated the upper Drau and Gail valleys in the heartland of Noricum Mediterraneum, although they did not fully secure these zones until the 620s.[34] Here the Romanic population sheltered not in the Roman towns but on defensive heights or *Fliehburgen*, such as the Karnburg, Lavant, Graz and Lienz, first occupied in the fifth century and presenting some evidence for Slavic activity, too. By *c.*600, therefore, the Slavs had reached the borders of Italy, and any Longobard military role that is claimed for sites like Kranj and Velike Malence will have ceased. Indeed, one small fortlet at Pivko, near

---

[33] Paul *HL*, II. 7. The *Codex Gothanus*, a ninth-century continuation of the *Origo*, puts a time limit of 200 years on this return clause.
[34] Paul *HL*, IV. 38. See Alföldy, *Noricum*, 213–27.

Naklo, 5 km north-east of Kranj, has been shown to have been overwhelmed by Slavs in this period on the basis of the numerous arrowheads recovered.[35]

Where Slavic control ended and Avar territory began is hard to define: some cemeteries show a symbiotic relationship, as at Devinska Nova Ves (west of Bratislava and east of Vienna), which combines Slav cremations with Avar inhumations. Generally, scholars view this situation as one of Avar military overlordship with a subordinate agricultural Slav population. In the 620s, however, many Slavic tribes rebelled against the Avars, carving out their own empire in Lower Austria and Moravia, which extended as far south as the Italian Alps. The Avars subsequently centred their resources on the Carpathian basin, but were still controlling lands up to the Julian Alps.[36] In effect the Longobards of north-east Italy were to face a dual threat, and Paul the Deacon's narrative for the seventh century certainly depicts frequent conflicts across the passes. But the Longobards were fortunate in that the Avars still focused their attention on the rich pickings of Byzantium, while the Slavs confronted the Franks. As we will see, what raids Italy did suffer were certainly not substantial enough to dislodge the newly-won Longobard kingdom.

[35] A. Valic, 'Gradisce nad Pivko pri Naklem', *Arheološi Vestnik, Acta Archaeologica, xix (1968)*, 485–508.
[36] Váňa, *Ancient Slavs*, 66–72.

3

The Longobards and Italy

The country that the Longobards now entered differed quite dramatically from the rich Roman province that had first lured the barbarian tribes over the *limes*. Town and civilian life was in serious decline, agricultural activity had been disrupted and trade badly reduced; plague, piracy and highway robbery were rife. The appearance of a new marauding invader, intent on settling, as well as looting, did little to restore the ailing peninsula, as witnessed by 30 ensuing years of conflict between Longobards and Byzantines. The picture is perhaps not altogether bleak, for excavations have shown a fairly good rate of urban survival and continuity, albeit at an impoverished level. Nonetheless, it is not until the second half of the seventh century or, more certainly, from the early part of the eighth century that we can observe a revival in Italy's domestic fortunes, marked primarily by renewed church and monastery building and embellishment. We will examine the physical character and contribution of Longobard settlement and society in the next chapters. Here, however, it is valuable to summarize the sequence and effects of the various phases of Longobard expansion in Italy. To introduce this, some comment on the nature of later Roman Italy is relevant.

Third-century invasions, by Alamanni in particular, prompted a first round of urban fortification in Italy, commencing in Verona in 268 and in Rome between

270 and 275. The construction of the Aurelianic walls around Rome is a clear statement of the anxiety of the State and an admittance of the fear felt towards the barbarians. Safeguards continued to be raised, notably in northern Italy in the fourth century, with Milan newly adopted as the imperial capital; barriers and forts were erected to control the Alpine passes, while further afield the frontiers were constantly reinforced and the army concentrated into roving mobile units. Despite all these measures Rome could do little to counter a series of devastating events at the start of the fifth century, culminating in the Visigothic occupation of Rome in 410. The weak emperor Honorius personifies this period, as he shifted the imperial seat from exposed Milan to sheltered Ravenna and ordered the execution of his able Vandal general Stilicho. Subsequently, from the 430s, the Vandals, who had displaced the Roman government in Africa, thereby depriving Rome of her principal grain and oil source, began telling raids on the Italian and Sicilian coasts, prompting renewed fortification of such sites as Naples. In 455 the Vandals even succeeded in occupying and pillaging Rome.[1] To this can be added Attila's incursion and the bloody internal Roman divisions as barbaro-Roman generalissimos selected and deselected puppet-emperors and watched as the western provinces slipped away from their control.

Stability was only re-established with the enforced retirement in 476 of the last western Roman emperor, Romulus Augustulus, by the federate commander Odoacer. Odoacer's own resources were too few, however, to counter a new flood of Germanic invaders, the Ostrogoths, whose king Theoderic founded a kingdom in Italy that lasted into the 530s. Theoderic was keen to promote Roman culture and administration and, like

[1] N. Christie, 'The Alps as a frontier, A.D. 168–774', *Journal of Roman Archaeology*, vi (1991), 413–24.

Odoacer before him, respected the role of the now impotent Senate; yet, at the same time, he sought to maintain Gothic cultural identity, leaving military affairs a Gothic preserve. Despite this, it is difficult to trace the Ostrogoths archaeologically in Italy: burial with grave-goods was restricted to females, and male dress items occur solely in hoards or as stray finds; what can be seen from the limited finds, however, is that Italo-Mediterranean traits become evident early on. Ostrogothic numbers were limited, and their forces were concentrated in northern, Padane Italy, with nominal presences only in the larger cities of the south, notably, Spoleto, Rome and Naples. The writings and letters collated by Theoderic's chief minister, Cassiodorus Senator, demonstrate that building activity was mainly limited to the royal centres of Pavia, Verona and Ravenna and that the major grain depots were sited in an arc across the north in the fortified towns of Tortona, Pavia, Trento and Treviso; Cassiodorus also refers to wall-building and to a likely revitalization of control of the Alpine passes. All this combines to suggest cautious logistical planning.[2] Theoderic seems to have been preparing for the day when the East Roman Empire would seek to claim Italy back. But even before his death in 526 the partnership between Goths and Romans threatened collapse, and subsequent rulers failed both to command wholesale loyalty within Italy and to uphold the network of strategic marriage alliances beyond the borders. This failure coincided with the accession of Justinian I (527–65) to the throne of the East Roman Empire. Having inherited full coffers and obtained peace on the Persian frontier, this ambitious emperor sought to alleviate civil tension at Constantinople by embarking on a project of restoration of the lost

---

[2] Bierbrauer, *Die ostgotischen Grab- und Schatzfunde*, 25–41, 53–69, 209–15; V. Bierbrauer, 'Aspetti archeologici dei Goti, Alamanni e Longobardi', *Magistra Barbaritas. I Barbari in Italia* (Milan, 1984), 445, 450; Wolfram, *History of the Goths*, 284–306.

West. In varying degrees this was a simple reassertion of rights over former territories, a religious crusade against Arian heretics, a search for personal glory and a hope for new economic gains and manpower to bolster the East Empire. The success of the primary campaign against Vandal Africa (533–4) prompted the expedition to Sicily and southern Italy in 535, with the rapid capture of Rome by early 537. As noted, however, the bulk of the Ostrogoths was settled in northern Italy, and, initially, Byzantine gains were illusory. The restricted number of imperial troops – perhaps no more than 25,000 men – reduced by the need to garrison captured towns and forts, was poorly supported logistically and only rarely bolstered by new Eastern forces; the 'guerrilla warfare' tactics adopted by the Goths and the besieging of enemy centres further delayed progress. Even so, the capture of Ravenna in 541 was viewed by Justinian as the mark of victory and prompted him to recall troops to fight in the East; but between 542 and 550 the Ostrogoths won back much of Italy, limiting the Byzantines to a few key sites. At the same time the Merovingian Franks, not obviously in alliance with either side, invaded northern Italy and took control of wide areas, almost preventing the arrival of a new Byzantine expeditionary force. Nevertheless, the Byzantines, led by Narses, fatally crippled the Ostrogoths in two field battles in 552–3. The Byzantine reconquest is often held to have been completed by 553; in fact, in 554 they faced a Franco-Alamannic invasion, which penetrated as far as the heel of Italy; then, between 555 and 563, they slowly expelled residual Franco-Gothic garrisons from sites both north and south of the River Po. Plagues, religious disputes, heavy taxation and an economy ruined by nearly three decades of warfare now haunted the peninsula.[3]

[3] Proc. *BG*; Agathias, I–II; C. Wickham, *Early Medieval Italy. Central Power and Local Society, 400–1000*, (London, 1981), 24–7; R. Collins, *Early Medieval Europe*, (London, 1991), 121–6.

Even if one near contemporary source vaguely speaks of Narses restoring the towns to their 'former splendour' (*Auctarius Havniensis*, IV), archaeologically there is nothing to show an upturn in fortune, and indeed most other sources speak only of the gloom and destruction wrought by the war.[4] Thus, at the eve of the Longobard march, Italy was poorly equipped to face a further round of military conflict. The loyalty of both soldiery and citizenry was suspect; troops were scattered and badly paid and border defences perhaps unmanned; many town walls were seemingly still in a state of decay; and agricultural activity was only just picking up again. Such a situation might even support the hypothesis mentioned above, that the Longobards were invited into Italy from Pannonia to help defend and cultivate the land, the blatantly debilitated state of which may have then prompted the Longobards to drop all thought of pacific settlement in favour of wholesale subjugation. Whatever the case, the events of 568–9 determined a divisioning of power in Italy that persisted well beyond the end of Longobard rule.

Conquest and Kingdom, AD 569–605

We have no detailed contemporary source through which to follow the initial Longobard advance. Local and western sources offer at best bare annalistic entries; only from the 580s, with popes Pelagius II and Gregory the Great, does more informative comment begin, although usually shrouded in religious discussion. Eastern Byzantine sources virtually ignore the vicissitudes in Italy and instead concentrate their attention on the wars in the Balkans and against Persia – as reflected in the fact that in 577–9 the emperor Tiberius II sent gold, but precious few men,

[4] Cf. N. Christie, 'The Archaeology of Byzantine Italy: A Synthesis of Recent Research', *Journal of Mediterranean Archaeology*, 2: 2 (1989), 263, 279, 282–3.

to the beleagured province.[5] Our earliest Longobard source, the *Origo gentis Langobardorum*, which forms the prologue to King Rothari's law code of 645, provides no more than a three-line summary of the early conquest: 'At Easter in the 1st indiction Alboin himself led the Longobards from Pannonia to Italy. In the 2nd indiction they began to overrun Italy. But by the 3rd indiction they had become masters of Italy' (V). For a coherent account we have to wait for Paul the Deacon's *Historia Langobardorum*, which, though composed in the late eighth century, incorporates details thought to derive from one or more lost Italian chronicles written close to the events portrayed. However, while events until the death of Pope Gregory the Great can be adequately pieced together from Paul the Deacon's account, his data for much of the seventh century are scattered and imprecise and restricted, geographically, to north-eastern Italy and the Duchy of Benevento. For the period 700–40, and in particular for the reign of King Liutprand (712–44), Paul the Deacon again has apparent access to competent sources (probably both written and oral) to create his narrative. However, his text terminates with Liutprand; it has been argued that he broke off deliberately, to avoid telling of his nation's fall. Thus, for the events of the second half of the eighth century, culminating in Charlemagne's conquest of the Longobard north, we rely on the largely hostile references in the Roman *Liber Pontificalis* and on Frankish annals and letters, supplemented by a series of *continuationes* and *vitae* (fig. 6).[6]

[5]　Menander, 22 and 24. Cf. V. von Falkenhausen, 'I barbari in Italia nella storiografia bizantina', *Magistra Barbaritas*, 310–12.

[6]　W. Goffart, *The Narrators of Barbarian History*, A.D. *550–800* (Princeton, 1988), 329–431; N. Cilento, La storiografia nell'età barbarica. Fonti occidentali sui barbari in Italia', *Magistra Barbaritas*, 330, 343–4. On Longobard history see, most recently, P. Delogu, 'Il regno longobardo', in P. Delogu, A. Guillou & G. Ortalli (eds), *Storia d'Italia, I: Longobardi e Bizantini* (Turin, 1980), 3–216; Collins, *Early Medieval Europe*, 183–203, 213–18.

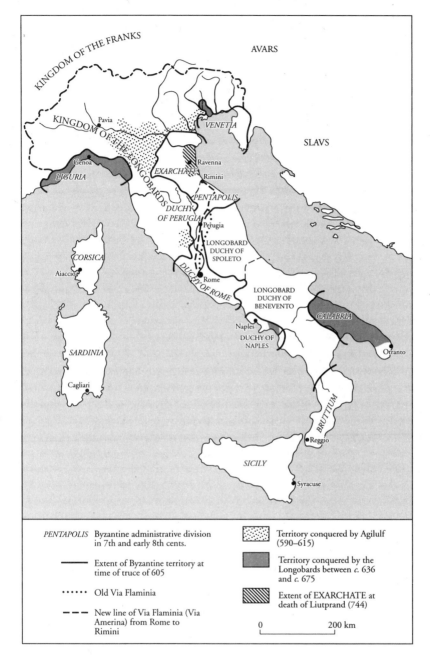

Figure 6 The conquest of Italy: Byzantines and Longobards
in Italy.

Legend:

PENTAPOLIS Byzantine administrative division
in 7th and early 8th cents.

——— Extent of Byzantine territory at
time of truce of 605

•••••• Old Via Flaminia

– – – New line of Via Flaminia (Via
Amerina) from Rome to
Rimini

Territory conquered by Agilulf
(590–615)

Territory conquered by the
Longobards between *c.* 636
and *c.* 675

Extent of EXARCHATE at
death of Liutprand (744)

0   200 km

It has already been noted that we have no documentary record of the Longobard migration meeting any military resistance in the Julian Alps. Archaeology has shown that the late-Roman defensive belt in this area, the *Claustra Alpium Iuliarum*, was inoperative after *c.*400 and that the Italian Alpine defence had shifted rearwards, taking the form of upland or strategically sited forts and settlements controlling the outlet of the pass routes. Paul the Deacon documents a number of such *castra* in the Trentino (*HL*, III. 31) and in Friuli (*HL*, IV. 37), but only one of these, *Ibligo* (Invillino), has been excavated (see chapter 5). Interestingly, finds from here indicate a first nucleation of settlement, *c.*400–30, of likely military character, on the prominent Colle Santino, which shows clear signs of maintenance into Ostrogothic, Byzantine and Longobard times, with no major structural modification to the site plan. Yet, like those of the Gothic and Byzantine phases, actual Longobard finds are few and do not seem to support the hypothesis of an ethnic Longobard garrison. Instead it is argued that Invillino and other such *castra* were native settlements, perhaps charged with military roles, but with only nominal Germanic supervision.[7]

There are no destruction levels to signify a bloody capture of the fort of Invillino by the Longobards in 569. A peaceful handover of control would, in fact, tie in with the story Paul the Deacon presents for the overall Longobard occupation of modern Friuli, carried out 'without any hindrance' (*HL*, II. 9–10, 12 and 14). The first step was the capture of the walled town of *Forum Iulii* (Cividale); immediately afterwards Alboin installed his nephew and shieldbearer Gisulf as duke of the region, charged with the defence of the Alpine borders. Gisulf

[7] V. Bierbrauer, *Invillino-Ibligo in Friaul. I: Die römische Siedlung und das spätantik-frünittelalterliche Castrum* and *II: Die spätantiken und frühmittelalterlichen Kirchen*, Münchner Beiträge zur Vor- und Frühgeschichte, xxxiii and xxxiv (Munich, 1987 and 1988).

was permitted to select the best of the leading kin-groups or *farae* to aid him in this task. Interestingly, a series of place-names derived from the term *fara* (e.g. Farra d'Isonzo, Fara di Soligo, Farra), fairly common in north-east Italy, illustrates the zones these groups came to occupy: many are rural locations, near roads and yet infrequently in vital strategic points. This leads us to assume that either in the early decades of conquest the Longobards preferred a rural lifestyle, or that these *farae* represent the Longobards' attempt at recolonizing depopulated or abandoned lands. Striking, however, is the immediate attachment of high-ranking Longobard nobles to towns as dukes and counts, paralleling the Byzantine military arrangement. Clearly the presence of extant city-based native populations – presumably at a greater level than that encountered in Pannonia – required resident Longobard supervision. In the case of Cividale the rapid development of Longobard cemeteries around the city, in part mingling with native burial grounds (pl. 13; see fig. 9), indicates the likelihood of a fairly substantial Longobard component from AD 569, which progressively fused with the Italians. Indeed, grave-finds throughout Friuli attest to a heavy immigrant settlement, in which a strong military element verifies the Duchy's major defensive role.[8]

The Longobards' slow advance westwards allowed for variable responses: Bishop Felix of Treviso parleyed with Alboin by the River Piave, surrendering his (ungarrisoned?) city without loss of blood; in contrast, Archbishop Paul fled from the exposed seat of Aquileia to the fortress of Grado, having time to take with him all the church treasury. Pushing almost due west into the Po plain, and thus striking at the economic heart of

---

[8] M. Brozzi, *Il Ducato Longobardo del Friuli*, Publicazioni della Deputazione di Storia Patriaper il Friuli, vi (Udine, 1981). On *farae* see C. Mastrelli, 'La toponomastica lombarda di origine longobarda', in *I Longobardi e la Lombardia. Saggi* (exh. cat., Milan, 1978), 37–8.

Plate 13 Migration-period Longobard stamped beaker vessel from Tomb 14 of the Gallo cemetery, Cividale. (Museo Archeologico Nazionale, Cividale.) The town of Cividale, elevated to a ducal capital in 569, has many graves that date to the early invasion years.

Byzantine Italy, Alboin's army captured Vicenza and Verona 'and other towns in Venetia', and by September 569 had entered the former imperial capital of Milan.[9] The flight of the Milanese archbishop Honoratus and his fellow Catholic clergy to Genoa signals the virtual cession of the northern Po plain to the invaders; presumably, this was accompanied by a movement of refugees to lands still in imperial hands. Paul the Deacon's narrative omits any reference here to Byzantine troop movement, although he does admit to Alboin's failure to capture southern Venetian towns like Padua and Monselice, which suggests that the Longobards – who were using the main roads of the region, most notably the *via Postumia* – merely controlled a broad east–west swathe of territory

[9] Paul *HL*, II. 10, 12, 14 and 25.

from the Julian Alps to Milan. Pavia is the one documented centre that resisted capture in this first Longobard wave of invasion, and its three year struggle must indicate at least some imperial military support. However, the Byzantines were seriously stretched on all fronts, so Alboin was able to maintain the initiative by sending raids out across the Apennines into Tuscany, extending control up to the fringes of the Alps, and continuing the process of establishing dukedoms. Paul informs us that the Byzantines were largely restricted to the coastal zones and that overall 'the Romans then had no courage to resist because of the pestilence which had occurred in Narses' time and which had destroyed very many people in Liguria and Venetia, and after the year of plenty [568], a great famine attacked and devastated all Italy' (*HL*, II. 26–7). In a similar vein, the *Liber Pontificalis* admits that the collapse of resistance on the part of many towns was due to the distresses of the famine. In effect, our sources do not put Longobard successes down to Germanic military prowess but rather to the debilitated state of the Italians. Furthermore, as noted, the Longobard arrival had come at a time of politico-military vacuum in Italy, the new Byzantine emperor Justin II (565–78) having dispatched the patrician Longinus to Ravenna as replacement for the nonagenarian Narses, then in retirement in Rome and Naples. In fact we cannot be certain that Longinus had even arrived in Italy by the time the Longobards seized Cividale. The insertion of the story of Narses' treacherous invitation to the Longobards in the *Liber Pontificalis* – probably around 625 – gave it an air of credibility, which such authors as Bede accepted and others, such as Paul the Deacon, inevitably elaborated upon, justifying as it did his nation's settlement of the peninsula.[10]

[10] *Lib. Pont.*, *v. Iohannes III*; Paul *HL*, II. 5. Cf. N. Christie, 'Invasion or Invitation? The Longobard Occupation of Northern Italy, A.D. 568–569', *Romanobarbarica*, xi (1991), 84–7, 103.

The westward momentum of the advance carried Longobard and Saxon expeditions into the Alps and past
Byzantine forts like Susa and Aosta into Frankish Burgundy, then under King Guntram (pls 14, 15). A series of
annual raids between 571 and 575 brought initial success, with much booty and the surrender of various
towns. The purpose of these incursions is not altogether
clear, whether as a show of force (some Longobards
knew how the Franks had benefited materially in Italy

*Plate 14 Migration-period S-brooch from Tomb 5 of the
Gallo cemetery, Cividale. (Museo Archeologico Nazionale,
Cividale.)*

Plate 15 Disc-brooch from the Cella cemetery at Cividale depicting one of the invaders' lance-bearing cavalrymen. (Museo Archeologico Nazionale, Cividale.)

during the Gothic War) or as an attempted annexation of land to secure control of the passes into Italy. Alternatively, the Saxon-Longobard forces might have been bribed into attacking Guntram's kingdom by Guntram's brother, King Sigebert, who later settled Saxons in the north of *Francia* and then re-enlisted them to fight his other brother Chilperic. The last major raid took place in 574 when three Longobard dukes, Amo, Zaban (*dux* of Pavia) and Rodan, divided up to penetrate as far as Arles, Valence and Grenoble, before being forced back by the Frankish general Mummolus with great loss of life and then being harried by the Byzantine commander Sisinnius at Susa. In defeat the Longobards were forced to pay a hefty annual tribute of 12,000 *solidi* to Guntram and at the same time cede the cities of Aosta and Susa –

though these probably still survived as Byzantine 'islands'.[11] Thus the Franks gained a valuable foothold on Italian soil. This was to be exploited not only in the following decades but also two centuries later when Peppin and ultimately Charlemagne defeated the *regnum Langobardorum*.

The involvement of such nobles as Zaban in these raids into *Francia* supports the view that these actions formed part of a wide-ranging campaign. Alboin himself, however, did not see it come to full fruition: in mid-572 he was murdered in his palace at Verona in a failed coup by his wife Rosemunda and her henchman Helmechis. Byzantine involvement is apparent from their subsequent flight to Ravenna, where Longinus sought to marry Rosemunda; the assassins, however, ended up killing each other, so, instead, the governor dispatched the royal treasure brought from Verona, as well as Alboin's daughter Albsuinda, to Constantinople. Longinus may have hoped to stem the Longobard tide by installing a pro-Byzantine or, at least, less aggressive faction on the throne; instead, Clef was elected king at Pavia and ferociously continued the struggle, although by the end of 574 he too had been murdered. The Longobards chose to elect no new monarch.[12] Despite the lack of a central figure, the dukes (now numbering over 30, according to Paul the Deacon) maintained the upper hand, to the degree that:

Many Roman nobles were killed for their wealth. The others, divided up amongst the conquerors, were made tributary, so that they paid the Longobards a third of their produce. Through the efforts of these dukes, in the seventh year since the arrival of Alboin and his whole people [575], having despoiled the churches, killed the priests, razed the cities to the

[11] Paul *HL*, III. 1–8; Greg. *HF*, IV. 42 and 44; Fredegar, III. 67–8 and IV. 45.

[12] *Origo*, V; ch. 96 in Agnellus, *Liber pontificalis ecclesiae Ravennatis*, ed. O. Holder–Egger, MGH, *SRL*, 273–391.

ground, exterminated the population, much of Italy, excluding those regions conquered by Alboin, was occupied and made subject to the Longobards. (*HL*, II. 28–31)

From subsequent chapters of the *Historia Langobardorum* it becomes clear that these conquests extended into Tuscany, threatening Rome, Umbria, and southern Italy, with important duchies being established at the cities of Lucca, Spoleto and Benevento. Thus, the imperial territories were splintered and had to rely on sea communications: only a narrow land bridge still connected the key seats of Rome and Ravenna (see fig. 6).

Paul's references here and in a later chapter (*HL*, III. 16) to *hospites* and *tertia* recall the terminology employed in the late Roman Empire when *hospitalitas* either signified the settlement on Roman soil of barbarian federates, who obtained a third part (*tertia*) of a landowner's property, or, alternatively, denoted the allotment of a third of a landholder's produce/income to federates settled in selected or designated zones.[13] Paul's imprecise comments and our own crude archaeological understanding of the post-Roman countryside necessarily leave us uncertain regarding this question and the broader one of the dislocation of Italian farmers. As noted already, however, the transition to Longobard rule was not destructive unless resisted. Most of the population, particularly in the north, no doubt still had strong memories of the strife of the Gothic War years, as well as a disaffection for the character of Byzantine rule. These sentiments, combined with the knowledge that the Longobards did not tax their subjects and were religiously flexible, may well have eased the way for the conquerors. The Longobards can have had little experience of the tactics of siege warfare, and yet few towns – nearly all were endowed with powerful circuit walls by this date – deigned to offer resistance. Indeed, the length of the siege

[13] W. Goffart, *Barbarians and Romans*, A.D. *418–584. The Techniques of Accommodation* (Princeton, 1980), 176–89.

at Pavia may indicate the Longobards' preoccupation
with extending their conquests and raiding further afield
rather than their lack of expertise. Centres with official
military garrisons were more prone to closing their gates.
The cases of Susa and Aosta have already been noted.
Elsewhere in the Alps the *Historia Langobardorum* hints
at some stubborn resistance from the Byzantines continuing into the 580s. Prominent is the defence of the island
fortress of Comacina in Lake Como, where the *magister
militum* Francio was finally forced to surrender his seat
and its rich treasury in 588 following a bitter six-month
siege – Francio was allowed to withdraw to Ravenna
(*HL*, III. 27). The strategic role enjoyed by this *castrum*
in controlling traffic along the lake, was probably maintained by the Longobards, although Comacina's subsequent usage by Longobard rebels and fugitives
eventually led to its destruction.[14] The reuse of similar
lake fortresses, whether islands such as San Giulio d'Orta
(pl. 16), or promontories such as Sirmione – all centres
with late Roman origins – seems to testify to a general
Longobard adoption of the existing defensive set-up after
the removal of the Byzantines.

This phase of Longobard expansion heralded a drastic
change in Byzantine tactics, following on from the
aborted counter-assault led by the general Baduarius,
son-in-law of the emperor Justin II, in 576. Subsequently,
with imperial military attention diverted to the Balkans
and the East, the emperors largely recommended the use
of gold to sue for peace, to subvert Longobard dukes to
the Byzantine cause or to hire the help of the Meroving-
ian Franks. They met with some success in bribing over
Longobard soldiery, but finite supplies of cash and the
fickleness of the mercenaries resulted in a complicated
game of switching sides, leading in some cases to disas-

[14] Refugees included Duke Gaidulf of Bergamo in 591: Paul *HL*, IV. 3;
King Cunincpert in *c.*670: *HL*, V. 38; and Ansprand in *c.*700: *HL*, VI. 19
and 21.

Plate 16 Isola San Giulio in Lake Orta, central north Italy: one of many island forts-cum-refuges that were elevated to semi-urban status.

trous imperial losses: notably, Faroald's seizure of Classe, the port of Ravenna, and his subsequent installation as Duke of Spoleto. Zotto, the first recorded Longobard duke of Benevento, may likewise have been a treacherous ex-imperial officer. Byzantium tried to curb this problem by sending Longobards to fight in the East; but loyalty there did not necessarily mean loyalty back in Italy, as shown by Ariulf, who, though recorded as a Byzantine commander against the Persians in 582, by 591 had raised himself to the status of Longobard duke of Spoleto. And yet other Longobard mercenaries remained steadfast allies to Byzantium. Paul the Deacon offers a rendition of the epitaph (no longer extant) of the commander Droctulft, 'the exterminator of his own people'. The inscription recounted Droctulft's Alamannic origins, his capture by the Longobards, his rise to the position of duke, his later defection to the Empire, his service against the Avars, his victory over Faroald at Classe, his stance against King Authari's forces at

Brescello on the Po and his final resting-place outside the
holy church of S. Vitale at Ravenna. However, his Ger-
manness was made clear: 'terrible of aspect but of kindly
mind, he had a long beard and a brave heart.'[15] This
example serves to remind us that the Longobards now
comprised a wide ethnic stock, which included Germanic
allies and subject tribal groups, Romanized Pannonians
and others. This smattering of types undoubtedly played
into Byzantine hands, and yet, despite the bribes and
despite the Frankish incursions, the Longobards emerged
after *c.*600 as the strongest of the rival powers. Indeed it
is a mark of notable resilience that the Longobards were
able to ride out the turbulent events of *c.*580–600, although the dukes felt the need to renew the kingship in
order to give their forces greater cohesion (584). Nonetheless, Longobard defections and rebellions continued
well into the reign of the forceful Agilulf (590–616), long
after the last of the Frankish invading forces was seen off.

Frankish co-operation with the Byzantines began as
early as 576 in conjunction with Baduarius' failed campaign. Franks are recorded as occupying the, most likely,
residual Byzantine fortress of *Anagnis* (Nanno) in the
Trentino, presumably as a preliminary for a southward
penetration along the Adige. They were countered briefly
by the local Longobard count *de Lagare*, Ragilo, and
then pushed back north by Duke Ewin of Trento. The
Frankish assault here had come via the Brenner pass and
is suggestive of actions by the Austrasian kingdom then
ruled by the young Childebert II – Frankish Burgundy,
meanwhile, seems chiefly to have abided by the treaty
made with the Longobards in 575. The episode of 576
may be that referred to in a passage recounting events of
584 in Gregory of Tours' *History of the Franks*: 'Some
years before, Childebert had 50,000 pieces of gold . . . to

15 Menander, 22 and 24; Paul *HL*, III. 13, 18 and 19 and IV. 16. See T. S.
Brown, *Gentlemen and Officers. Imperial Administration and Aristocratic
Power in Byzantine Italy*, A.D. *554–900*, (London, 1984), 70–4.

rid Italy of the Longobards.' In 584, to make amends for the earlier aborted mission, Childebert's troops invaded once more. According to Gregory, the Longobards, fearful of the Frankish army, submitted immediately to Childebert's authority, loaded him with gifts and then 'as soon as he had achieved all that he had intended, Childebert returned to Gaul'. Yet in Paul the Deacon's account, the Longobards simply entrenched themselves in their fortified towns, bought off Childebert with gifts and signed a treaty. Imperial embassies encouraged further incursions in both 587 and 588, the latter resulting in a defeat in which 'the slaughter of the Frankish army was such that nothing like it could be recalled'.[16] The loss of Isola Comacina coincides with this disaster; most probably, any other remaining Byzantine-Frankish outposts were swept away at this time.

The best documented invasion is that of 590, where extant correspondence of the Byzantine governor (exarch) makes plain the Byzantine view of the 'master plan' to eject the Longobards. The imperial troops are recorded as capturing the towns of Modena, Altino and Mantua and pushing north towards Verona, in theory to combine forces with the main body of Franks under Duke Cedinus before marching on Pavia. In the meantime the Longobard dukes of Parma, Piacenza and Reggio had rebelled and joined the imperial side, allowing for the movement of a fleet along the Po. To the east, Duke Grasulf of Friuli was defeated and succeeded by the pro-Byzantine Gisulf. North of Milan, the rebellion of dukes Gaidulf of Bergamo and Mimulf of San Giulio d'Orta can also be linked with the Franco-Byzantine venture. In sum, it appeared that substantial territorial gains had been made, seriously threatening the Longobard position. The result was, however, largely dependent on the faithfulness of the Franks to the cause and the

---

[16] Greg. *HF*, VI. 42, VIII. 18 and IX. 25; Paul *HL*, III. 17, 22 and 29.

military ability of their leaders.[17] Gregory of Tours gives
an honest commentary on events and, surprisingly, lies
blame where blame was due. Twenty dukes were dispatched by Childebert, but such was their troops' lack of
discipline that at first they were busy 'ravaging their own
regions . . . and only afterwards made an attempt to beat
the real enemy'. A force of seven dukes pushed as far as
Milan and despite rampaging through the countryside
they made little material impact. The other larger force,
commanded by Duke Cedinus, established control of the
upper reaches of the Adige valley by capturing a series of
castella. Paul the Deacon, clearly utilizing a local source –
presumed to be the lost *Historiola* of Secundus of Trento
– supplements Gregory's description by providing the
names of thirteen forts 'demolished without resistance',
whose occupants were made prisoners as the Franks
pushed south towards Verona. The Longobard duke
Ewin of Trento nonetheless resisted Cedinus's forces, by
holing himself up in the massive natural fortress of Verruca (pl. 17) and by bribing the Franks away. The same
tactic was employed elsewhere, quickly bringing disaster
upon the Franks:

For nearly three months the [Frankish] troops wandered
about in Italy, but they achieved nothing and inflicted no
losses on the enemy, who had shut themselves up in strongly
fortified places. And they failed to capture the king and avenge
themselves on him, for he was safe inside the walls of Pavia.
Overcome by hunger and decimated by dysentery prompted
by the climate, they turned homewards. Before reaching their
native lands, the Franks suffered such hunger that to get food
they had to sell their clothes and then their weapons too. (Paul
HL, III. 31)

Gregory of Tours states that the first Frankish force near
Milan waited for six days for the proposed link-up with

---

[17] MGH, *Epistolae Austriacae* III. 40 and 41. Described also in Greg. *HF*,
X. 3, and Paul *HL*, III. 31 and IV. 3.

Plate 17 Verruca *('the wart'): the hill opposite Roman Trento on the Adige, in the central Alps, documented as an Ostrogothic and Longobard fortress.*

the Byzantines, but he omits mention of a similar plan for Cedinus's troops. Yet letters by the Byzantine exarch, which barely conceal his anger and outrage under diplomatic phrases, accuse Cedinus of totally failing to comply with the terms of the alliance, indeed, of making his own peace with King Authari, for personal gain.

We do not know what settlement the Franks would have received from the Byzantines if the 590 campaign had been successful. What we do know, however, is that the Franks from now on received large annual subsidies from the Longobards, and that the Frankish military threat dissipated in a series of desperate civil wars.[18] The physical consequences within Italy were even more telling. The new king Agilulf respected the treaty made with the Franks and forcefully quashed remaining Longobard insurrection before dislodging the Byzantines from their gains of 590. The Byzantines, no longer able to afford to pay allies to make incursions and in any case no longer daring to trust the Franks, were forced to employ their own poor logistics to attempt to restrict Longobard

[18] Greg. *HF*, IV. 4 and 14.

encroachments. In the end it was the geography of Italy, rather than superior Byzantine military training, that allowed the imperials to retain a precarious foot-hold in the peninsula.

A major struggle raged over control of the land link between Rome and Ravenna: the Longobard possession of Spoleto effectively meant that they controlled the old *via Flaminia*; the eventual recapture of Perugia by the Byzantine exarch Romanus caused the *via Amerina* to emerge as the new north–south line of imperial communications.[19] This fragile 'corridor', which may have been no more than an interlinked line of fortified road stations, at least managed to isolate the southern Longobard territories (Spoleto and Benevento) from the *Regnum Langobardorum*, with its royal capital based at Pavia. The *Letters* and *Dialogues* of Pope Gregory I (the Great) (590–604) illuminate this phase of the conflict, with Gregory tirelessly searching for peace with the 'most hated' Longobards, treating with embassies, writing to the king and his dukes or to the Byzantine emperor and the exarch, and in constant contact with his fellow bishops. His letters reveal how civil, and to some extent military, authority now devolved around the figure of the pope, who often was forced to act independently of the exarch, and who occasionally even had to help pay the garrison of the Rome duchy. Papal diplomacy could not always halt Longobard military manouevres, and the enemy managed to bring the combat almost to the gates of Rome between 592 and 594, first under Ariulf of Spoleto and then under King Agilulf. The struggle was hard, but for once Longobard inroads were countered.[20] However, to the north of Rome, imperial Tuscany was progressively taken over by the campaigns of the Longobard dukes of Lucca and Chiusi, which

---

[19] Paul *HL*, IV. 8; *Lib. Pont., v. Gregorii.*
[20] Greg. *Reg.* II. 23 and 45 and XIII. 36.

isolated such regions as Liguria and towns as Pisa from land support from Rome. Few details exist for southern Italy, although it seems likely that the Beneventan dukes gained control of extensive territories. Throughout, the Byzantines were forced back onto the coast, with key centres at Naples, Gaeta, Otranto and Taranto; Sicily remained Byzantine and relatively healthy, allowing for vital supplies of staple products such as grain, wine and oil to reach the rest of beleagured imperial Italy (see fig. 6). In the Po valley a complicated series of offensives eventually resulted in further Longobard encroachments, with the surrender of Cremona, Mantua, Brescello and the *castrum Vulturina* in 601–2; further east, Padua and Monselice also fell to Longobard assaults, while Byzantine Istria (north–west coastal Croatia) was devastated by Longobards, Slavs and Avars. Despite taking Agilulf's daughter and her husband hostage, the exarch Smaragdus was forced in 603 to draw up a truce, which was renewed in 604 and bolstered by the large subsidy of 12,000 *solidi*. Repeated in 605, the treaty was ratified and extended by the emperor Phocas. The Byzantines had finally admitted their inability to rid Italy of the Longobards.[21]

Consolidation and Stability, AD 605–700

It is difficult to determine the full effects of the sixth-century wars on the Italian landscape and its population. For areas which had become border zones between Byzantine and Longobard duchies, old Roman farming and settlement patterns – disrupted in any case since the fourth century – may have totally disappeared or been reduced to meagre, scattered and inward-looking farms and villages in sheltered locations. Our most vivid

[21] Paul *HL*, IV. 20, 23–5, 32 and 35.

pronouncement comes from Gregory the Great (*Dial.*, III. 38): 'Now the cities have been depopulated, fortresses razed, churches burned down, monasteries and nunneries destroyed, the fields abandoned by mankind, and destitute of any cultivator the land lies empty and solitary. No landholder lives on it; wild beasts occupy places once held by a multitude of men.' Whilst charged with high rhetoric, the claims seem not altogether inaccurate. As will be shown later, archaeologically, the countryside appears to be virtually deserted between *c.*600 and 750, with continuity provable at no Roman villa site and the overall material culture at an almost prehistoric level. Gregory in fact documents the transfer of depopulated or exposed settlements and bishoprics to fortified centres on promontories or hilltops, such as Bagnoregio.[22] Many of these safe havens were tiny and could have held only a small community. At the same time there is no material evidence to suggest that any of the larger walled towns took in masses of refugee farmers, since towns also decline dramatically in this period, in terms of building activity and standards, amenities and hygiene; in contrast, our data point to major urban depopulation. In the case of Rome, Procopius, in relating the numerous sieges suffered by the city in the course of the Gothic War, claims a population at one point of just 500 persons. It can never have sunk quite so low, but an estimate in terms of tens of thousands or even just of thousands may not be far off the mark. By the time of Gregory, however, matters had improved, and Rome did not suffer the same rapid swapping of masters as she had sixty years previously. At best we can argue for a maximum of *c.*70–100,000, a tenth of the figure estimated for Rome under Augustus.[23] It is, of course, impossible to estimate popu-

---

[22] *Reg.* II. 17 and 42 and X. 13. J. Richards, *Consul of God. The Life and Times of Gregory the Great* (London, 1980), 100–2.
[23] Proc. *BG*, III. 20–4. Cf. R. Hodges & D. Whitehouse, *Mohammed, Charlemagne and the Origins of Europe*, (London, 1983), 51.

lation figures in Italy as a whole, for our sources nowhere offer figures – even wild guesses – for either urban or rural contexts. What can perhaps be argued, however, is that if figures like Procopius' 50,000 for the numbers of peasant farmers carried off by plague in the 540s in Picenum are at all accurate, then the persistent warfare and pestilence attested for Italy between 540 and 600 must have had a calamitous effect on the peninsula. In effect, Gregory's woeful words may not be very far from the truth.

Data for the Longobard regions are even less coherent, even though Paul the Deacon provides rare snippets of seemingly relevant information. For the 580s and 590s, and thus in the context of the Franco-Byzantine offensive, Paul claims various natural disasters: floods and fires, parched fields, epidemics, swarms of locusts (handily side-stepping crops in the Trentino) and portents in the sky – but these are nothing out of the ordinary for an early medieval chronicler seeking to highlight his narrative at suitable moments. All we can argue is that the fertile Po plain cannot have gone uncultivated and the Longobards themselves will not have sought to dislodge the native farmers here; indeed, the Longobards' ability to hide away in the towns during the Frankish invasion of 590 speaks of ample food stores to counter long sieges, while the famine and dysentery encountered by the Franks were largely self-inflicted, caused by mindless ravaging of the land.

The Byzantine–Longobard treaties of the early 600s by no means marked the cessation of hostilities and despite a lack of good sources for the period *c*.605–60, following the death of Gregory the Great, we may visualize persistent raids and squabbles between the two sides. Northeast Italy forms the principal theatre of activity, centered on the Duchy of Friuli. Prominent is the Avar incursion of 610–11, with Cividale its target, when once again the Longobards (and natives) took shelter behind town and fort walls.[24] In this episode, however, Cividale fell – or rather, its gates were opened to the enemy – and traces of a destruction level plus the occurrence of Avar-style stirrups would seem to confirm their destructive presence within the walls. Paul devotes a lengthy chapter to the saga of Romilda, widow of the defeated Duke Gisulf and alleged betrayer of Cividale, who, with her family, was dragged off into captivity and humiliated. Several members of her family – including Paul the Deacon's great-grandfather (minus, of course, the impaled Romilda) – escaped back to Friuli to revive the fortunes of the Duchy. The account of the Avar incursion is unusual in that Longobards and Avars otherwise appear to have maintained reasonably good diplomatic ties – though this need not exclude the possibility of periodic small-scale raiding. Noticeably, however, there is nothing archaeological to prove a cultural exchange on any scale between the Avars and the Longobards, even though the nomads appear to have quite readily adopted Gepid and Byzantine stylistic traits in their metal-work.

A greater threat to Longobard Italy was provided by the Slavs to the north: we hear of the Friulian dukes Taso and Cacco establishing a bridgehead across the Alps in Slavic Noricum-Carinthia and obtaining an annual tribute (paid well into the eighth century). Continued Byzantine intrigue is meanwhile recorded in the death of the two dukes at the hands of the general Gregory at Oderzo, and later in the account that Duke Arichis of Benevento's son Aio was made to drink a potion that drove him mad. This affliction little helped Aio when the Slavs, 'with a multitude of ships', raided the Adriatic coasts of Italy, beached at Siponto and killed him in a skirmish.[25]

[24] Paul *HL*, IV. 37.
[25] Paul *HL*, IV. 38, 42 and 44. Aio's death was avenged by the Slavic-speaking Friulian Raduald: *HL*, IV. 46.

New territorial gains were made under the strong Arian king Rothari (636–52), a former duke of Brescia, who secured his position by marrying the widowed queen Gundeberga, daughter of Agilulf. If the sequence of events outlined in the *Origo gentis Langobardorum*, the prologue to Rothari's own law edict, is accurate, then the King's first aggressive move was a rapid and conclusive campaign against the isolated Byzantine coastal province of Liguria. Whereas the Longobard sources provide only bald statements regarding the victory, the Frankish historian Fredegar recounts a particularly savage conquest:

. . . Rothari went with his army and took from the Empire the maritime cities of Genoa, Albenga, Varigotti, Savona, Oderzo, and Luni. He ravaged and destroyed them and left them in flames; and the inhabitants, stripped of their belongings, were seized and condemned to servitude. He ordered that these cities should be known only as villages in future; and he razed their walls to the ground. (IV. 71)[26]

Excavations in such towns as Albenga and Ventimiglia give some support to this description of wholesale devastation; certainly it is the case that Longobard Liguria is totally anonymous until the reign of Liutprand (712–44), when we hear of the foundation of a series of small monasteries.[27]

Soon afterwards Rothari terminated the Byzantine control of Oderzo, which since 568 had hindered Longobard communications in the north-east. Subsequently – though we do not know how much later – the King attacked the Exarchate, then governed by Isaac: the clash of the armies on the River Scultenna resulted in the death of the exarch and 8,000 of his men. That Rothari did not push home his advantage and attack the Byzantine capital may signify that the Longobard army also had

[26] Cf. *Origo*, VI; Paul *HL*, IV. 45.
[27] N. Christie, 'Byzantine Liguria: An Imperial Province Against the Longobards', *Papers of the British School at Rome*, lviii (1990), 229–69.

suffered heavy losses. The Greek epitaph of Isaac survives on a sarcophagus now preserved inside the church of S. Vitale at Ravenna. This speaks generously of his efforts to hold West and East together and of his military prowess – yet it omits mention of his plundering of the Lateran episcopal palace in Rome and his exiling of many of the Roman clergy, all actions which contributed to the growing rift between papal Rome and imperial Ravenna.[28]

Byzantine interest in the peninsula had flagged badly since the treaty of 605, primarily because of serious new pressures on Constantinople from Avars, Bulgars, Persians and, later, Arabs, all of whom threatened the very existence of the Eastern Empire. Inevitably, hardly any support for Italy was forthcoming. In the meantime, imperial officials like Isaac did little to endear themselves to the Italo-Romans: in 615 the exarch John was assassinated, and his successor, Eleutherius, executed various nobles in Ravenna; in 618 Eleutherius set himself up as king, only for his troops to mutiny; and in *c.*640 the *chartularius* Maurice, the man who had prompted Isaac to plunder the Lateran, briefly rebelled against the exarch. In the 650s the exarchs were called upon by Byzantium to force religious reforms on the pope and the Italian clergy, culminating in Pope Martin's arrest and his subsequent exile and death in the Crimea (655).[29] In part to restore Italian allegiance, in 663 the Byzantine emperor Constans II and his army arrived in Rome. Initially Constans duly worshipped in the city's main churches, but soon he outstayed his welcome, stripping Rome of all her bronze and denuding her churches of

---

[28] *Corpus Inscriptorum Graecorum*, IV. 9869; *Lib. Pont.*, *v. Severini*. Interestingly, *Lib. Pont.*, *v. Theodori* reports Isaac dying from a stroke in Ravenna and omits mention of Rothari and the Scultenna bloodbath. Cf. O. Bertolini, 'Il patrizio Isacio esarca d'Italia', in *Scritti scelti di storia medievale*, i (1968), 65–8.

[29] *Lib. Pont.*, *v. Deusdedit – v. Martini*.

their sacred vessels. He fixed his base at Syracuse in Sicily and viciously burdened his subjects for many years with 'intolerable tributes, poll-taxes and ship-money'. Constans was murdered in his bath in 668/9 by Mezezius, who was himself killed, soon after, by units of the Italian army; the booty gathered up by the Emperor fell into Arab hands.[30]

Constans had, in fact, made some attempt to dislodge the Longobard duchy of Benevento before despoiling Rome. After reaching Taranto, on the 'instep' of Italy, his army successfully captured a series of fortified towns, destroyed Luceria, vainly attacked Acerenza and besieged Benevento and its young duke Romuald. There is a possibility that Constans had persuaded the Franks to cause a diversion by invading northern Italy at the same time, although they were defeated near Asti by King Grimoald. Grimoald had himself only just obtained power in a bitter civil war, seeing off the sons of the late king Aripert and their supporters, and needed time to settle affairs in northern Italy. Forceful measures freed his hand and enabled him to assist Benevento. Significantly, Grimoald had been a duke of that city; if this connection had not existed, Constans's expedition may have met with greater success. In the event, Grimoald marched south (despite desertions from the ranks) and forced Constans to raise the siege and retire to Naples. Romuald's victory over the general Saburrus in a skirmish shortly afterwards persuaded Constans to abandon his attempts against the Duchy and to turn instead against the monuments of Rome.[31]

Grimoald's absence prompted a rebellion at Pavia led by Duke Lupus of Cividale, who withdrew to his duchy at the king's return. While we cannot exclude that Lupus was in league with the Byzantines, his earlier raid on

[30] *Lib. Pont.*, *v. Adeodati*; Paul *HL*, V. 11–13.
[31] Paul *HL*, V. 1–10.

imperial Grado suggests rather a personal bid for power. Surprisingly, Grimoald, 'not wanting to stir up civil war amongst the Longobards', summoned the Avars to intervene by raiding the Duchy of Friuli. Not surprisingly, once the Avars had defeated Lupus, captured Cividale and overrun the region they were unwilling to depart. Only a ruse on the part of King Grimoald saved the day and prompted an Avar withdrawal. Recriminations against other disloyal nobles followed, alongside the capture and destruction of the Byzantine town-fortresses of Oderzo and Forlimpopoli.[32]

A fascinating passage in the *Historia Langobardorum* records a group of Bulgars under their duke Alzec requesting lands from Grimoald in return for military service. They may have been ex-Byzantine federates already stationed in Italy, but Grimoald readily welcomed these cavalry troopers and settled them in the badly depopulated territories of Sepino, Boiano, Isernia 'and other towns' in the northern part of the Duchy of Benevento. Paul the Deacon recounts that in his own day these people spoke Latin but still used their native tongue. The settlement of these federates – much in the manner of Roman policy in the late fourth and fifth centuries – will have aided in repopulating the land, in defending the northern and western borders of the Duchy and perhaps also in securing royal Longobard control in central Italy. Archaeological confirmation of the Bulgar presence may in fact come from the localities of Vicenne and Morrione, near Campochiaro, between Boiano and Sepino, where, since 1987, excavations by the Superintendency of Molise have uncovered over 120 burials, including a set of ten horse burials characteristic of nomadic, steppe tribes such as the Avars and Bulgars (pl. 18). The W–E aligned graves, set in rows, are mainly earth-cut, but occasionally contain traces of coffins; male

[32] Paul *HL*, V. 17–21 and 26–8.

Plate 18 The warrior and horse burial at Vicenne, near
Campochiaro in Molise: a descendant perhaps of one of
Duke Alzec's federate troops. (Soprintendenza Archeologica
per i Beni Ambientali Architettonici, Artistici e Storici di
Campobasso.)

burials are equipped with weapons, including arrow-heads and stirrups (both elements rare in Longobard contexts), and personal dress items such as belt-fittings and even earrings. The combined warrior and horse graves are amongst the best-furnished in the cemeteries and should undoubtedly be viewed as housing members of the high-born warrior class. Of particular interest in this respect was the presence in Tomb 33 of a gold ring with an engraved Roman gemstone on the upper face and, in contact with the finger, an inset gold copy of a later seventh-century Beneventan coin. As we will see later, similar seal-rings recovered from the seventh-century Longobard cemetery of Trezzo sull'Adda near Milan have been interpreted as symbols of state office. If so, we could tentatively identify the officer buried in Tomb 33 at Vicenne with the documented duke/*gastald* Alzec or one of his successors. Finds overall represent a mixture of cultural styles and of Avar-Byzantine and Italo-Longobard types, and are datable, on the basis of metalwork and coins, mainly to the period 650–700. We can note that there are indications that the nearby towns were not totally uninhabited by this date: excavations in the forum and theatre at Sepino and in the amphitheatre at Larino have revealed a number of tombs of post-Roman date set into or over the decayed Roman struc-tures but containing few, if any, grave-goods. Although these tombs cannot be closely dated, they do at least indicate that people were still eking out an existence within the shells of the old Roman centres.[33]

Grimoald died in 671 and was buried in his church of S. Ambrogio in Pavia. Although exiled in the coup of 662, Perctarit, after spells of refuge in Gaul and Britain, returned to reclaim the throne. Welcomed with open

[33] Paul *HL*, V. 29. See V. Ceglia, 'Lo scavo della necropoli di Vicenne', *Conoscenze*, iv (1988), 31–48, and various contributions in *Samnium. Arche-ologia del Molise* (exh. cat., ed. by S. Capini & A. di Niro; Rome, 1991), 329–65.

arms (perhaps a sign that Grimoald's reign had been oppressive), Perctarit held the throne for sixteen years, after 679 combining with his son Cunicpert and, according to Paul the Deacon, in that time building a nunnery and church near Pavia and a 'Palace Gate' within the capital. The *Carmen de Synodo Ticinesi* bolsters the image of this glorious phase in the architectural history of Longobard Pavia, and speaks highly of the piousness of recent kings (including Perctarit who had slain unrepenting Jews). Perctarit's reign also marked the signing of a formal peace treaty with Byzantium (680), although this event is only cursorily signalled by the sources. With Cunicpert's accession a sizeable rebellion by Duke Alahis of Brescia threatened extended civil war in northern Italy (689–90), but a swift campaign against opposing towns such as Vicenza and Treviso led to Cunicpert's victory. The Friulian duchy did not join in the fighting; however, soon after this a certain Ansfrit, Count of Ragogna, a fort near the ducal capital, removed the duke Rodoald and threatened to seize the kingdom, but he perished before achieving his aim. With the rebel's death, Cunicpert installed a temporary governor or *loci servator*.[34] All these events distracted the King from the southern Longobard duchies, which began to pursue more autonomous courses: Benevento, in particular, extended its territory at Byzantine expense, occupying the vital southeastern ports of Taranto and Brindisi, and thereby limiting the Greeks to the very heel of Italy, centred on Otranto; subsequently, the dukes pushed northwestwards into Campania, capturing forts at Arce, Arpino and Sora, thus driving a wedge between Rome and Naples and presaging the further decay of imperial lands in the eighth century.[35]

[34] Paul *HL*, V. 38–41 and VI. 3.
[35] Paul *HL*, VI. 1 and 27.

Longobard Revival and Demise, AD 700–780

In the *Historia Langobardorum*, eclipses, plague, omens, the eruption of Mount Vesuvius, Saracen victories in Africa, civil war in Byzantium and the resurrection of Frankish rule all precede a period of bitter strife in the Longobard kingdom, with a succession of minor kings, usurpers, rebel dukes and internecine warfare within duchies. That the Kingdom survived was due to the emergence of an aggressive new king, Liutprand (712–44), who, after establishing his own position, began to move against the Byzantine exarchate: in the 720s he attacked Ravenna, destroying Classe, and occupied an array of powerful forts, including Bologna and Osimo; moves against Rome included the temporary capture of Sutri. Further gains were made in the Pentapolis in the later 730s.[36] Still Byzantium did nothing to improve its own standing in Italy: in 726 the Emperor Leo promulgated an Empire-wide ban against the worship of icons or images of Christ and the saints (Iconoclasm), creating much distress in Italy (on both Byzantine and Longobard soil), where the rite of icon adoration was most popular. An attempt by the exarch Paul to impose the imperial ban by ejecting the pope was, in fact, countered by Longobards, mainly Tuscans and Spoletans, near Rome. Certainly, from this time on the relationship between Rome and the Longobards becomes quite complex and fluid, partly as a result of anti-imperial sentiment and partly through the variable aims of Longobard duchies such as Spoleto and Benevento. King Liutprand himself is seen as a deadly foe, however, although his withdrawal from Sutri and the donation of the Cottian Alps to the Roman Church indicates some diplomatic manoeuvring. Liutprand attempted to counter Longobard independence in

[36] Paul *HL*, VI. 5–38.

the south *c.*740 by dispossessing Thransamund of Spoleto and installing his nephew Gregory at Benevento. Thransamund, using Roman help, regained his duchy and attacked the King's forces in the Pentapolis; Liutprand responded by recapturing Spoleto, sending the rebellious duke to a monastery, installing another nephew, Agiprand, and then occupying Benevento, which had fallen into the hands of one Godescalcus – the latter was soon killed, but his wife fled to Constantinople; yet another royal nephew, Gisulf, took over the running of the Beneventan duchy.[37]

The failure of the alliance with Spoleto, the territorial isolation of the Exarchate, and religious alienation from Constantinople forced Rome to look elsewhere for succour. The Franks were now once more a powerfully organized nation and had successfully prevented – unlike Byzantium – Arab inroads; spiritual ties already existed between the Catholic Frankish court and Rome and the popes eagerly pursued these. Liutprand, however, had maintained a good alliance with the Franks and had even assisted in removing Saracen troops from Provence in 739. The King's death in 744 probably saw a flurry of embassies from Rome to Francia, leading eventually in 752 to papal recognition of the Carolingian dynasty as the true kings of Francia.[38]

Paul the Deacon's narrative terminates with the end of Liutprand's reign and avoids telling of the Kingdom's final decades. Nevertheless, a sufficient number of ninth- and tenth-century *Continuationes* from (former) Longobard zones exist, and these, in addition to details furnished by Roman, Ravennate and Frankish sources, allow for a reasonably coherent picture of the period 750–80. These reveal the maintenance of a hostile policy under the Longobard King Ratchis, formerly Duke of

---

[37] Paul *HL*, VI. 49 and 55–8.
[38] Paul *HL*, VI. 53–4; Einhard *V. Car.*, 3.

Friuli, who assailed both the Exarchate and the Duchy of Rome (pl. 19). His laws, issued in 746, echo those of Liutprand in terms of seeking to strengthen royal power against the dukes and *gastalds* who controlled towns, forts and lands within the kingdom; Ratchis is also shown as establishing tighter security controls along the frontiers, primarily against Francia – a sure reflection of the growing fear of a Romano-Frankish alliance. Ratchis was retired in 749 to the monastery of Montecassino and replaced by the ambitious Aistulf. In his own laws Aistulf stressed the Longobards' military obligations, presum-

Plate 19 The Altar of Ratchis, c.745. (Museo Cristiano, Cividale.)

ably hoping to build up army numbers against the imminent Frankish threat. Yet he pushed on with plans of total conquest in Italy: the Duchy of Spoleto, again part of the *Regnum*, was deprived of its duke; Ravenna, the final official Byzantine stronghold in the north, was occupied and briefly made the Longobard capital; in 752 Aistulf pushed against Rome and captured a series of border fortresses. When negotiations with the 'hated' Longobard king broke down, Pope Stephan II appealed to the Frankish king Peppin III: in 754 the Carolingians invaded, defeated Aistulf in battle in the Susa valley and forced terms on him, in particular requiring him to cede the Exarchate to Rome.[39] A repeat performance was needed in 756 when Aistulf again threatened Rome.

In that same year Aistulf died, and Ratchis briefly returned to Pavia – perhaps against his wishes. The *dux* of Tuscia, Desiderius, certainly made him regret the move by deposing him in 757. Since neither the Pope nor the Franks followed up the successes of 754–6, Desiderius was able to bide his time and build up his kingdom's internal resources, notably through securing Spoletan and Beneventan allegiance. Yet, despite Peppin's death and disputed successions both in Francia and in Rome in 768–9, Desiderius made no immediate move. His daughter was in fact married to Charles (Charlemagne) in 770, and this may well have smoothed over relations with Carolingian France. However, by the end of 771 the Frankish king had rejected Desiderius' daughter, a move which may have enraged the Longobard monarch, since in 772 he marched on Rome. A new man, Hadrian, now occupied the papal throne: although wise and resourceful, and much akin to Pope Gregory the Great in terms of organizational abilities and piousness, he lacked the military logistics to repulse Desiderius, and he, too, was forced to turn to Francia. Charlemagne had renewed the

[39] Einhard, *V. Car.*, 6; Fredegar, *Cont.* 37; Agnellus, *liber pontificalis*, 155, 159.

military vigour and ambitions of the Franks and brought
economic stability and a desire for expansion to his
united kingdom; Italy offered itself as a most tempting
prize, and Charlemagne undoubtedly knew from his
uncle's previous victories over the Alps of the relative
weakness of the Longobard army and of the strong de-
pendence of papal Rome on his nation for her survival.
Charlemagne hesitated briefly, but soon enough crossed
the Alps, defeating some lack-lustre Longobard border
troops before advancing into the Po plain and besieging
first Pavia and then Verona (773–4). The Monk of St
Gall, in the 880s, provides a powerful visual image of an
iron-clad Frankish king and his iron-clad army marching
ominously and menacingly on Pavia, scaring the Longobards half to death. Resistance overall was short-lived:
the Longobard strongholds caved in, and in June 774
Desiderius surrendered and was promptly exiled.[40]

Despite insurrections in Friuli, northern Italy lay
securely in Charlemagne's hands and he duly annexed it
as a sub-kingdom. Charlemagne's policy was to allow
Longobard dukes – if willing to be loyal – to retain their
posts, and only to replace them with Frankish functionaries at their death; this allowed for a gradual integration
with the Frankish state with minimal disruption to the
existing set-up. There was some disruption even so, notably in the flight of a number of Longobards south to
Benevento, and in hardship in the north created by the
Frankish army's depredations. Charlemagne's own visits
to Italy were infrequent, and there is little to show an
influx of northerners into the new Kingdom of Italy.
Even later on in the ninth century, when Frankish kings
were actually based in northern Italy, the physical and
political impact of the Carolingians remained restricted,
primarily owing to the recurrence of internal divisions
within the Carolingian realm. As we shall see, it is only

[40] Notker, II. 15–17; Einhard *V. Car.*, 6; Paul, *Pauli continuatio tertia*,
52–3; Agnellus, *Liber pontificalis*, 160.

on the cultural plane that Carolingian influence is evident, and then primarily only for the period up to *c*.830.

Against an ever weakening imperial hold in Italy the Longobard kings had long had the edge. In military terms the two sides were little different,[41] but geographically the Longobard territories possessed the better economic back-up, while the Byzantines more than felt the pinch once the Arabs had extended their control throughout much of the Mediterranean. In theory, the Longobards were still a martial society, but a settled existence within towns in Italy, Christianization, intermarriage with native Italians and an overall diminishment of military threats had led to a decline in standards and in centralized administration; at the same time many nobles had become unwilling to bear arms – witness Ratchis's and Aistulf's laws and the record that several aristocrats made their wills before joining Aistulf's army in the Susa Valley in 754. The strength and the resilience that had enabled the Longobards to counter repeated Franco- Byzantine invasions and campaigns between 580 and 590, and to conquer Ravenna and threaten the capture of Rome after 720, were lacking by the mid-eighth century. If Rome had been conquered, a Carolingian invasion would undoubtedly have followed, and the results would have been the same; if it had been anyone other than Charlemagne, things may have come out differently; but such speculation is, of course, pointless.

In any event, an independent Longobard state did survive the northern kingdom's fall. Desiderius had made his son-in-law Arichis II duke of Benevento early on in his reign, and Arichis, by minting his own gold currency, issuing his own laws and declaring himself prince after 774, clearly viewed himself as an autonomous ruler, if

---

[41] Cf. Brown, *Gentlemen and Officers*, 82–101; N. Christie, 'Longobard Weaponry and Warfare, A.D. 1–800', *Journal of Roman Military Equipment Studies*, ii (1991), 9–20.

not necessarily the rightful heir to *Langobardia*. Hadrian I encouraged Charlemagne to intervene in the south, and his appeals culminated in an invasion in 787. In the same year Arichis died, and his son and heir Grimoald was taken hostage. Grimoald was, nonetheless, employed to defeat a Byzantine task force called in by Arichis before his death and headed by Desiderius's son Adelchis. Afterwards, Charlemagne chose to install Grimoald as duke: as time went on Grimoald III's allegiance to the Franks became less than nominal, but distractions elsewhere, notably in Saxony and Hungary, prevented further, concerted Carolingian intervention. The final chapter will follow the fate of Longobard Benevento.

4

Society and Economy

The half century of Ostrogothic rule in Italy (489–535) was perceived by contemporaries as a virtual golden age, a period of prosperity and peace contrasting strongly with the bloody machinations that had marked the last decades of Roman rule. Success was due, primarily, to the long authoritative reign of Theoderic, his diplomacy, his choice of allies and in particular his use of skilled Roman administrators. The Ostrogoths were a dominant minority, dependent on the passive support of the vast native Italian population: whilst keen to keep Ostrogothic martial values and mores distinct, Theoderic clearly looked up to and thus sought to maintain the complex Roman civilian infrastructure. The literary output of his minister Cassiodorus Senator, the evidence of traded manufactures from across the Mediterranean and the apparent vitality of urban and rural life all testify to the construction of a successful Romano-Gothic state edifice. Its foundations were fragile, however, and – even before the bonding force of Theoderic disappeared in 526 – Ostrogothic–Roman hostilities had begun to surface, with the imprisonment of such prominent Roman officials as Boethius prompting preliminary appeals by the Romans to Constantinople. With the Byzantine threat looming large, the Ostrogothic nobility rejected over-Romanized royals such as Amalasuntha and Theodahad; as war broke and continued 'every new king henceforth seemed more and more obviously a rough untutored barbarian', and numerous outrages were perpetrated against the Roman nobility.[1]

Too often the Byzantine reconquest is viewed as a regeneration of Roman society, and imperial Italy is contrasted with the bleak militaristic regime of the Longobards. Yet the disastrously prolonged Gothic War and the rapaciousness of Byzantine tax-collectors allowed little scope for a prosperous Italy. The Longobard invasion set the seal on this: resources were necessarily diverted to aid the war effort, civilian offices were made subordinate to the military, and insecurity emptied the fields. The scattered nature of the imperial territories after *c.*590 hindered the effectiveness of an already weak and divided central authority. Continued neglect led to increased militarization of society and to the localization of power, with clergy and military coming to vie for supremacy both within towns and outside.[2] The seeds of feudalism were thus already being sown in seventh- and eighth-century Italy. But how far does this picture differ from that of the Longobard areas? How easily did Longobard society adapt to the residual complexities of urbanism in Italy? And to what degree did the Longobards seek to shield their ethnic identity from the inevitable flow of *romanitas*?

The Longobard Laws and the Evolution of Longobard Society

Like the Ostrogoths before them, the Longobards, in their occupation of Pannonia, had come face to face with many pockets of Romanized population, based mainly in strongly walled centres. We have shown how it is difficult to define the conqueror–conquered relationship in

---

[1] Wickham, *Early Medieval Italy*, 24. Ostrogothic rule in Italy: *ibid.*, 21–5; Collins, *Early Medieval Europe*, 99–104, 110–13, 121–2.
[2] See Brown, *Gentlemen and Officers*.

the absence of detailed urban excavation, although the
close proximity of Longobard cemeteries to such
'Roman' sites probably signifies direct supervision of
native activities. The Pannonian cemeteries overall reveal
little in terms of immediate Roman cultural influences,
and it is unlikely anyway that the local population had
much to offer – instead, Longobard funerary rites, dress
styles and weaponry lean westwards, towards the Franco-
Thuringian orbit, rather than southwards towards the
Mediterranean. But the increased involvement of the
Longobards with Byzantium, first as nominal allies and
subsequently as mercenaries, fighting in Italy and even in
the East, must have introduced subtle changes, particularly through their receipt of sizeable subsidies of Byzantine gold, usually in the shape of coin, which was not
used as money, but to denote wealth and status amongst
the elite. These influences may well have instigated a
redefinition of Longobard social rankings, much in the
same way as early Germanic tribes close to the Rhine
limes were affected by Roman commercial contacts in the
first centuries AD. Various Longobard necropoleis in
Hungary reveal evidence of planning of plots, perhaps
for use by extended family groups. Within these there is
a fairly consistent hierarchy of grave-finds, which materially implies social stratification, clearest at the top and
bottom of the scale. Correlation is often made between
Pannonian burial groupings, defined by associated weapon finds, and later Italian social divisions as defined by
mid-eighth-century law codes,[3] but how plausible is this
argument? No real clues can be extracted from the *Historia Langobardorum*: Paul the Deacon confines himself
to the leading royal, ducal and religious protagonists,
only rarely touching upon the bit players. His most useful contribution is his definition (II. 9) of *fara* as a family
or kin group in the context of Gisulf's installation as

[3] Bóna, *Dawn of the Dark Ages*, 73–82.

Duke of Friuli and his selection of the best *farae* to settle
and defend the territory. In fact, a near contemporary to
the invasion of 569, writing in Avenches, speaks of Longobards occupying Italy in *farae*. Here at least we glean
something of Longobard invasion-period military and social organization. The incidence of place-names in Italy
derived from the term *fara* may, thereby, represent col-
onies of such kin groups in strategic points. Logically, we
should envisage a like mode of settlement for Pannonia –
but there the uprooting of population in 568 seems to have
removed all toponymical trace of the Longobards. The
fact that Paul the Deacon needs to translate the term *fara*
indicates that he is referring to an old, probably long
defunct Germanic institution. Indeed the eighth-century
Longobard laws omit any mention of the *fara*, while the
mid-seventh-century Edict of Rothari alludes to it just
once (Roth. 177). In this instance royal permission is
required for any possible transfer of a *fara* from one duchy
to another: this implies that such groups were by then
fairly static. In the conquest years dukes and their *farae*
had ranged far and wide, maintaining military mobility;
but clearly peace after 605 led to more stable settlement
patterns, and so the *farae*, as military groupings or units,
lost their prominence. This is not to say that there was a
concomitant demilitarization of the Longobard people,
for, as we have seen, the kings Rothari, Grimoald, Liutprand and others continued to fight with success against
the Byzantines; rather it is the case that the strengthening
of royal power in the seventh century sought to counter
fratricidal conflict within the Kingdom through closer
supervision of the dukes and their retinues.

It is the Longobard law codes that provide by far the
most comprehensive source of information regarding the
structure and evolution of Longobard society in Italy.[4]

---

[4] Translation and commentary by K. Fischer Drew, *The Lombard Laws*
(Philadelphia, PA, 1973); cf. A. Cavanna, 'Diritto e società nei regni ostrogoto e longobardo' in *Magistra Barbaritas*, 351–79.

These were issued in Latin between AD 643 and 755, the bulk of the titles being promulgated by Rothari in 643 (388 laws) and by Liutprand (713–35) throughout his reign (153 titles); in between, nine were issued under Grimoald (668), and the last laws were passed by Ratchis in 745–6 and Aistulf in 750 and 755 (although the independent princes of Benevento in the south issued supplementary laws after 774). Rothari's Edict was offered as a near complete code of law, being arranged in a roughly systematic manner; the later laws were mainly gap pluggers or updatings and are rarely ordered. Rothari's code admits to being a revision of primitive Longobard oral laws, prompted by over 70 years of settlement within Italy. Title 386 states that:

With the favour of God and with the greatest care and most careful scrutiny, obtained by heavenly favour, after seeking out and finding the laws of our fathers which were not written down, and with the equal counsel and consent of our most important judges and with the rest of our most happy nation [*exercitus*] assisting, we have established the present lawbook containing those provisions which are useful for the common good of all people. We have ordered these laws to be written down on this parchment, thus preserving them in this edict so that those things which, with divine aid, we have been able to recapture through careful investigation of the old laws of the Longobards known either to ourself or the old men of the nation, we have put down in this lawbook. Issued and confirmed by the formal procedure [*gairethinx*] according to the usage of our nation, let this be strong and stable law ... (Fisher Drew 1973)

The evolution of Longobard state and society is neatly revealed in the changing character of the various royal prologues: under Rothari, the king requires the deliberation and sanction of the judges and the assembly; and, as an Arian, Rothari – perhaps for diplomatic reasons – only fleetingly refers to the aid of God. By contrast, in 713, Liutprand has a totally different pitch: 'This Catholic

Christian prince has been influenced to promulgate these laws and to judge wisely not by his own foresight but through the wisdom and inspiration of God: he has conceived [these laws] in his heart, studied them in his mind, and happily fulfilled them in his word' (Fisher Drew 1973). He is backed up in his task by the judges of northern Italy and by his sworn followers (*fideles*) who have given their approval to the King (Prologue, AD 726). Divine inspiration similarly aids Ratchis and Aistulf in their provision of new titles, some of which go against the judges themselves. Here, therefore, the laws begin to offer a guide to major social changes. The eighth-century laws in particular highlight the progressive breakdown of royal control within the kingdom, with dukes, *gastalds* and lords taking increasingly independent stances or at least failing to adhere to written codes of conduct – kings, dukes and lords alike found that they needed retinues of sworn followers (*fideles* or *gasindii*) in order to maintain their positions (Ratchis 1, 9, 10, 13–14). This is true even under Liutprand, though his long reign briefly stemmed the break-up of central authority (cf. Liut. 35, 59). Certainly the laws of Ratchis and Aistulf demonstrate a high level of insecurity – within the palace, within duchies, on the frontiers and in the army – a prelude to the conflict with the Franks.

By contrast, Rothari's laws depict a relatively harmonious kingdom, bar instances of personal injury and property infringements. Surprisingly, despite its scope, the Edict provides a somewhat restricted picture of the contemporary political scene and its institutions and allows for only a vague understanding of the make-up of Longobard society. At the top of the hierarchy stood the king and his court, based in Pavia. State offences – rebellion, collusion with the enemy, spying – met with capital punishment, while disturbances in the presence of, near or against the king met with death or onerous fines (Rothari 1–7, 9, 17–18). Of the court, nothing is said except for the presence of notaries and, later on, of a chancellor and cellarer (Ratchis 12). The king himself appears as a rather shadowy figure, relying on his judges to mete out justice but occasionally listening to appeals; this remains true into the eighth century, although Ratchis (1, 2, 11) had to legislate against the by-passing of local judges ('because we cannot attend any celebration or ride anywhere without being besieged by the appeals of many men'), whilst simultaneously demanding that the judges themselves held court and saw that their subordinates did their duty too. These judges comprised town- or fort-based dukes (the old aristocratic clan chiefs) and *gastalds* (royal appointees). The two often resided in adjoining palaces, and both oversaw cases relating to their administrative district (*civitas* or *iudiciaria*), and possessed combined military and civil powers. By the eighth century the *gastalds* had displaced the dukes in all but the larger ducal centres (e.g. Cividale, Trento, Brescia and Spoleto) – dukes are not mentioned in the laws of Liutprand. Under Rothari the struggle between ducal and royal authority was already under way: the dukes are still seen as army commanders and thus exercise military justice over the soldiers (Rothari 6, 20–2), but appeal could be made to the *gastald* (23–4). Fines, however, were paid both to the king and to the duke. How well this dual system of judicial administration functioned is unclear, but, despite the progressive ousting of the dukes, the king merely replaced one locally powerful figure with another by enhancing the powers of the *gastalds*, who, by Ratchis' time at least, paid as little heed to the king as the dukes had once done (Liut. 59). Local uprisings against judges (Liut. 35; Ratchis 10) and the gathering of sworn bands of followers (*gasindii*) around the person of the judge point to oppression and distrust (Ratchis 11, 14). Rebellions by dukes such as Lupus of Cividale and Alahis of Trento in the second half of the seventh century, although rarely successful, denote armed opposition to royal interventions in the more powerful duchies. Royal strength within these duchies is documented in the early eighth century, when Duke Corvulus of Cividale, after offending the King, was blinded and replaced by Pemmo, who was more amenable and 'useful to the kingdom' – until removed by Liutprand.[5] Royal authority did not extend consistently in the south: though the duchies of Spoleto and Benevento adopted the system of appointing *gastalds* for local administration, these officials were subject to the dukes and not to the king.

All these judges were powerful land-owners, and office-holding brought with it grants of royal land – though it is unclear whether this returned to royal control at the official's death (Roth. 375; Liut. 59). Nor is it clear whether these posts were fixed-term appointments. The king stepped in to remove rebellious or inefficient dukes and judges, but this does not exclude the possibility of life-long offices (Ratchis 1). While in the case of dukes it is possible to trace some dynastic lines, clearest in Cividale, our documentary sources do not yet reveal hereditary lines of *gastalds*. Such appointments were no doubt the preserve of the Longobard nobility, but feuds, disfavour and shifting royal patronage all appear to have made for a certain level of fluidity in Longobard power politics.

The judges supervised a series of lesser officials within their designated districts. Top of the ladder was the *sculdahis*, administering justice over a *sculdascia* (roughly equivalent to a parish) and dealing with a variety of cases such as violation of graves, disturbances in churches and sorcery (Roth. 15, 35; Liut. 85). Below the

---

[5] Lupus: Paul *HL*, IV. 18; Alahis: *HL*, IV. 36–41; Corvulus: *HL*, VI. 25; Pemmo: *HL*, VI. 26 and 51. Interesting is *HL*, VI, 3 where Rodoald of Cividale is ousted by Ansfrit, commander of a nearby fort, but 'without the king's agreement'. On dukes and *gastalds* see Fischer Drew, *Lombard Laws*, 23–4; Wickham, *Early Medieval Italy*, 41–2.

sculdahis we find reference to the *saltarius* or forester and the *deganus*, both active in policing village territories (Liut. 44, 85), while vaguer roles are offered to the, most likely, town-based *centenarii* ('hundred-men') and *locopositi* ('local officials') (Ratchis 1; Liut. 96). Most of these men brought local disputes to the attention of the *sculdahis*, of the judge or even of the king himself.[6] Again we can only guess at the efficiency of this network of minor public officials, none of whom are noted in the earlier laws of Rothari.

Clearer distinctions are made amongst individuals as members of classes. The status of the freeman or freewoman was dominant, who must have been viewed, at least initially, as of 'pure' Longobard stock. Rothari's laws show how injuries, insults or damage inflicted on the person or the property of this class resulted in the highest tariff of penalties, assessed on the basis of the *wergeld* – a monetary value fixed to a person's life according to rank (*in angargathungi*). Ranking occurred even within the freeman class: Liutprand, title 62, states that custom dictated that lesser freemen should have a *wergeld* of 150 *solidi* and first class freemen one of 300 *solidi*. Here the distinction is probably based on wealth in terms of property (Aistulf 2). A member of a lord's or the king's retinue (*gasindii*), meanwhile, held a minimum value of 200 *solidi* 'because he serves us' and a maximum of 300. The murder of a freeman entailed loss of property and payment of the *wergeld*, or if the murderer lacked the means to pay, slavery to pay off the debt (Liut. 20; Roth. 11, 14). However, the murder of a lord (*dominus*) – presumably a duke, *gastald* or count – meant execution (Roth. 13). Rothari's laws impose massive fines of 900 *solidi* in certain homicide cases and for violation of graves (13–15). Freewomen, although legally totally dependent on husbands or male kin, appear well protected:

[6] Fischer Drew, *Lombard Laws*, 23, 26; Wickham, *Early Medieval Italy*, 42.

huge fines were imposed in cases of abduction or rape (900 *solidi*) and of murder (1200 *solidi*) – though a woman who killed her husband was herself automatically killed (Roth. 186, 191, 200–1, 203). In contrast, rape of half-free, freedwomen and female slaves merited fines of just 20–40 *solidi* (Roth. 205–7).

The freeman class formed the backbone of the Longobard army. Their role is reflected in their name, with the Latin *exercitalis* (soldier) and the German *arimannus* (army man) being used interchangeably with freeman (*liber homo*); the Longobard nation as a whole was termed *exercitus* (army). Military service was both a privilege and a duty and was carried out at the summons of either the duke or the king. But at the time of Rothari's laws there are already a few signs of unwillingness to serve in the time-honoured Longobard way (e.g. 20–2) and harsh justice is meted out to rebellious or cowardly troopers (Rothari 3–7). In the earlier eighth century Liutprand barely mentions military matters, perhaps reflecting the overall stability of the Kingdom. By contrast, Ratchis (4) and Aistulf (2, 3) are forced to remind freemen of their responsibilities:

We decree that every freeman [*arimannus*] should carry a shield and lance for himself when he rides out with his judge. And when he comes to the palace with his judge, he shall be likewise equipped. We order this to be done so because the times are uncertain and it cannot be known what orders he will receive from us or where they will be asked to ride. (Fisher Drew 1973)

Aistulf spells out the equipment required of each man: wealthy *arimanni* should have horses, mailcoat, shield and lance; lesser freemen at least a horse, shield and lance; those without horses at least a shield, bow and arrows. Merchants too are told to arm themselves. Men may have been happy to render service to their judges as *gasindii*, but on a national level the kings found it hard to muster a full mobilization of troops. Wickham has shown how gifts of land from king to judges to lesser officials initially came with appointment to a post; but how, over time, such land-giving became the prime means of securing loyalty, reinforced by oath, as illustrated in the growing use of retinues. Yet it was far easier for the various lords to secure firm local and territorial roots than for the king to harness the ambitions of these scattered judges.[7] The *arimanni* nonetheless retained public responsibilities and overall allegiance to the state, and this relationship was maintained even under the Carolingians after 774, disappearing only as state control weakened and lordly powers intensified.

The laws of both Rothari and Liutprand testify to the firm land base of the freemen, describing the often complicated means of inheritance between male heirs and other relatives (Roth. 153–75, 181–2); disputes over damage to or theft of property, property markers and livestock (Roth. 236–41, 285–302, 309–51; Liut. 45–7, 115–16); the use of slaves, oxen or sheep as pledges (Roth. 249–52); and the welfare of farm-workers (Roth. 130–7). Various levels of dependants existed, composed chiefly of residual Germanic peoples conquered and incorporated by the Longobards before 568, notably, Rugi, Heruls and Suevi. Those with most rights were the half-free or *aldii*, with a *wergeld* set at 60 *solidi*. Marriages could occur between freeman and *aldia* and freewoman and *aldius*, often with the status of the latter partner being raised to allow the children to become legitimate and free; also, *aldii* could marry slaves, but here children tended to assume the lowlier status (Roth. 216–19). Under Rothari *aldii* are equated with household slaves (*servi ministeriales*), who were 'taught, nourished and trained in the home' (Rothari 76–102). Duties are not stated, although King Grimoald's law 1 implies that an *aldius* held his own property: *aldii* may

---

[7] Wickham, *Early Medieval Italy*, 131–7.

have served as heads of household staff, as farm over-
seers and as agents for their lord. Tenant slaves (*servi
massarii*) likewise held plots of land, which they farmed
for their master, employing subordinate field slaves. Ox
ploughmen, swine-, cattle-, goat- and ox-herders could
also possess houses on their lord's land and oversee
subordinates (Roth. 131–7). Slaves possessed no rights
and were the property of the lord, who received the
payment of any fines if the slave was abused by others;
yet there is ample evidence for the manumission of slaves
to dependent free or half-free status (Roth. 224). Despite
this, it is noteworthy that the law concerning the striking
of a pregnant slave that resulted in miscarriage or death
is listed in Rothari's Edict amongst laws on animals
(334). The treatment of slaves obviously will have varied
greatly, and laws dealing with the flight of slaves, and
even seditious acts by gangs of field slaves, indicate a
ready level of discontent (Roth. 269–80; Liut. 44, 143).

References to Romans and non-Longobards are surprisingly rare. Liutprand 127 says Longobard women
who marry Romans will live by Roman law. This does
not signify moving outside of Longobard territory, but
rather implies that 'Romans' lived side by side with the
Longobards. A large percentage of the peasant population in Longobard lands must have comprised native
Italians, for, unlike the Roman high nobility, the
native small farmers had little to lose by staying put and
in fact gained because the Longobards did not tax as
heavily as the Byzantines. Accordingly, we can assume a
coexistence of Roman and Longobard law codes: this
may have separated the two peoples, at least nominally,
but intermarriage was clearly taking place, and as we will
see, in archaeological terms, Longobard tomb-finds show
a progressive uptake of 'Italian' traits.[8] Furthermore, by

---

[8] Cf. M. Brozzi, *La popolazione romana nel Friuli longobardo (VI–VII
sec.)*, Publicationi della Deputazione di Storia Patria per il Friuli, xix (Udine,

this date the Longobards were predominantly Catholic, thus rid of another barrier between themselves and the Italians. Strikingly, the Longobard laws encompass many Roman legal norms, for example in reference to property owning. This in itself suggests the survival of Roman farmers and land management. Likewise, for the Longobards to occupy Roman urban centres must have required the survival and maintenance of Roman infra-structures.[9] Longobard law was written in Latin for an Italianized Longobard population to understand and for Longobardized Italians to recognize. Written Roman law was not modified after the *Codex Justinianus* of the 540s but must have evolved, at least verbally, to face the new circumstances of Longobard rule – there was much give and take, and in Longobard territories we can prob-ably assume that most 'Romans' followed Longobard law.

Some elements of this Longobard acculturization pro-cess have already been noted, notably the restricted mobility of the *fara* and reduced individual military co-operation. Further signs include the use of monetary reckoning in the evaluation of the *wergeld* and fines assessed from this, which presupposes the availability and circulation of coin – a situation that would have been largely alien to the Longobards before the end of the sixth century, and thus an indication that a more primitive means of reckoning was being replaced. The alternative to fines was the blood-feud (*faida*), but it is clear from Rothari's Edict that the King viewed this feud as disruptive to the fabric of the new, more civilized Longobard state; obviously, he was seeking to break

1989); C. La Rocca Hudson & P. Hudson, 'Riflessi della migrazione longo-barda sull'insediamento rurale e urbano in Italia settentrionale', in R. Fran-covich (ed.), *Archeologia e Storia del Medioevo Italiano*, Studi nuova Italia scientifica archeologia, iii (Rome, 1987), 29–38.

[9] Wickham, *Early Medieval Italy*, 64–71; Cavanna, 'Diritto e società . . .' in *Magistra Barbaritas*, 362–4.

from the traditional means of seeking justice, though without being able to legislate directly against it (Roth. 45). This seems no easy task, and the large number of laws dealing with personal injuries and affronts (Roth. 45–138, 236–41, 285–302) suggests that disputes and retribution were generally settled physically: Rothari details at length the fines applicable to crimes ranging from killing a person to physical mutilation (from eyes to teeth to arms down to little toes) and to intrusion, disturbance or breakage of personal property or space. Tariffs were dependent on the status of the aggrieved: mutilation of a man's big toe carried a fine of 16 *solidi* if the man was a freeman, 4 *solidi* in the case of an *aldius* and 2 *solidi* for a field-hand. Rothari 377 certainly implies that quite a few one-eyed freemen and slaves were hobbling around the kingdom in the mid-seventh century. The lack of follow-up by Liutprand to these injury laws may, however, indicate that Rothari's stiff penalties had had the desired effect and far fewer mutilated members of the Longobard race were about in his day.

'Civilizing' tendencies are witnessed also in the need for the numerous legal modifications issued under Liutprand, testifying to an increasing complexity in Longobard society. A useful example in this respect is the constant insertion of new titles relating to the possibilities of property inheritance by women. As noted above, in Rothari's code it is made abundantly clear that the freewoman played a quite subordinate role, possessing no legal competence and being constantly under male protection (of father, husband or guardian) and unable to inherit property even if male heirs were lacking (Roth. 204). In marriages, contracts were drawn up between father and groom and the groom made a payment (*meta*) for the transfer of legal authority; the father then provided a gift (*faderfio*) at the ceremony, and the morning after, in appreciation of pre-marital virginity, the groom gave the bride a gift (*morgengab*), often consisting of property (Roth. 178, 181–4). An alternative type of marriage was one where no *meta* was paid, and the woman remained under her father's legal control. Girls could be married off after they reached the age of 12 (Liut. 12); for boys the age of legal responsibility had risen to 18 under Liutprand, from 12 under Rothari (Roth. 155; Liut. 19, 117).[10] A wife's property was, however, inalienable and could not be broken up without her permission. Also, a freewoman's *wergeld* was the same as that of a freeman – though if injuries were inflicted on a freewoman, any fines would be paid not to her but to her legal guardian (Roth. 205–10). Come the eighth century, Liutprand's first round of laws allows for the inheritance of property by daughters 'as if they were legitimate sons', but only in the absence of any legitimate male heirs; not long after we see how daughters may inherit some property even when male heirs exist (Liut. 102) and how women become able to sell their property or to pass some on to the Church (Liut. 22, 29, 101). The woman's material and legal position nonetheless remained limited, and it is no surprise to hear of women taking vows to join nunneries (Liut. 30, 76, 100–1).

A further aspect to note is the growth in literacy, or rather in the use of the written word in daily life (pl. 20). In AD 643 the notary Answald is credited with the written compilation and distribution under seal of Rothari's Edict from the palace at Pavia (Roth. 388). From the outset of Longobard settlement in Italy churchmen, ambassadors and judges had all attended the king's court; under Agilulf we know of the Italian bishop Secundus of Trento, who composed a short *History*, and we have extant correspondence between king and Byzantine emperor and between queen and pope; early on interpreters, diplomats and scribes were essential. It is impossible to

---

[10] The earlier age of 12 for male adulthood may have been linked to the weapon-bearing age of the Longobard youth. If so, this too marks a change from primitive mentality.

Plate 20 Longobard graffiti on one of the columns of the church of SS. Felice e Fortunato in Vicenza.

assess how far literacy extended beyond the court – indeed we cannot even be certain that the kings were literate. Rothari's Edict in size and scope implies a fairly competent set of judges and support staff able to read and interpret the law and to record cases. The Italian population was long used to the concept of written documentation regarding transactions of property, and there are signs of this rubbing off on the Longobards: Rothari 227 allows for the existence of sale or lease documents, but in their absence relies on the traditional method of oath-giving. Pledges are frequent (Roth. 245–52) in cases of debt, but with no apparent back-up by documentation. Yet title 243 does indicate that paper was used: 'he who forges a charter or other kind of document shall have his hand cut off'. By Liutprand's reign, charters, wills and forgeries are commonplace and attest a healthy range of legal disputes, primarily concerning property sale and inheritance (Liut. 22, 29, 54, 91, 115, 116). Title 91 states:

In the case of scribes we decree that those who prepare charters should write them either according to the law of the Longobards – which is well known to be open to all – or according to that of the Romans; they shall not do otherwise than is contained in these laws and they shall not write contrary to the law of the Longobards or of the Romans. If they do not know how to do this, let them ask others, and if they cannot know such laws fully, they should not write such charters. He who presumes to do otherwise shall pay his *wergeld* as composition. (Fisher Drew 1973)

The mid-eighth-century crisis brought with it strict border control with letters bearing the royal seal required for natives wanting to leave Longobard soil or for merchants trading within the kingdom, while passports were issued to pilgrims travelling through *Langobardia* to Rome (Ratchis 13; Aistulf 5, 6). Here of course the kings were reliant on the scrutiny and goodwill of their judges in ensuring their security.

Though we can identify fairly easily the intrusion of 'civilizing' trends within Longobard law through long-term settlement in Italy, it is much harder to pin down secure pre-invasion-period social traits. Many of the recorded official positions, such as that of *centenarius* or of *deganus*, are obviously novel, designed to oversee fixed population groups; posts such as the *gastald* and *sculdahis*, though endowed with Germanic names, need not have a pre-Italy origin. By contrast, the use of the terms 'duke' and 'count' dates back to the Longobard sojourn in Pannonia, where it was, clearly, conscious Roman borrowing and indicated the Longobard willingness to adapt to new social and military forms. We have seen how the *fara* was rapidly deprived of its military function, and how the *faida* (blood-feud), the age-old Longobard system of justice, had been all but rejected by the royalty in the mid-seventh century, replaced by fines calculated with Roman coin. It is argued that the inbred militarism of the Longobards is reflected in the character of their public officials, making them markedly different to the Roman civilian institutions in both town and country. But against this we should note that society in Byzantine-controlled Italy was now equally militarized, in order to counter the Longobard threat. Certainly there was little difference between the two sides by the mid-eighth century, as shown by the alliances between popes and Longobard dukes in central Italy against the king.[11]

Archaeology and Society

In this light we should be cautious in accepting the concept that the social classes and their related weaponry requirements listed by Aistulf mirror the hierarchy of burial types identified in Pannonia: two centuries separate finds and documents, and, as we have seen, two centuries had greatly altered the primitive nature of the Longobard tribe. By the time that Aistulf's laws were promulgated in AD 750, the Longobards had been, largely, Catholic for almost two generations. Amongst other things, conversion put a virtual stop to the provision of funerary gifts with the deceased, and as a result there are

[11] Compare Cavanna, 'Diritto e società . . .' in *Magistra Barbaritas*, 364–7, and Brown, *Gentlemen and Officers*. Often quoted is the reference to the citizen body of Byzantine Comacchio as *milites* ('soldiers'). Cf. Wickham, *Early Medieval Italy*, 71–7. On literacy and acculturation, see B. Luiselli, *Storia culturale dei rapporti tra mondo romano e mondo germanico*, Biblioteca di Helicon (Rome, 1992).

no convenient mid-eighth-century weapon burials to corroborate the laws. Stray finds of early eighth-century silver-inlaid spurs or belt-fittings are known, but these merely help chart the decorative evolution of certain military and dress items. Changes in Longobard beliefs and burial rites must have already begun in the early invasion years, through the occupation of heavily Romanized lands, the incorporation of Catholic natives and the interaction with the Byzantines. To some degree the grave finds do allow us to identify some of these changes: adoption of and cross-fertilization with Mediterranean dress and decoration types, loss of the provision of food offerings and intrusion of Christian symbols.

Again, it must be stressed that as is the case with most of the peoples of early medieval Europe, we know far more about the Longobards in death than in life. Whereas secure Longobard settlement structures remain elusive, some thousands of burials are known: among these such large individual cemeteries as Testona, near Turin, with roughly 350 graves and Castel Trosino in eastern central Italy with 257 graves, as well as more than 500 Longobard tombs in the region of Friuli, with a high concentration around Cividale (figs 7 and 9).[12] The numbers are impressive, and yet the majority of graves were excavated before the 1950s, anthropological analysis is extremely restricted and only in rare instances are data such as the position of the skeleton and of the grave-goods recorded. For too long the grave-goods alone were

[12] The principal cemetery reports comprise: O. von Hessen, 'Die langobardischen Funde aus dem Gräberfeld von Testona (Moncalieri–Piedmont)', *Memorie dell'Accademia delle Scienze di Torino. Classe di scienze morali, storiche e filologiche*, iv, 1971, 1–120; R. Mengarelli, 'La necropoli barbarica di Castel Trosino, presso Ascoli Piceno', *Monumenti antichi della Reale Accademia dei Liucei*, xii (1902), 145–380; P. Pasqui and R. Paribeni, 'La necropoli barbarica di Nocera Umbra', *Monumenti antichi della Reale Accademia dei Liucei*, xxv (1916), 137–362. For Friuli see Brozzi, *Il ducato longobardo del Friuli*. Broader surveys are Kiszely, *Anthropology of the Lombards*; Melucco Vaccaro, *I Longobardi in Italia*, 85–116.

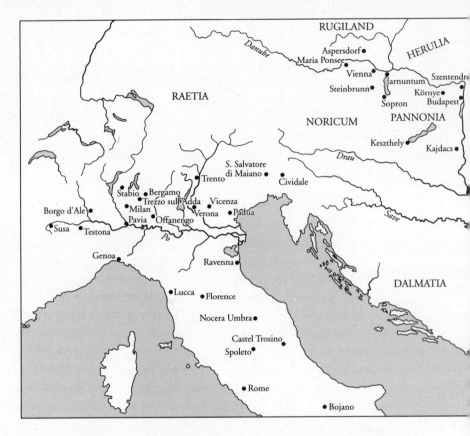

*Figure 7 Principal Longobard and Byzantine sites in
Pannonia and Italy.*

deemed worthy of attention, and Longobard studies centred largely on the evolution of metal-work decorative
styles[13] – essential, of course, for establishing chronological frameworks, but often achieved without sufficient
social interpretation. Social analysis from grave-goods is
in itself problematic, and recent studies recommend caution in compiling status tables and in claiming ethnic

[13] For example, J. Werner & S. Fuchs, *Die langobardischen Fibeln aus
Italien*, (Berlin, 1950); Roth, *Die Ornamentik der Langobarden*.

associations.[14] In the case of Italy we cannot be fully certain of the rate and mode of Longobard conversion to Catholicism nor of the impact on the grave ritual of interaction with Catholic Italians, particularly in the wake of the decline in the Byzantine–Longobard conflict after 605. For instance, we may note that Friuli possesses a high percentage of weapon graves, which extend well into the seventh century, mainly because of the military role of the frontier duchy and the concentration here of *farae*. Further south, however, as in the Duchy of Spoleto, a lesser density of Longobard colonists appears to merge more quickly with the indigenous population.

We know little of the graves and bones of the Longobard kings and queens. Seventh-century monarchs, as well as dukes, chose Roman style burial in sarcophagi below ground: those that have been located have generally been pilfered, either by medieval clergy for relics or by their modern discoverers. The opening of the sarcophagus believed to house the remains of Queen Theodelinda in Monza Cathedral in 1941, for example, revealed only fragmented skeletal remains and goods, but with enough small gold elements, such as brocade, to justify an association with Agilulf's queen. According to tradition, Theodelinda, Agilulf and their son and successor Adaloald were buried in the same tomb – but a tooth and a lancehead were all that survived to suggest a male presence.[15] The so-called 'Tomb of Gisulf' at Cividale, comprising a stone sarcophagus with marble cover and with a scratched (modern) graffito reading *Cisul*, could, plausibly, be identified with an actual duke because of the presence of a jewelled gold-sheet cross, weaponry, parade shield, belt fittings and a seal-ring.[16] More securely

---

[14] R. Samson, 'Social structures from Reihengräber: mirror or mirage?', *Scottish Archaeological Review*, iv/2 (1987), 116–26.

[15] G. Haseloff, 'Die Funde aus dem Sarkophag der Königin Theodelinda in Monza', *Germania*, xxx (1952), 368–77.

[16] *I Longobardi*, (exh. cat., ed. G. C. Menis; Milan, 1990), 470–5.

Plate 21 Funerary inscription, c.763, of Audoald, 'Duke of Liguria'. (Musei Civici di Pavia, Castello Visconteo.)

identified although no finds survive, is the bath-like sarcophagus housed in Vicenza Cathedral and bearing the epitaph of the *gastald* Radoald. From the eighth century, inscriptions (pl. 21), as well as occasional reliefs (pl. 22) resurface as funerary memorials, again in Roman style.

Easiest to identify are graves of the office-bearing nobility, bedecked with rich weaponry sets, high-class dress fittings and jewellery in precious metals. Prominent examples are the five male burials excavated in 1976–8 at Trezzo sull'Adda near Monza.[17] Each tomb, built of

---

[17] E. Roffia (ed.), *La necropoli longobarda di Trezzo sull'Adda*, Ricerche di archeologia altomedievale e medievale, 12–13 (Florence, 1986).

Plate 22 Roman-style tombstone relief walled into the precinct wall of the cathedral at Gemona in Friuli. Its date is disputed, but an eighth-century Longobard context is not unlikely.

stone slabs, within this presumed family group contained striking collections of weaponry, comprising long sword (*spatha* – some pattern-welded), short sword (*scramasax*), lance, parade shield and spurs (pl. 23), plus quality dress items such as gold belt sets, gold-sheet crosses, brocade from garments, boot fittings and rings. Coins from two of the graves, plus the decorative motifs on the crosses and spurs, help allocate the burials to various phases in the period 600–60. The most illuminating finds here were the three seal-rings, one containing a Roman gemstone, the other two bearing presumed royal

*Plate 23 Spur, decorated with silver inlay, from Tomb 2 at
Trezzo sull'Adda. (Archivio Fotografico della
Soprintendenza per i Beni Archeologici
della Lombardia.)*

portraits and the name of the owners – Ansuald and
Rodchis *vir illustris* (cover photograph). These rings
(only four others are known in Italy) represent the badges
of office given to royal appointees, perhaps *gastalds*,
charged with managing the extensive royal estates
around Monza. The discovery of a group of closely similar tombs is, most likely, an indication that office-
holding, if not hereditary, was very much the preserve of
certain noble families.

The graves at Trezzo sull'Adda also indicate that the
nobility might bury their dead away from urban centres,
within their own family estates. But the nobility also
lived in towns and fortresses, and so it is usual to find an
incidence of similar high-status burials, often acting as
focuses for family groupings, in larger cemeteries. The
use of gold, full weapon sets and fancy goods such as
saddle fittings, stools and drinking horns again should
indicate status, though we must bear in mind that it was
the deceased's relatives who were responsible for the
burial and the provision of grave-goods – hence we cannot be certain of the assumed equation of wealth with
office. Yet the quality and quantity of grave-goods must
bear some relation to the status of the deceased and/or to
that of his immediate kin, and it seems logical to view
expressions of wealth as expressions of authority – in this

world and the next (pl. 24). The provision of weaponry can reasonably be tied in with the eighth-century laws of Aistulf: sword, spear and shield remain constants and probably relate to the main body of Longobard freemen; the presence of spurs and bronze – as opposed to iron – belts denotes a slightly higher level of wealth; while the 'parade' style weaponry of Trezzo and elsewhere marks

Plate 24 Detail of the hilt of the nobleman's sword from Tomb 3 at Nocera Umbra. (Museo dell'Alto Medioevo, Rome.)

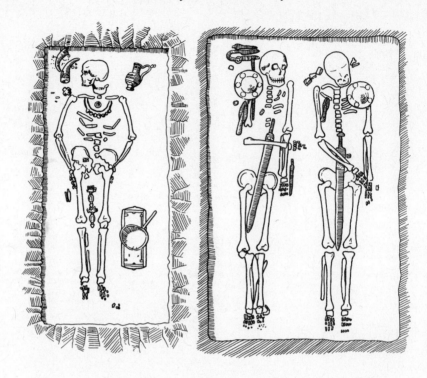

*Figure 8 Plan of the rich female grave 17 and the double
warriors' grave 111 from Nocera Umbra, in central Italy.
Two of the high-quality illustrations from the exemplary
excavation report of a Longobard cemetery examined at the
end of the last century (Pasqui and Paribeni 1916).*

the high nobility and large landowners (fig. 8). Bows and
arrows are a rare find, and occur either in poorly furnished graves (sometimes with swords) or in rich graves
(such as in Castel Trosino graves 90 and 119), where
they presumably indicate a use in hunting rather than in
war.[18]

It is harder to carry over this form of social ranking to
the other types of grave finds, except in the case of
metals, which can be ranked in terms of their material

[18] Christie, 'Longobard weaponry and warfare', 1–26.

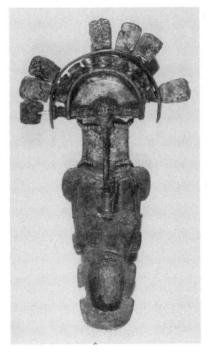

*Plate 25 Bow-brooch (front and rear) from Tomb 3 at
Nocera Umbra. (Civiche Raccolte Archeologiche
Numismatiche, Milan.)*

value. Personal and dress items do, however, allow for some discussion of the effects of 'Romanization' on the Longobards, although the general lack of coins as dating evidence in graves means that the chronological context for many of the visible changes is not secure. Hence, one model holds that Mediterranean dress styles were adopted fairly swiftly at least amongst the women, indicating a willing Italianization, whilst another argues for a stubborn resistance to change.[19] As noted above though, there are many variables, largely dependent on geography (i.e. proximity to trade contacts) and on the density of Longobard/native settlement, so we should not expect a single neat model. A clear sequence has nonetheless been presented for Castel Trosino, where the earliest women's graves, commencing *c.*580, retain old style Migration-period bow-brooches in the first Animal Style, but lack the pair of S-brooches which come to be replaced by a single disc-brooch (designed to fasten a garment at chest level; pls 25, 26). A second phase, from *c.*600–10, sees the Roman style disc-brooches as dominant, and the bow-brooches (numbering just seven in all for the cemetery) gone. In this or the following phase (from *c.*625) animal and cross-brooches appear, which are also items of Mediterranean-style jewellery (pl. 27). These then tail off as brooch-pins briefly make an appearance before burial with grave-goods ceases (*c.*650).

For male burials our main guide is the belt set, comprising buckle, strap-end and attachments. The earliest of these is the 'quintuple belt' with chunky oval buckle and triangular plate and counterplate with decorative studs:

[19] Compare Bierbrauer, 'Aspetti archeologici dei Goti, Alamanni e Longobardi' in *Magistra Barbaritas*, 469–508, with L. Jørgensen, 'AD 568: A Chronological Analysis of Lombard Graves in Italy' in L. Jørgensen, ed., *Chronological Studies of Anglo-Saxon England, Lombard Italy and Vendel Period Sweden, Arkaeologiske Skrifter*, v (Copenhagen, 1992), 94–122.

Plate 26 Seventh-century gold Byzantine disc-brooch from the Benevento region. (Ashmolean Museum, Oxford.)

these first occur in gold, silver and bronze in the later sixth century and from 600 are decorated in the second Animal Style. From *c*.600–20 at Castel Trosino 'multiple belts' appear, adaptations of a Byzantine belt set borrowed from the Avars. Early belts of this type show Byzantine motifs, but later iron versions feature silver-inlay zoomorphic designs. Changes are thus evident, partly to be explained by 'Romanization' and partly assimilated through service in Byzantine ranks. But male dress – in death at least – was basically military and conservative, in keeping with Longobard warrior tradition, and it is hard to see whether modifications in weaponry and fittings were made for military purposes or if they were a sign of a more 'Mediterranean' attitude.

Plate 27 Silver native-style horse brooch from Tomb 121 at Castel Trosino. (Museo dell'Alto Medioevo, Rome.)

Two other classes of finds are of relevance here. Firstly, the gold-sheet crosses: thinly cut, stamped crosses, usually with small holes at the end of each arm allowing

Plate 28 Gold-sheet crosses: the Clef cross from Lavis (Museo Provinciale d'Arte, Sezione Archeologica, Trento) and a cross from Caravaggio, Bergamo (Civiche Raccolte Archeologiche Numismatiche, Milan).

them to be sewn onto the funerary shroud, located either on the forehead or on the chest. Decoration is largely in the writhing second Animal Style with occasional human faces, animals and inscriptions (pl. 28). They appear only from *c*.580 and continue to be used into the mid-seventh century, as attested at Trezzo sull'Adda. In shape they are obviously Christian – either Arian or Catholic – but ornamentation is heavily Germanic, if with Mediter-ranean intrusions. The second relevant find type is pot-tery. In sixth-century tombs, pots are an important element of the grave ritual and are still produced in the Pannonian tradition: handmade vessels with stamped or wavy-line decoration.[20] But after *c*.600 we begin to lose sight of this ceramic type, chiefly because of its absence from graves – certainly the seventh-century Trezzo tombs do not contain any pots. These Longobard ceramics cannot have been replaced by local wares or imports because by this era the latter seem to have stopped circu-lating inland; rather, they probably continued to be used at a domestic level, but no longer served a function as part of a funerary meal ritual. This of course implies a notable modification in belief, again to be linked to a 'Romanization' of Longobard society. The sequence and rate of this process will continue to be debated, but that there was change cannot be doubted. It is difficult there-fore to claim 'ethnic markers' or items imbued with tribal spirit amongst the seventh-century Longobards – none of the brooch types persist long enough to suggest ethnic symbolism, and indeed few of the migration-period arte-facts extend even beyond *c*.600. Italy was a new world and one to which the Longobards had to adapt; this willingness to adapt is clearly attested in the goods taken to the grave.

[20] O. von Hessen, *Die langobardische Keramik aus Italien* (Wiesbaden, 1968).

Trade and Exchange

Longobard-type parade shields and gold-sheet crosses are encountered over the Alps in Franco-Alemannic lands in the seventh century and presumably signify trade communications rather than booty or tribute gifts. The intensity and character of such contacts remain vague at present, but study of the data will no doubt in time yield important information regarding transalpine communications and exchange. Archaeology's contribution is vital here, since trade and commerce play a low-key role in the Longobard laws and in other documentation: no mention at all is made of traders (*negotiatores*) in the seventh-century legal titles, while under Liutprand we find only a restriction on the amount of time traders could spend away from their home or country (Liut. 18). Yet an indication that traders formed a reasonable percentage of the population is given by the harsh measures exacted by Aistulf, who banned trade with the Romans, ordered merchants to carry letters showing royal approval and instructed them to equip themselves with weaponry suitable to their status and wealth (Aistulf 3, 4 and 6).

This rather minimal picture of commercial activity agrees with the documentary and archaeological data available for Byzantine Italy. Excavations at the port of Classe, attached to the imperial capital of Ravenna, have uncovered a fascinating sequence of changing commercial activities from the fifth into the eighth century. The excavations show a major downturn in Mediterranean commerce from the late sixth century, with virtually no activity identifiable after AD 700, by which date the shops, warehouses and roads are redundant. What is true for the Byzantine capital must be doubly true for the rest of Italy, and the absence of any coherent potting industry in Italy for the period from 625 to 750–75 is a clear indication of how low things had sunk in economic terms.

The loss of an international market may have removed the exotica, but day-to-day trade in foodstuffs, timber and livestock persisted throughout, even if scaled down in intensity. Surpringly, markets are mentioned only once in the Longobard laws, in the context of the purchase of a horse (Liut. 79). Whether this was an urban or rural market is not made clear, but the implication is that the goods sold were mainly livestock or agricultural produce. In their fleeting mentions of commercial travellers, the laws say nothing of the types of goods carried or their points of destination, bar that dealings were going on with the Romans. Probably, most merchants plied their trade mainly in the larger urban centres, leaving the rural districts much to their own devices. Barter must have been the essential means of exchange within each district, for both foodstuffs and such craft products as wooden or metal tools, barrels, leather-work or larger items as wagons; eighth-century charters suggest that each village or estate possessed its own specialist craftsmen. These and later documents, in addition to the law codes, point to the use of coin at least in terms of rent- and fine-payment and major purchases, and it is logical to argue that coin circulated at some level within the market system. Yet the laws speak almost solely of *solidi*, high value gold coin, of little relevance to everyday market transactions; the only smaller denomination mentioned is the silver *seliqua*, of uncertain value (Rothari 253–4), but again probably well in excess of simple day-to-day purchase requirements.

This picture does not tally with that gleaned from actual coin finds within Italy, the most striking discrepancy being the relative paucity of *solidi* and the frequency of lighter gold *tremisses* (pl. 29). Studies in the 1980s have greatly clarified the evolution of coin production within Longobard Italy, identifying three distinct monetary zones: northern Italy, Tuscany and Benevento.[21] Benevento, like the Duchy of Spoleto, was separated from the Kingdom by the Byzantine presence across central Italy, and so was forced to fend for itself; in the case of Spoleto there is no indication that it ever struck its own coins. Initially Benevento too seems anonymous, but from the early eighth century greater trade interests with Arabs and Byzantines encouraged local minting of good quality *solidi*, perhaps in response to a tail-off of Byzantine gold within Italy. These Beneventan *solidi* continued to be minted until the mid-ninth century, when political fragmentation deprived the principality of its former economic stability (see chapter 7). The northern and Tuscan mints, by contrast, issued almost exclusively gold *tremisses* (where one *tremissis* equalled one-third of a *solidus*). Between *c*.570 and 690 these *tremisses* were of pseudo-imperial type, copies of current Byzantine coins minted at Rome and Ravenna, and as such they bear imperial busts and legends. A high percentage of these are copies of coins issued by Justinian I, Justin II and Maurice Tiberius and suggest a greater frequency of coin movement in the last decades of the sixth century, presumably linked to Byzantine attempts to buy up Longobard mercenaries and the Longobard kings' attempts to counter these moves (pl. 29a). Noticeably, the seventh-century issues show a progressive inability or unwillingness to reproduce faithfully the imperial legends or images: busts are stylized, and mere lines replace legible characters (pl. 29b).

The symbolic importance of coinage is recaptured only from the late seventh century, when true Longobard silver issues appear, bearing the king's bust and a Victory or St Michael on the reverse (pl. 29c). Circulation in this period cannot have been great, but was undoubtedly

[21] E. Arslan, 'La monetazione' in *Magistra Barbaritas*, 425–44; P. Grierson & M. Blackburn, *Medieval European Coinage. I The Early Middle Ages (5th–10th centuries)* (Cambridge, 1986), 55–71.

*Plate 29 Longobard-period coins: (a) pseudo-imperial
tremissis of Maurice Tiberius (548–602); (b) tremissis of
Constans II (641–68) with illegible legend; (c) royal
Longobard tremissis of Liutprand (712–44); (d) follis issued
by Aistulf (749–56) from the Ravenna mint. (Fitzwilliam
Museum, Cambridge.)*

sufficient for coin to pass through the hands of the
nobility to help them recognize the kingdom's figure-
head. Minting was carried out in various cities and fortresses such as Pavia, Milan, Ivrea, Castelseprio and

Pombia, and most of the coins bear the stamp *Flavia* to indicate at least nominal royal supervision. One striking issue is the bronze *follis* of Aistulf at Ravenna, commemorating his capture of the old Byzantine capital in 751: a full frontal bust depicts a confident ruler threatening even greater conquests (pl. 29d). Yet it seems that these coins were not circulated outside of Ravenna, and they may have merely served an internal, symbolic purpose. In conclusion, the laws speak chiefly of *solidi*, whereas the 'national Longobard coinage' is predominantly silver *tremisses*, of no value in the diminished world of Mediterranean trade. Indeed, it appears that even smaller silver issues circulated, as attested in a hoard of 1,600 coins dating from 680 to 730 found at Biella, but the name of these thin issues is unknown, and there is nothing to show their use in everyday exchange. In the second half of the eighth century coin weight and silver content were in fact badly reduced, suggesting economic fragility and matching a debasement made elsewhere in the Mediterranean and in Europe. Whilst apparently pointing to decay and despondency, this debasement in fact coincides, as we will see (chapter 6), with a major artistic and architectural flourish in Longobard Italy, a burst of promise that endured even beyond Charlemagne's conquest.

5

Settlement and Defence in Longobard Italy

Until recently, any discussion of Longobard settlement patterns within Italy would have centred totally around the distribution of grave-finds, backed up by place-names and by information on cities stored in Paul the Deacon's *Historia Langobardorum*. This creates a badly imbalanced picture, hardly connected with the patterns of the fifth and sixth century AD. Only in the last decades have settlement sites themselves come under detailed archaeological scrutiny, yielding vital data on the evolution of Longobard material culture and, more importantly, new perspectives on Longobard relationships with the native Italian population. However, work is still at a preliminary stage, so this chapter can only give an interim interpretation of the modes of settlement and defence within the Longobard territories of Italy.[1]

Royal Capitals and Ducal Centres

Alboin fixed the first capital of the newborn kingdom at Verona, which had, perhaps significantly, been the last seat of Ostrogothic resistance against the Byzantines in the 560s (pl. 30). Endowed with powerful third-century

[1] A useful summary of recent research is S. Lusuardi Siena, 'Insediamenti goti e longobardi in Italia settentrionale', *XXXVI Corso di cultura sull'arte ravennate e bizantina: Ravenna e l'Italia fra Goti e Longobardi*, (Ravenna, 1989), 191–226.

Plate 30　Verona: the view across the River Adige from the Roman theatre. Verona was the first capital of the Longobard kingdom in Italy.

circuit walls and an array of well-preserved Roman public buildings, including a palace which had been restored under Theoderic the Great, Alboin's choice indicated the Longobards' immediate acceptance of a town-based *Regnum* and of pre-existing administrative focuses. However, shortly after the 574–84 dissolution of the monarchy, the capital was shifted westwards to Milan, the former imperial capital. This huge city offered far more centralized control of the Kingdom, being located at the intersection of a wide network of roads and in close contact with the vital Alpine routes. Agilulf crowned his son and successor Adaloald in the circus at Milan in 604 – a spectacle watched by Frankish ambassadors; north-east of the city, Agilulf's queen Theodelinda, a Catholic Bavarian by birth, established a royal palace at Monza.[2] Subsequently, in the 620s, the capital shifted once more, this time to Pavia, south of Milan, an equally favoured Ostrogothic residence and military headquarters, but at the same time a more compact Roman town. Pavia remained the preferred royal seat until the Kingdom's demise, and still retained its prominence under Carolingian rule.

Yet, apart from the documented building works at Monza and the Arian episcopal church at Pavia built under Rothari, we know almost nothing of the Longobard structural contribution or embellishment of these royal capitals before the later seventh century. After this date kings exhibited their Catholic piety in Pavia by constructing small chapels, churches and monasteries inside and outside the city walls, or occasionally adding to the existing palace complex. Such documented building works show not merely the impact of the Catholic Church on the Longobard kings but also the signs of economic upturn, in part brought on by the formal cessation of hostilities with Byzantium. Yet there is noticeably little to match this activity in later seventh-century or even eighth-century non-Longobard Italy: neither Rome nor Ravenna offer much in the way of even small-scale church construction, and sources like the *Liber Pontificalis* and Agnellus record only tiny gifts such as curtains or church plate – though of course both cities had a number of existing churches, whose upkeep alone swallowed up much of the meagre papal and imperial

---

[2] Paul *HL*, IV. 22.

resources. We lack documentation to show similar maintenance procedures for churches in Longobard-controlled
regions, although these must be expected if we assume that
a reasonably large native Catholic population was still
resident after the Longobard conquest. In the northern
territories, for the most part, the survival of bishops documents the upkeep of at least the episcopal churches and
their baptisteries; in the south, urban decay since the fifth
century had led to the progressive abandonment of episcopal seats, and the Longobard occupation will have done
nothing to alleviate the decline. In the eighth century the
number of royal religious foundations continued to multi-
ply; we also gain the evidence of inscriptions and decorated sculptural elements, such as choir screens and
pilasters, to supplement the charters. Pavia in particular
appears to have been chock-full of small churches.[3] Papal
Rome, by contrast, needed the forging of close political,
religious and economic ties with Francia from 774 to
allow for the repair and embellishment of many churches;
but for Ravenna, the brief Longobard rule and the period
of nominal papal control gave no scope for revitalization
– indeed Charlemagne requested marble-work and ornaments from palaces and churches here and in Rome to
decorate his capital at Aachen.[4]

Longobard ducal centres likewise boomed in the
eighth century – though in fact, any substantial building
activity in stone after the hiatus of *c*.500–700 could be
classified as a 'boom'. The data are best summarized by

[3] For urban public building from the 6th to 8th centuries see B. Ward-
Perkins, *From Classical Antiquity to the Middle Ages. Urban Public Building
in Northern and Central Italy*, A.D. *300–850* (Oxford, 1984. For Pavia there
are valuable surveys by D. Bullough, 'Urban change in early medieval Italy:
the example of Pavia', *Papers of the British School at Rome*, xxxiv (1966),
82–130; and C. Maccabruni, *Pavia: la tradizione dell'antico nella città
medievale*, (Pavia, 1991).

[4] Ward-Perkins, *From Classical Antiquity to the Middle Ages*, 205, 238–
9, 242–3; P. Delogu, 'The Rebirth of Rome in the 8th and 9th Centuries', in
(eds) R. Hodges & R. Hobley, *The Rebirth of Towns in the West*, (London,
1988), 32–42.

Ward-Perkins, who gives particular emphasis to the Tuscan city of Lucca, whilst stressing that Lucca is exceptional only for its wealth of extant charters of eighth- to tenth-century date: 'Here, in the eighth century at least, the building activity and charitable endowment was just as frenetic as in the three capitals. The only differences are in the scale of individual buildings, in the absence of imperial or royal patronage, and in the scarcity of the patronage of court officials.'[5] Bishops, governors (dukes or *gastalds*) and local urban aristocrats all contributed to church building, reviving a mode of patronage all but extinguished by the economic crises of the sixth and seventh centuries. For Lucca, private charters commence *c*.720 and record in the period to 774 the foundation or endowment of various small churches, monasteries and *xenodochia* (hostels). As with Rome, however, more extensive works were not undertaken until the first phase of Carolingian domination (774–825), when a prominent role was played by the Lucchese bishop James, whose epitaph of 818 lists many foundations. After the 820s, declining Carolingian authority is reflected in declining patronage, although gifts of church furniture continued to be made into the late ninth century. With the tenth century, however, patronage almost completely ceases. In terms of location it is interesting to note that the royal palace, mint and cathedral at Lucca lay within the Roman walls and near the old forum, while the ducal palace lay outside the walls, along with roughly a third of the attested churches. This perhaps indicates a shift in settlement out of the rubble strewn *civitas*, and indeed documents show flourishing suburbs, housing craftsmen, moneyers, goldsmiths and merchants. The transformation of the amphitheatre into a solid ring of houses, fronting onto a market area in the arena, may relate to this period of urban growth and renewal (pl. 31).

[5] Ward-Perkins, *From Classical Antiquity to the Middle Ages*, 52, 51–84, 245–9.

Plate 31 Lucca: view of the arcading of the amphitheatre, converted into housing from the early medieval period.

Of like value are rare panegyrics, such as the *Carmen de Synodo Ticinesi* of *c.*690, the *Laudes Mediolanensis Civitatis* (*c.*740) and the *Laudes Veronensis* or *Veronae Rythmica Descriptio* (*c.*795–800), which provide us with poetical glorifications of their respective cities. These concentrate primarily on the Christian shrines and their saints and relics, but they also celebrate prominent antique elements, in particular the late-Roman defensive circuits with their towers and gates. Of other survivals the Milanese poem records that 'the building on the forum is most beautiful, and all the network of streets is solidly paved; the water for the baths runs across an aqueduct'.[6] The poems may gush with civic pride, but

---

[6] J. Hyde, 'Medieval descriptions of cities', *Bulletin of the John Rylands Library*, xlviii (1966), 311–15; Ward-Perkins, *From Classical Antiquity to the Middle Ages* 224–7. Comparable is Theoderic's call in 510 for servicing 'of the glorious sewers of the city of Rome, which cause such amazement to

reveal through the vagueness of their descriptions a lack of much to talk about. At the same time the author of the *Laudes Veronensis* is at pains to contrast pagan and Christian, happily praising the functionality of the pagan legacy but stressing the glory of the modest but Christian present. Of course, the panegyrics' rhetoric does not provide fully accurate contemporary depictions of the cities: the poems may be paying most attention to the former monumental zones, whilst quietly overlooking the dilapidated and dangerous structures dotted around elsewhere and the crude housing erected amongst the ruins. The holiness of the shrines obscures the likely squalor of some of the worshippers.

This state of affairs existed already in fifth-century Rome: laws in the *Codex Theodosianus* and royal recommendations under Theoderic the Great demonstrate that there was an abundance of decayed public and private buildings, often occupied by squatters, and that monuments were quarried for building materials. The vastness of imperial Rome and her suburbs and the rapid population decline attested there from the fifth century could suggest treating the city as an exceptional case, however, sufficient documentary and archaeological evidence exists to prove otherwise. This decay cannot have been countered to any degree in the following centuries, and we must assume a widespread need to demolish edifices that were beyond repair and even to abandon parts of the city endangered by decayed monuments. Indeed, in many centres settlement became focused around one or two serviceable *insulae* (the Roman units of division of an urban space) or in the less built-up suburbs, and usually around churches. Hence, the *Laudes Mediolanensis* and *Veronensis*, by following round the points of holy pilgrimage, were effectively picking out those areas still humming with life.

beholders that they surpass the wonders of other cities' (Cassiodorus, III. 30).

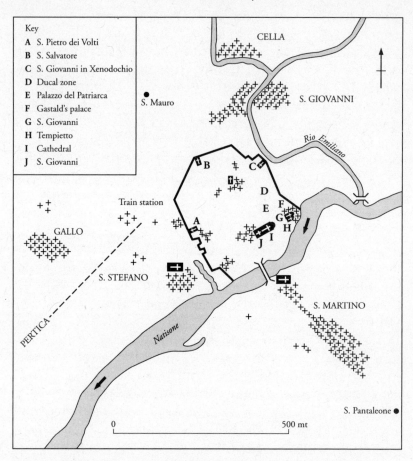

Key
A S. Pietro dei Volti
B S. Salvatore
C S. Giovanni in Xenodochio
D Ducal zone
E Palazzo del Patriarca
F Gastald's palace
G S. Giovanni
H Tempietto
I Cathedral
J S. Giovanni

CELLA
S. GIOVANNI
Rio Emiliano
S. Mauro
B
C
D
E
F
G
H
Train station
A
I
J
GALLO
S. STEFANO
S. MARTINO
PERTICA
Natisone
S. Pantaleone

0   500 mt

Figure 9 Cividale: town plan and distribution of cemeteries
(after Brozzi 1981).

There are enough eighth- and ninth-century charters
and capitularies from northern Italy to indicate that the
upkeep of city walls, bridges and roads had long been a
public duty of the citizens. Such a practice, on paper at
least, helps explain the survival of so many Roman features in Milan at the time the *Laudes* were composed,
and how so many towns preserve coherent traces of the
gridded Roman road system. City walls had of course
become integral elements in urban identity since the late

third century, owing to barbarian incursions and civil insurrections. Many Roman circuits, few of which have been studied in such detail as to provide indications of early medieval repair, survived almost intact into the thirteenth and fourteenth century, when major urban expansion and changing defensive requirements necessitated the building of new, more substantial circuits. It can further be noted that in the early medieval period districts within towns came increasingly to be named after gates, with less emphasis being given to the old Roman road divisions, which again highlights the prominence of the town walls.

Of value is a survey of *Forum Iulii* (Cividale), the ducal capital of Friuli. Here, elements of the defensive curtain survive, delimiting a horseshoe plan, bounded to the south by the steep gorge of the river Natisone (fig. 9). The circuit is generally ascribed to the period of the Marcomannic invasions of northern Italy of AD 168–9; undoubtedly, however, reconstructions and repairs occurred in the late-Roman, early medieval and medieval epochs, since Cividale has only recently expanded beyond the compact Roman confines. Roman remains within the walls are limited to part of the baths and the so-called 'Ipogeo Celtico', interpreted as subterranean Roman-period dungeons. Retention of the major gateways means that the lines of the main Roman roads (the *cardo* and *decumanus maximus*) are largely preserved; but little of the internal layout of the town otherwise survives. Various sources combine to illustrate the monumental make-up of the ducal centre: seventh- and eighth-century Longobard churches of royal and ducal foundation are attested in various quarters, namely S. Pietro dei Volti, S. Giovanni in Xenodochio (founded by Duke Roduald), S. Maria in Corte, S. Giovanni and S. Maria in Valle (founded by Queen Piltrude), S. Giovanni Battista near S. Maria (beneath the present cathedral) and another of unknown dedication in Piazza Paolo

Diacono. Of these, S. Maria in Valle survives as the stunning 'Tempietto' overlooking the Natisone (pl. 37); the much-rebuilt cathedral houses the baptismal font and canopy of the bishop Callistus, as well as the Altar of Ratchis (pl. 19), and the Museo Nazionale contains a wide collection of sculptural material from obscured or demolished eighth- and ninth-century edifices. The name S. Maria in Corte clearly alludes to the chapel belonging to the duke's court and residence sited in the east of the town; Paul the Deacon in fact mentions the eighth-century palace and an older, adjoining structure called the *domus Agonis* (Ago was duke of Cividale in the 650s). Close by, in the south-east corner of the town lay the seat of the king's representative, the *gastald*, in an area now enclosed by the Monastero Maggiore. This palace possessed a church dedicated to S. Giovanni, next to which was founded a nunnery whose chapel was formed by the 'Tempietto' of S. Maria. Large, squared masonry in the outer wall of the Monastero Maggiore has been interpreted as part of the defensive fabric of the *gastald's* palace.

Significantly, small groups of rich Longobard graves have been discovered near to all of the documented churches – and given that many of the finds stem from the later sixth and the first half of the seventh century, it is plausible that many of these churches have much older origins. The bulk of the Longobard and native Italian population buried their dead in cemeteries gathered around the roads leading out of the town: those to the north and across the river to the south show continuity from Roman times; the western cemetery, by contrast, seems predominantly Longobard and features the remains of the church of S. Stefano in Pertica, whose appellative records a tradition, noted by Paul the Deacon, of having empty graves marked by wooden posts topped by carved bird figures (*perticae*) to commemorate people who had died abroad or whose bodies could not be recovered. As we have seen, these cemeteries provide abundant data on Longobard material culture from the early invasion period on.[7]

At present, we rely heavily on burials as archaeological guides to the vitality of these Longobard centres, but detailed archaeological excavation alone will reveal the complexities of late and post-Roman urban evolution. Modern redevelopment, drain-laying and, in the case of Milan, construction of an underground train system provide scope for study, though results are obviously largely dependent on the time and area available for excavation and the level or depth of destruction caused by medieval and modern foundations and cellars: too often only isolated pockets of intact stratigraphy survive, making for a fragmented understanding of a site sequence.[8] If one adds to this the major facts that building in stone was largely limited to churches, themselves demolished and reconstructed frequently, that technical expertise was restricted due to limited patronage, and that the material culture for the period *c*.600–800 was impoverished and thus barely legible archaeologically, then the task becomes even more arduous. Only in a few rare instances so far, has a wide enough and relatively undisturbed plot of ground been presented for examination. And, even on these occasions, conclusions on early medieval settlement can be vague or open to debate.

Best published and most informative of these studies are the excavations at Brescia and Verona in central north Italy, both ducal seats of some importance in the Longobard period.[9] At Brescia, excavations since 1958,

[7] *Perticae*: Paul *HL*, V. 34. Topography and cemeteries of Cividale: Brozzi, *Il Ducato longobardo del Friuli*, 19–31.

[8] G. P. Brogiolo, 'Le città tra tarda antichità e medioevo', in *Archeologia Urbana in Lombardia*, (Modena, 1985), 48–55.

[9] G. Panazza & G. P. Brogiolo, *Ricerche su Brescia altomedievale. I. Gli studi fino al 1978. Io scavo di via Alberto Mario* (Brescia, 1988); G. P. Brogiolo, 'Trasformazioni urbanistiche nella Brescia longobarda' in *I Longobardi* (exh. cat., 1990); C. La Rocca Hudson, ' "Dark Ages" a Verona

but chiefly since 1980, have examined an area of over 7,500 sq. m in the eastern part of the city, covering the *insulae* of S. Giulia and Ortaglia, which from *c.*760 were dominated by the monastery of S. Salvatore, founded by Desiderius (see fig. 13, p. 194). The S. Giulia excavations revealed a single Roman *domus* of 120 m by at least 60 m, presumably an aristocratic residence, containing over thirty rooms on two floors. The *domus* fell into decline in the fifth century, with hearths and beaten earth floors set over Roman mosaics and with post-holes cut down into these, sometimes to support the masonry walls, elsewhere to create crude partitions. The signs are of a disintegration of *domus* ownership and a drastic technical and economic decline. This is further borne out by the failure to revive after an extensive fire, whose destructive traces are known throughout the city and which is broadly dated to the mid-sixth century, most probably in the context of the Gothic War or its aftermath. The later sixth and early seventh century marked a levelling and clearance of collapsed rubble layers in parts of the *insulae*, followed by construction of a scattered group of at least twelve houses, timber-built or with stone footings that utilized surviving stumps of Roman wall. Floors were of clay or beaten earth, while two huts featured sunken interiors – a format well known in Anglo-Saxon and other Germanic contexts but, until this discovery, unknown in Italy. Small yards lay between the houses, and these were generally used as rubbish tips and, occasionally, even for burials. Between the *insulae* a hut with dry-stone footings was located facing onto a road which had been fairly competently recobbled. This zone contained a series of contemporary and later burials, mainly

Edilizia privata, aree aperte e strutture pubbliche in una città dell'Italia settentrionale', *Archeologia Medievale*, xiii (1986), 31–78. Comparable excavations in southern Italy are rare, but A. Staffa, 'Scavi nel centro storico di Pescara', *Archeologia Medievale*, xviii (1991), 201–367 offers new data on late Roman to medieval Pescara.

in graves with tile and stone-built sides and with slab or tile covers. Anthropological analysis identified a combination of Nordic and Italo-Alpine Mediterranean characteristics in the bones retrieved, suggestive of a merging of locals and Germans. Interestingly, palaeopathological evidence indicated a high incidence of malnutrition and anaemia, resulting in short lifespans. The excavators took this as support for their view of Brescia as a run-down urban centre lacking effective systems of food supply. The difficulty lies, of course, in determining whether the community represented by those graves is typical for all of Brescia or if, in fact, it is just an impoverished urban-labourer group eking out an existence amongst the ruins; similarly we do not know if this community relied on food grown outside the town walls or indeed within them – possible areas of cultivation were in fact identified in the Ortaglia *insula*.

A contrast may be drawn with Verona, where excavations in the town centre, at the Cortile del Tribunale, suggested a replacement of a large Roman *domus* with a series of planned buildings facing onto the streets, with yards set behind; in Via Dante the continuity of location of one or more houses from the fifth into the twelfth century is evident in the successive raising of the house façade, fronting onto a rising street level. Although the Tribunale excavations did reveal some timber structures, Longobard-period buildings for the most part featured stone foundations and stone façade elevations – perhaps denoting high status residences.

At Brescia a striking fact is that the *insulae* of S. Giulia and Ortaglia were in royal ownership, certainly by 753–6 when King Aistulf granted the land to Duke (later King) Desiderius to construct a monastery dedicated to S. Salvatore. In diplomas of 759–60 Desiderius distinguishes between the wide-ranging property of the royal court, that of the ducal court and his own private property gained whilst duke – all together these cover roughly a third of Roman Brescia, with control centred on the west gate (ducal court) and east gate (royal court). How far back this fiscal control went is unclear, but datable occupational debris associated with the buildings, which were largely made of timber, runs only to *c*.650. Some demolition and levelling then occurred to make way for a T-plan church with horseshoe apses, roughly dated on the basis of its three floor levels to the latter half of the seventh century. Slightly later in date is a complex of three stone-built structures gathered around a courtyard, with a cistern-well sited in the north: the largest building here was 33 by 10 m, with an ambulatory set parallel to an arcaded façade, elements of which remain visible – a unique preservation of the elevation of a non-religious Longobard building. The remains overall suggest either a palace or a monastic complex and bear witness to an economic vitality and, quite possibly, to royal intervention.

Subsequently, in 755, the monastery was built: this entailed the rebuilding and enlargement of the T-plan church and the courtyard/cloister structures to the south, and the addition of cloisters to the north, with a like arrangement of rooms, one of which contained a hypocaust. Roman-style lead piping reveals a revamping of the old Roman aqueduct to supply water to the monastery: four charters record the laying of the pipe, running from the *Porta Mediolanensis* and cutting through privately owned land within the town. The prestige of the monastery was enhanced by Desiderius' promotion to king, his daughter's role as first abbess and by the arrival in 760–2 of the body of St Giulia from Gorgona, housed in a newly inserted crypt. Tradition later records the church as the burial place of Queen Ansa. The Queen's extant epitaph – attributed to Paul the Deacon – speaks poetically of her piety and energy in helping rebuild a city damaged by war (a civil conflict? Or the result of Peppin's invasion of 756?). Even if vague as a text, the epitaph at least highlights the sense of urban identity and pride emerging in later Longobard Italy.

The evidence from both Brescia and Verona provides vital new insights into the question and level of urban continuity: at each there are signs of maintenance of Roman roads both as surfaces and as property markers, though at Via Dante in Verona only half of the original road width was reused, the other half having its paving ripped up to form thresholds in the façades of the fifth- to sixth-century houses. Habitational activity fronted directly onto the streets; yet the interiors of many *insulae* seem to have become dilapidated, being used for burials or for vegetable plots and, later, for the building of churches and monasteries, as indeed at S. Salvatore, Brescia. The forum was no longer a focal point for urban life – this role had already lapsed in fifth-century Italy and the process of decay merely continued under the Longobards with demolition and stripping of the Roman square and its adjoining public structures (as at Piazza Maffei, Verona). Indeed, the Longobard phase marks no major transition: although at Brescia the final destruction of the S. Giulia *domus* by fire and the later insertion of sunken timber huts and other crude houses suggest a traumatic breakdown, by *c.*500 the *domus* had already sunk into a collection of small hovels, paying scant regard to the Roman fittings. Along Via Dante in Verona the intrusion onto the Roman road and the first phase of related house building is also set around AD 500. Here construction was largely with reused Roman materials (*spolia*), bonded with clay, but with, most likely, timber superstructuring to the side and rear walls.

Large quantities of brick, cut stone and marble must have been readily available in most towns: church building swallowed up only a small proportion of this, particularly the finer quality *spolia*. The likelihood is that the control of *spolia* and of ruinous public, and perhaps also private, buildings lay in State hands, continuing the pattern documented in the late Empire by the *Codex Theodosianus* and under the Ostrogoths by Cassiodorus' *Variae*. Unfortunately, direct evidence for the period 550–800 is lacking: documents that refer to centralized supervision of ancient buildings within the area of the *Regnum Langobardorum* post-date 800. Yet, given the Carolingian practice of limited initial interference in the State machinery in Italy, such control can probably be interpolated back in time.[10]

The later seventh- and eighth-century programme of church, monastery and palace building hints at a renewed urban and socio-economic vitality, expressed primarily in construction in stone and brick, with much of the brick and tile newly fired. Building and artisanal skills had never died out in Italy, but merely lacked an adequate level of patronage: in fact, from the time of King Rothari we begin to find occasional references to a distinct class of specialists, the *magistri commacini*, initially itinerant craftsmen (trained where?) but with time becoming increasingly dependent on the royal court. Rothari's laws 144 and 145 mention such *magistri* with building partners; the *Memoratorio de mercedes commacinorum*, most likely of Liutprandine date, fixes prices for their work: for one- and two-storey houses, wall styles ('Roman' or 'Gallic' type), roof construction and extras such as wells, shutters or marble ornamentation – all clearly pitched at an aristocratic market. At Brescia the S. Giulia palace/courtyard structures, combined with elements such as the hypocaust and the aqueduct, point to specialist involvement: interestingly, the later addition of porticoes to the mid-eighth-century cloisters was crudely achieved, and is viewed as the work of poorly trained local builders, a cheap alternative to the *magistri commacini*. By the mid-ninth century, however, these *magistri* all but disappear from the documentary record. In their

[10] Ward-Perkins, *From Classical Antiquity to the Middle Ages*, 203–18.

place large landowners, notably monasteries, lay claim to various specialist craftsmen, including carpenters (working with both wood and stone), who provide for the immediate needs of individual estates. This situation neatly reflects the break-up of royal control and the rise of private and monastic power, particularly in a rural context, after the initial decades of Carolingian rule.

Palaces

Each Longobard ducal centre possessed a palace for its royal appointee, and some also held residences for the occasional royal visit. We can assume, in the absence of direct evidence, that most palaces dated back to late Roman times or were reworkings of aristocratic *insulae* or *domus*. Royal summer retreats and hunting lodges are also attested in the countryside near to the capitals. Evidence for these is usually restricted to documentary references or to toponymic traces, as with the palace complex built under Theodelinda and Agilulf *c.*600 at Monza, north-east of Milan. Paul the Deacon records how this palace was decorated with fine figured murals still visible in his day (enabling him to describe the primitive dress of the Longobards); he adds that Theoderic, too, once had a summer palace at Monza. The Catholic queen Theodelinda also oversaw construction of the generously endowed palace church of S. Giovanni Battista: this basilica, remodelled in the Romanesque period, preserves the Queen's sarcophagus (see chapter 4) and, in the treasury, gifts presented to Theodelinda by Pope Gregory the Great in respect of her efforts to convert the Longobards to Catholicism (see pl. 35).[11]

In the case of Corteolona, east of Pavia, medieval and later buildings have partly fossilized the plan of the

---

[11] Paul *HL*, IV. 5–6 and 21–2.

palace of Liutprand and its church of S. Anastasio. These suggest an arrangement of rectangular buildings around a central courtyard, thus bearing striking similarities to the excavated complex at S. Giulia, Brescia, dating to the late seventh century, and to the Ostrogothic rural palaces at Palazzolo, near Ravenna, and Monte Barro, near the south-east tip of Lago di Lecco.[12] For Corteolona two inscriptions, now lost, relating to the foundation of the palace recorded how Liutprand obtained a rich array of mosaics, marbles and columns from Rome to adorn his 'paternal seat' and how the King initially planned to build some baths there, but, piously, changed his mind to found a soul-cleansing monastery instead. Only a few scattered fragments of quality marble-work – of types poorly attested at nearby Pavia – have been recovered from the unexcavated site, though one figured fragment depicting a horse's head appears to be a contemporary manufacture. Carolingian and later documentation reveals how Corteolona continued as a *curte regia* or *palatio regio* into the late ninth century, when it was fortified and became *castrum Ollone*; after the 930s the site slipped into a slow decline, and both monastery and palace were certainly ruinous by the twelfth century.

From Towns to Farms

We know all too little of the character of the lesser towns and their satellite villages in Longobard Italy. Church dedications, toponyms, stray or reused early medieval church sculpture (screens, pilasters, etc.) and chance finds of burials or their scattered contents often provide the sole available clues, but these rarely indicate more

[12] Corteolona: C. Calderini, 'Il palazzo di Liutprando a Corteolona', *Contributi dell'Istituto di Archeologia*, V (1975), 174–203; Ostrogothic period sites: G. P. Brogiolo & L. Castelletti, *Archeologia a Monte Barro. I. Il grande edificio e le torri*, (Lecco, 1991), 26–50.

than a survival of activity within or around a given settlement; they do not enable us to assess the levels of settlement continuity. For the most part the old Roman road system had survived intact and, thus, remained vital in influencing the distribution of settlement. It seems probable that these smaller, generally open sites would have been most affected by the warfare and insecurity that plagued Italy from the fifth century on. Since there are no signs of hordes of displaced refugees taking shelter in the larger towns, we can envisage a slow movement of people away from exposed locations to more secluded, upland or hilltop sites. This shift perhaps first affected the poorer farmers, those who had always lived on the land and who shared little in Roman or post-Roman culture. Larger landowners, those who did not still live in towns, occasionally may have fortified their sites, shifted them to secure hilltops, or encouraged local dependent farmers to settle in the immediate proximity for mutual protection, creating incipient nucleated villages – these are transformations encountered in Gaul, and yet they remain to be fully recognized in Italy. Only the incidence of early medieval churches amidst the ruins of larger Roman villas give support to this hypothesis of nucleation.

Villas generally show a persistence of life into the fifth–sixth century, before giving way to the 'squatter activity' syndrome, where the blocking of doors, crude repairs and hearths and occasional burials are dismissed as signs of shepherds sheltering in villa ruins (pl. 32). In reality, however, archaeologists have largely failed to address the question of post-Roman survival and the reuse of villas, concentrating their efforts too much on clarifying merely the tidy classical layers. The application of field survey/walking has been of value in elucidating the character of late-antique rural settlement. The results of many field surveys have indicated a progressive decline in the number of rural sites of all sizes throughout

Plate 32 Desenzano. Roman villa: the fifth-century apsidal hall with post-Roman burials cut into its patterned floors.

Italy beginning as early as the third century but accelerating in the fifth and sixth centuries AD. Here the problem becomes increasingly one of actually being able to locate sites in the field given the decline in the production and distribution of imported and datable pottery types – clearly the poorer and middle range farmers, who were always dominant in numbers in the countryside, were the first to lose out in this shrinking market. A return to a pre-Roman style of self-sufficiency, wattle-and-daub timber huts and handmade pots effectively removes them from the archaeological record.[13] In some cases there is a datable shift to other sites: in such regions as Liguria, on the north-west coast of Italy, or Apulia, in the south-east, caves were reused as habitations from as early as the fifth

[13] On problems in identifying post-Roman rural settlement: T. W. Potter, *The Changing Landscape of South Etruria*, (London, 1979), 139–46; G. P. Brogiolo, 'La campagna dalla tarda antichità al 900 ca. d.C.', *Archeologia Medievale*, x (1983), 73–88; Christie, 'The Archaeology of Byzantine Italy'.

century, having not seen permanent occupation since the Bronze Age or earlier; the presence of medieval finds may indicate continuous and materially impoverished activity in such caves throughout the early Middle Ages. Elsewhere hilltops are settled: in some instances these dominate road and river lines and, thus, have an ostensible military purpose: the supervision of strategic or defensive points; others, equally defensible, lay off the beaten track and probably represent refuges or new focuses of settlement with no predetermined military role. In some zones reduced urban communities fled to the hills: in the Carnic Alps, in Friuli, the inhabitants of *Iulium Carnicum* (Zuglio) appear to have transferred in the fifth century to the hill and church of San Pietro overlooking the old *municipium* (pl. 33); the community nonetheless retained its bishop into the eighth century. Only rarely can these shifts in location be dated, although it seems reasonable to argue that the shift of settlement upland occurred earliest in the Alpine regions, since they were the first on the path of external invader.

For Friuli, an adequate picture of the distribution of both Longobards and natives can be assembled on the basis of numerous grave finds, from which it can be argued that the Longobard settlement had not caused a major disruption of the native population. Of note are the results of small-scale excavations carried out in the 1940s near Farra d'Isonzo, close to the Slovenian border. The name Farra clearly derives from *fara* and denotes an early, official Longobard station, here designed to control an important bridge across the Isonzo. A number of early medieval tombs were discovered, but the few finds, comprising iron knives and simple, bronze earrings broadly datable to the sixth–seventh centuries, and the form of grave construction in fact seem to relate to the indigenous population rather than to Germans. The excavations also revealed part of a Roman bath-house with coins datable into the fifth century. In effect, the Longo-

Plate 33 Iulium Carnicum *(Zuglio), Friuli: view from the
Roman forum to the hill of San Pietro.*

bards established a *fara* and strengthened control of an
existing river crossing, without displacing the residual
local Romans.[14] It can be noted that the Friulian dialect
has its fair share of Longobard loan-words, which, as

[14] See Brozzi, *Il Ducato Longobardo del Friuli* and *La popolazione romana nel Friuli longobardo*; F. Dreossi, 'Farra d'Isonzo (Gorizia). Scavi
eseguiti: in località Monte Fortin', *Atti della Accademia Nazionale dei
Lincei. Notizie degli Scavi di Antichità*, iv, 3–4 (1943), 189–98.

elsewhere in northern Italy, are generally linked with daily life, such as house and furnishings, farming, hunting and fishing, or with dress and moods. These would appear to be a sign that the Longobards fitted in and integrated with the locals at a grass-roots level. Other Longobard words have become fossilized as place-names, notably *sala* (farm/house), *braida* (plain), *gaggio* (enclosed woodland), and *staffolo* (boundary ditch/fence). A combination of incidences of names would suggest relatively healthy Longobard settlement on what had probably been uncultivated land; status of the related settlement may be indicated by place-names of institutional character such as *fara, gastald*, or *sculdascio*.[15] However, despite the grave-finds, which are often accidentally exposed by agricultural work, farm building and road-cutting, Friuli, too, like the other regions occupied by the Longobards, needs long-term, systematic excavation projects to reveal the contemporary timber-built houses and farms.

In Britain timber-built Anglo-Saxon farms, villages and palaces, too, have been identified through detailed aerial photographic survey. Such techniques have yet to be widely applied scientifically in an Italian context, although air photos have done much to reveal neolithic and Roman-period farming activity in south-east Italy, as well as the ground plan of the Byzantine-period lagoon site of *Heraclea* (Cittanova) in the Veneto. Despite our data bank being accordingly somewhat crude and restrictive, some attempts have been made to work out the make-up and density of rural settlement in the Longobard period. Important in this respect are the studies undertaken of a zone west of Turin (centring on the vast Longobard necropolis of Testona), and in the modern

[15] C. Mastrelli, 'La toponomastica lombarda di origine longobarda' in *I Longobardi e la Lombardia* (exh. cat., 1978), 35–49; M. Arcamone, 'I Germani d'Italia: lingue e "documenti" linguistici' in *Magistra Barbaritas*, 399–404.

provinces of Brescia and Verona.[16] These analyses recognized two principal Longobard cemetery types: smaller units of up to 50 burials relating to nearby village communities or representing family plots near towns; and large 'official' or 'authorized' cemeteries used by a range of neighbouring and dispersed sites (e.g. Testona and Calvisiano, with *c*.450 and 500 tombs respectively). The Longobard cemeteries frequently lie in areas preserving Latin toponyms; the admixture of Alpine and Mediterranean individuals and native-style personal goods further indicates a merging with, rather than dislocation of, the indigenous population. In a few cases the Germanic input is stronger, as in parts of the Veronese such as the upper Valpolicella, and this tends to suggest Longobard settlement of zones only limitedly used in the Roman period. Some of these hypotheses remain tentative, particularly because few Longobard-period cemeteries have seen modern systematic excavation and post-excavation analysis. A further limitation is that the Longobard cemeteries and stray finds that provide most of the dots on distribution maps relate, almost wholly, to the later sixth and seventh centuries: the full conversion of most Longobards to Catholicism by *c*.700 put a stop to the provision of gravegoods, whilst the processes of acculturization make it hard to distinguish Longobards and natives through bone types – yet the law codes continue to offer a distinction between Longobard and Roman law. With Christianization we do of course gain the evidence of churches, but so many of these now underlie Romanesque and later successors that, at best, occasional sculptural fragments survive to hint at Longobard roots. Clearly, only new field studies can hope to provide adequate data for discussion of the sequence and level of

---

[16] La Rocca Hudson & Hudson, 'Riflessi della migrazione longobarda. . .' in Francovich (ed.), *Archeologia e storia del medioevo italiano*, 29–38.

German–native interaction and the relationship of cemeteries to settlements.

Accordingly, it is difficult to tie in the physical evidence with the documentary texts. Paul the Deacon, as noted, in relating the Longobard seizure of land in the later sixth century, confusedly mentions a form of *hospitalitas*. Their law codes show that status, amongst the Longobards, was chiefly reflected by landed property, and our eighth-century charters substantiate this view in both urban and village contexts. In the invasion years the nobility undoubtedly obtained prized landed properties for themselves and their heirs through the bloody removal of Roman aristocrats and rural gentry. In time, appointment to office brought with it suitable land grants to help provide financial and economic support – a precursor, indeed, to later feudal arrangements, since the nobility was often the recipient of royal gifts of land designed to secure support within the kingdom. The king, of course, remained by far the largest landowner, his properties being administered by an array of officials headed by the *gastalds* – as noted, the rich burials at Trezzo sull'Adda probably belong to a family of *gastald* status, who had supervised the extensive royal domains around Milan (see chapter 4).

On royal, aristocratic and monastic lands lay various farm units and estates, farmed by half-free tenants and slaves. Charters document numerous village settlements, termed *vici, loci, casalia* and *villae*, in Longobard lands, relating perhaps to extended family groups or nucleated groups of scattered farmsteads. Money and produce rents were fixed, and some labour service was required. But, for the most part, villagers and peasant farmers merely provided for themselves, and each unit seems to have possessed artisans, notably carpenters and metalworkers, with trade specializations often handed down in families. Documents make plain the fact that building activity in the rural context was almost exclusively in timber, illustrating Germanic and native rural building traditions, and perhaps signifying that the woodlands had regenerated since the late-Roman period.[17] Some woodland clearance was certainly under way in the fairly prosperous eighth century, but it would be the ninth-century growth of monastic land-control, linked with a likely population increase, that would mark the major phase of systematic land clearance. Crops grown by the Longobards seem to have differed very little from those of Roman times, chiefly corn and vines, while Rothari's laws give some emphasis to stock-raising, particularly cattle and pig. However, we await the excavation of suitable village rubbish pits to gauge the accuracy of the texts.

Fortifications

Although no accurate figures can be given as to the numerical strength of the Longobard invaders, the probability is that it was insufficient for them to defend their new territories and to pursue new conquests on their own. In effect, an immediate involvement was required on the part of the subject Italians, in order to maintain Longobard rule. As with the Ostrogothic invasion of 489, the swift and apparently painless occupation of populous fortified centres such as Cividale and Verona in 569 seemingly confirms the natives' ready acceptance of the new ruling elite and, simultaneously, the conquerors' own willingness to adapt to and maintain the existing administrative and military structures. Unlike the Ostro-

[17] Wickham, *Early Medieval Italy*, 97–107; P. Galetti, 'La casa contadina nell'Italia padana dei secoli VIII–X' in Francovich (ed.), *Archeologia e storia del medioevo italiano*, 97–111. On tools in this epoch: M. Baruzzi, 'I reperti in ferro dello scavo di Villa Clelia (Imola). Note sull'attrezzatura agricola nell'altomedioevo', also in Francovich (ed.), 151–70; *I Longobardi* (exh. cat., 1990), 344–9.

goths, however, the Longobards had to maintain a military attitude, with warfare continuing until the early seventh century in many regions of Italy. As a result they seem not to have had the time to carry out modifications to the defensive set-up, such as had been possible under Theoderic the Great.

Paul the Deacon (*HL*, III. 31 and IV. 37) provides detailed descriptions of two invasions by enemy forces from beyond the Alps into northern Italy. For each episode he lists a series of *castra* or fortresses: in the first, in 590, the Franks, in collusion with the Byzantines, penetrated into the Trentino in the central Alps and captured and destroyed 13 forts, taking their 'inhabitants' as prisoners; Duke Ewin and his garrison of 600 men evaded capture by holing out inside the *castrum Ferruge* (*Verruca*), opposite Roman Trento. Eventually, once the Franco-Byzantine alliance had collapsed, the Longobards regained their lost territory. In the second, in 610–11, Avar troops defeated Duke Gisulf and forced the Friulians into flight:

The Longobards took shelter within the nearby fortresses, namely Cormons, Nimis, Osoppo, Artegna, Ragogna, Gemona, and also Invillino, whose position is quite unassailable. In the same way they sheltered within all the other fortifications to avoid falling prey to the Huns, or rather, the Avars. These Avars, raiding the whole territory of Cividale and setting fire to everything, put Cividale under siege, ranging all their forces against the city . . . (IV. 37)

Despite the strengths of the circuit walls, the gates were opened through treachery and the city ransacked and burnt, its inhabitants killed or carried off. The other forts resisted and survived.

Local scholars have identified many of the documented Alpine fortresses, frequently placing them in an extensive system of control of natural and man-made communications lines leading towards the Italian plains, achieved

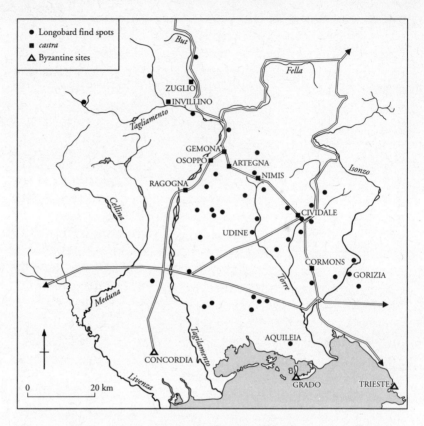

- Longobard find spots
- *castra*
- Byzantine sites

Figure 10 Fortresses named by Paul the Deacon and other main sites in Longobard Friuli.

through the occupation of strategic hilltop and spur sites (fig. 10). While stray finds from in or around these locations readily attest Longobard period activity, the coincidence of late Roman material, often structural, recommends much earlier origins. Indeed, the likelihood is strong that the bulk of the defensive arrangements utilized by the Longobards – as also by the Byzantines and Ostrogoths before them – was, in fact, installed in the later fourth or in the fifth century to counter the break-up of Roman control beyond the Alps. Most pertinent is the collapse of the frontier rigged across the pass routes running over the Julian Alps beyond Friuli: the *Claustra Alpium Iuliarum*, probably initiated under Constantine the Great in the 320s, had failed repeatedly to stem enemy (both barbarian and rebel or legitimate Roman) incursions, and in the early 400s no reference is made to its garrisons during the invasions by Alaric and the Visigoths. Excavations at the principal fort of *Ad Pirum* (Hrušica) have, indeed, confirmed a destructive termination to its military role in *c.*395. Roman attempts to restore defensive control in the Alpine sectors provide the politico-military context for the erection of many of the *castra* and *castella* recorded by Paul the Deacon.[18]

A large-scale, systematic excavation, to verify the origins and character of these Longobard fortresses, has only been made on one site, namely the 'unassailable' fort of *Ibligo* (Invillino) in the northern reaches of the Duchy of Friuli (fig. 11). In most cases the medieval reuse, expansion or reconstruction of many of the castle sites has left only limited archaeological accessibility; Invillino, fortunately, escaped this fate, thus allowing a clear recognition of the early medieval and other structures.[19] The site consists of a 630 m long, steep-sided hill rising *c.*60 m above the flood plain of the River Tagliamento, near the modern village of Villa Santina. The *castrum* covered a level area of 200 by 100 m at the west end of the hill: steep slopes provided a natural defence, reinforced by a quadrangular tower overlooking the approach; no certain traces of circuit wall were identified. Of the three settlement phases, the first comprised a small, unimpressive group of first- to fourth-century houses; in the second phase, running from *c.*350 into the first half of

[18] L. Bosio, 'Le fortificazioni tardoantiche del territorio di Aquileia', *Il territorio di Aquileia nell'antichità, Antichità Altoadriatiche*, xv (1979), 515–36; Christie, 'The Alps as a frontier', 410–30.

[19] Bierbrauer, *Invillino-Ibligo in Friaul. I & II*. A major earthquake in Friuli in 1976 partially destroyed many of the fortifications – restoration programmes at many sites such as Ragogna, still in progress, have allowed for some limited investigation.

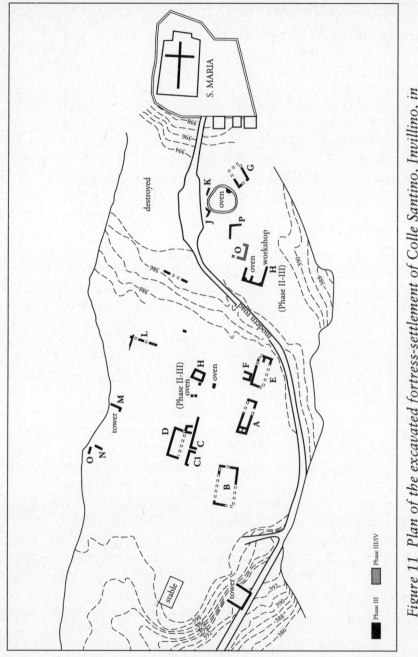

Figure 11 Plan of the excavated fortress-settlement of Colle Santino, Invillino, in Friuli, showing the sixth- to eighth-century house plans and the late eighth-century church of Santa Maria (Bierbrauer 1988).

the fifth century, there was no structural change but some industrial activity commenced and imported ceramics appeared. The mortar-bonded buildings of the first two phases were replaced, in the first half of the fifth century (Phase III), by several individual houses and workshops built of timber over dry-stone footings, while the construction of a substantial tower indicates defensive requirements. There is held to be continuity of population from Phase II, with some increase in numbers. Settlement continues into the seventh century, but features no clear Ostrogothic or Byzantine input, while a Longobard presence is suggested primarily on the basis of a sword pommel. Finds can largely be attributed to the Romanized native population, with only stray Germanic hints. To support this view, there is a Christian church and cemetery on Colle di Zuca (locally called 'Cimitero dei Pagani'), upstream of Colle Santino, also dating from Phase III: noteworthy are the building's size (39.50 m length) and the well-executed mosaics.

Problems exist in dating some significant episodes: a siege of the settlement, as revealed by the distribution of catapult shot; a destructive fire in the church; the abandonment of the settlement. The first two events broadly fit the period 550–600 and conceivably tie in with the Longobard invasion; however, the catapult shot might be Byzantine, and the church's destruction may have been accidental. As regards the decline of the *castrum*, this coincided with the construction of the extant church of S. Maria Maddalena on the rise east of the settlement plateau – an inscription from the church, recording the priest Ianuarius, can be roughly dated to the first half of the eighth century. By this phase burials had begun to be made in and around the ruinous houses, suggesting that the former residents had moved down to the plain. The Colle di Zuca church perhaps also persisted to this period. It is thus possible to argue that the site lost its military role around 700–25. A link exists with the apparent decline of Zuglio, to the north, whose bishop had been moved to Cividale by the 730s. Perhaps this relates to a relaxation in Longobard frontier control in the Friulian Alps coinciding with territorial gains against the Slavs in Carinthia. Yet, surprisingly, there is no sign of revitalization at Invillino in the 750s or 770s, when the Carolingian threat loomed large. Invillino may of course be atypical in being quitted so early, in having few man-made defences and in having a native garrison, but exca-vations elsewhere are needed to prove this case.

The terminology offered by Paul the Deacon and by contemporary sources for Longobard and Byzantine for-tifications creates confusion: *castrum* predominates for fortress and equally for fortified towns like Cividale and Pavia, while *castellum*, infrequently used, signifies a smaller defensive location. Invillino itself cannot easily be classified as a sizeable fortress and, as noted, its artificial defences are minimal, and yet it is still called a *castrum*. In effect, we have a major blurring or simplifica-tion of terms, with *castrum* referable to any fortified site, military or civil; some *castra* were of episcopal status (such as Bomarzo or Bagnoregio in the Duchy of Rome), others not; some, such as Castelseprio or Sirmione, pos-sessed an extensive administrative district, which could enclose a series of lesser *castra*; and occasionally a *castrum* lay within a fortified town or *civitas* (like Verona) or close to one (for example *Verruca* and Trento). Whether an official hierarchy of site labels (per-haps based on the status of the commander – *dux* for town and larger fort, count or *gastald* for lesser forts) existed in this, or even in the late-Roman period, cannot be determined. Size seems largely irrelevant; more signi-ficant was the level of strategic importance of a specific fortress.

An interesting case for study is provided by the site of *Sibrium* (Castelseprio), located in the sub-Alpine foot-hills north-west of Milan and west of Como (fig. 12).

There is a reasonable amount of documentation regarding *Sibrium*, attesting that its territory extended as a wedge between lakes Como and Maggiore north into Canton Ticino; we hear also of a parish church and a mint, functioning from the eighth century. Documentation is particularly good for the period 1000–1250, centring on the territorial conflict with Milan, which culminated in 1287 with the destruction of all but the religious edifices on the promontory of Seprio. Surviving elements today comprise the fragmentary church remains of S. Giovanni Evangelista and S. Paolo, the intact church of S. Maria Foris Portas outside the *borgo* west of the *castrum*, with its stunning and enigmatic cycle of, most likely, eighth-century frescos, and the contemporary monastic complex (still in use in the 18th century) of S. Maria di Torba, located within a fortified annex at the eastern base of the promontory.

Castelseprio has seen various excavation campaigns since the 'rediscovery' of S. Maria Foris Portas in 1944, but the limited publication of all but the most recent makes it difficult to assess fully the character of the site over time.[20] The overall chronology, however, seems fairly clear. The first historic phase, of later fourth-century date, involved the erection of three watch-towers, designed to oversee approach routes from the north and to signal south to the military command at Milan. In the course of the fifth century this military role was consolidated by the foundation of a *castrum*, girded by an extensive circuit wall, built of river cobble and *spolia*, that follows the sinuous course of the hilltop; within the walls lay a large cistern and the adjoining baptismal

[20] M. Dabrowska et al. 'Castelseprio: scavi diagnostici, 1962–63', *Sibrium*, xiv (1978–9), 1–128. Excavations since 1977: G. P. Brogiolo & S. Lusuardi Siena, 'Nuove indagini a Castelseprio', *Atti del VI congresso internazionale di studi sull'alto medioevo* (Spoleto, 1980), 475–99; M. Carver, 'S. Maria Foris Portas at Castel Seprio: A Famous Church in a New Context', *World Archaeology*, xviii 3 (1987), 312–29.

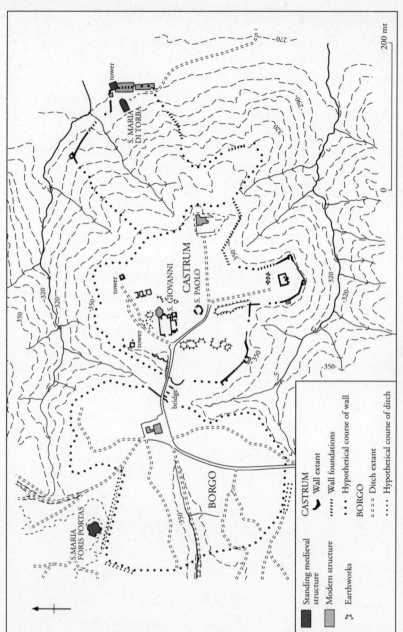

Figure 12 Plan of the late antique and early medieval castrum of Castelseprio, Lombardy (Carver 1987, fig. 2; reproduced by kind permission of Routledge).

church of S. Giovanni. The site may have been largely self-sufficient, since few imports occur here in the fifth and sixth centuries – an important observation given Castelseprio's undoubtedly high military status, and one that also helps to demonstrate the shrinkage in overseas trade activity. Longobard occupation is marked by a remodelling of S. Giovanni, by extramural growth in the area of the *borgo* and by intramural house construction in stone and timber with clay bonding. However, as at Invillino, specifically Longobard elements, such as stamped wares and weaponry, are mostly absent, and instead artefacts of late-Roman tradition persist. Problems in dating these undistinguished ceramics, combined with a stratigraphy disturbed by earlier excavations, mean that the Longobard–Carolingian transition phase is currently obscure. To offset this we have the church of S. Maria Foris Portas, built in mortared rubble and of trilobate form with atrium. The date of its foundation and of its internal decoration is much disputed, ranging from the mid-sixth century to the early ninth century. Graves around and within the church, however, suggest use from the eighth into the thirteenth century; though two built tombs, one with a sword-like cross engraved on its cover slab and fragments of gold braid inside and the other with the inscription *Wideramm* on top, could recommend a seventh-century origin. A 4 m wide ditch created an artificial promontory around the church area in the twelfth century, perhaps following an earlier cutting: the excavators suggest this formed a property boundary, possibly linked to a count, *gastald* or bishop's residence. If so, S. Maria may have been a private church, hence its extramural location; its survival in 1287 suggests that it had remained a prized jewel and had come into the possession of the Milanese bishop or count.

Thus, from the fifth century on, naturally defensible sites, such as hilltops, spurs and promontories, came to form the links in the Italian 'body armour', contrasting

*Plate 34 The meandering late-Roman circuit walls on the
promontory of Sirmione on Lake Garda.*

strongly with the large, inviting walled cities of the
plains. All routes of penetration were guarded: such promontories as Sirmione (pl. 34) and islands as San Giulio
(see pl. 16) and Comacina were fortified to provide both
military control of the northern lakes and compact strongholds and treasuries. The size and the location of the sites
virtually repeat a pre-Roman, Iron Age settlement pattern, indicating, thereby, a general decay in strong, centralized administrative and military control. In Etruria,
for example, many Etruscan hill-forts (*oppida*), depopulated since late Republican times, were revitalized by a
revamping of the old defences; in such Alpine regions as
Liguria, the Trentino and Veneto, many protohistoric
castellari or *castellieri* were reused. The sequence of flight
to the hills is attested earlier across the Alps, particularly
in Austria and former Yugoslavia, along the main routes
of access to Italy. Some sites appear to be the direct

successors of low-lying towns, as shown by the provision of sizeable church complexes and wall circuits; others were simply refuges. Too frequently, local scholars have elevated all such hilltop sites into the planned elements of an elaborate defensive screen, controlling and defending all communication lines. The evidence for such orchestration is minimal, and, while we must assume some degree of military forethought, the personal safety of the various civilian communities was perhaps the dominant factor.[21] The evidence from Invillino meanwhile offers a new reading, namely one of civilian settlements, possibly charged with military duties, but lacking an obvious 'official' presence. As noted, the Longobards were numerically dependent on the native Italians for support: Invillino documents this tacit co-operation.

This pattern can be extended to cover the rest of Italy: the Longobard failure to conquer the whole peninsula required the supervision of the borders with the residual Byzantine territories. Natural topographic features such as mountain ranges, rivers or marshes formed the main lines of division, which were reinforced by watch-towers and forts. Our knowledge of these borders is extremely limited, although reasonable reconstructions can be made for Byzantine zones, such as Liguria and the Duchy of Rome.[22] In each instance material traces of hilltop occupation are fragmentary and difficult to date, and we are partly reliant on toponyms as guides. In the case of Byzantine Liguria, tiny garrisons were installed in

[21] S. Johnson, *Late Roman Fortifications* (London, 1983), 218–20, 226–44.

[22] Christie, 'The Archaeology of Byzantine Italy', 274–8; cf. G. Schmiedt, 'Le fortificazioni altomedievali in Italia viste dall'aereo', *XV Settimana di studio del Centro Italiano di Studi sull'Alto Medioevo* (Spoleto, 1968), 859–927. For the Duchy of Benevento, relevant are the studies in Molise: R. Hodges et al. 'Excavations at D85 (Santa Maria in Cività)', *Papers of the British School at Rome*, xlviii 48 (1980), 70–124; and in Campania: P. Peduto, 'Archeologia medievale in Campania', *La Voce della Campania*, 10 (1979), 250–3.

observation posts overlooking passes, road and rivers, and these signalled back to *castra* or coastal towns. Along the Po, by contrast, defence was probably articulated between riverine *castra* of urban status (such as Ferrara, traditionally founded by the Byzantines in *c.*604) and small *castella*. Paul the Deacon fails to relay any real information regarding border skirmishes, though these must have been fairly frequent. Byzantine military treatises of the early seventh century, in fact, make reference to such raids and recommend suitable strategies to combat them. In Italy we have no evidence of successful Byzantine responses – not unexpectedly, Paul the Deacon prefers to highlight the Byzantine failure to stem major Longobard assaults, for example in Liguria in 643, when the imperial defences totally caved in.[23] Again, considerably more archaeological study is required before we can obtain even a rough understanding of the mechanics of Longobard – Byzantine border control in sixth- to eighth-century Italy.

[23] Liguria: Paul *HL*, IV, 45. On Byzantine and Longobard military organization: Brown, *Gentlemen and Officers*, 82–108; O. Bertolini, 'Ordinamenti militari e strutture sociali dei Longobardi in Italia', XV *Settimana di studio del Centro Italiano di Studi sull'Alto Medioevo*, 429–607.

6

Religion, Architecture and Art

From Arian to Catholic

The prologues of the Longobard law codes offer us a transition from a casual, passing acknowledgement of God by the Arian king Rothari to the profuse bestowal of thanks by the devout Catholic Liutprand. Somewhat surprisingly, there is little within the laws in the way of comment regarding Longobard religion, whether primitive pagan or civilized Christian. The most specific reference occurs in laws issued by Liutprand in 727 when 'in defence of our Christian and Catholic law we make provision that no one may presume to wander from the faith of Christ' through penalties against pagan rites:

He who, unmindful of the wrath of God, goes to sorcerers or witches for the purpose of receiving divinations or answers of any kind whatsoever from them, shall pay to the royal fisc as composition half of the price at which he would have been valued if someone had killed him, and in addition, shall do penance according to the established canon. In like manner, he who, like a rustic, prays to a tree as sacred or adores springs, or who makes any sacrilegious incantation, shall also pay as composition a half of his price to the royal fisc. . . We decree that each judge and sculdahis shall undertake to send a warning to those who, whether male or female, have in the past done such unspeakable deeds [i.e. sorcery] that they shall not do them in the future. If they do not do them in the future, they shall not be offered for sale. (Liut. 84–5).

The law is pitched at freemen and lords. The phrase 'like a rustic' implies that at serf level paganism was still practised and probably overlooked. Clearly, though, as in the last centuries of Roman rule when many senators and aristocrats still clung to the old gods, the conversion to Catholicism of the Longobard nobility or free class was neither wholesale nor effective. Indeed, the warning given out by Liutprand (85) to the judge and lesser officials of each district to suppress witchcraft may be a comment on their own illegal participation in these rites. Rothari's laws 197–8 certainly admit the possibility of freewomen, *aldiae* or slaves being accused of being witches, vampires or enchantresses, yet law 376 dismisses the existence of such creatures: 'No one may presume to kill another man's *aldia* or woman slave as if she were a vampire, which the people call a witch, because it is in no wise to be believed by Christian minds that it is possible that a woman can eat a living man from within.' A mingling of primitive and contemporary beliefs and superstitions is also shown in the mode of oath-taking: either on consecrated weapons or on the holy gospels (Roth. 363) – but there is no indication that the use of consecrated weaponry lasted into the eighth century.

In Rothari's laws churches are mentioned mainly as places of public assembly and worship, and fines were imposed for creating a disturbance in them; fugitive bondsmen might take refuge there, but these renegades had to be handed back to their lord by the priest (Roth. 35, 343, 272). By Liutprand's reign the Church was the recipient of bequeathed lands, in part because women seemed frequently to enter nunneries (Liut. 30, 95, 100–1). Church influence increased dramatically under Liutprand, but its landed power was restricted, in strong contrast to the situation in Byzantine zones. In fact, greater landowning was allowed only to churches and monasteries founded by the kings, who placed them under palace protection (Aistulf 19). Members of the clergy, however, were subject to Roman law and thus are only shadowy figures in the Longobard codes. The Church's popularity amongst women and the paucity of references to men entering the service suggest that its appeal to male Longobard minds must have been rather lack-lustre.

Our other documentary sources provide variable insights into Longobard religion. Of greatest value are the letters of Pope Gregory the Great (590–604), revealing his indefatigable attempts to unite and fortify the Italian Church against the heretical or pagan Longobard intruders. Before the invasion the bishops of northern Italy had sided with the supporters of the so-called Three Chapters schism, against papal wishes; on their arrival, the Longobards had allowed the Catholics to continue their worship unharmed (few bishops actually fled their sees), and, indeed, their presence helped harden the schismatics' resolve. Gregory only fleetingly comments on heathen practices, but concentrates on attacking the Arian heresy professed by most leading Longobards. In the bitter war years, King Authari had in fact forbidden the sons of Longobards to be baptized in the Catholic rite, fearing, according to Gregory, 'Catholicism as an instrument of the Empire, sapping the warrior vitality of his people'. Authari's death and the outbreak of plague in 590 were joyfully proclaimed by Gregory as clear signs of God's punishment of Arianism, and he urged the northern bishops to preach the true word.[1] This episode alone shows that many of the Longobard nobility were Arians, but that Catholicism was already making its presence felt. Authari's marriage in 589 to the Catholic Bavarian princess Theodelinda marks a point of transition; her marriage after 590 to Agilulf led to an increasing Catholic influence at court, and this rubbed off on Agilulf, to the extent that their son Adaloald was baptized

---

[1] Greg. *Reg.*, I.17. See Richards, *Consul of God*, 191–4.

Plate 35 The Hen and Chicks, *most probably one of the gifts sent by Pope Gregory the Great to the Catholic Longobard queen Theodelinda. (Tesoro del Museo del Duomo, Monza.)*

a Catholic.[2] Gregory duly sought to exploit Theodelinda's faith and position, sending her letters and gifts (pl. 35) and willing her to drop her allegiance to the Three Chapters. She countered by asking that Rome accept the Three Chapters – Gregory claimed that ill health prevented his reply, and, indeed, his death shortly afterwards terminated their intriguing exchanges. Gregory's efforts extended elsewhere, even within imperial Sicily and Campania, to counter the pagan worship of 'stones and trees'. As implied by Liutprand's law 84, such rites were generally being performed by 'rustics', though a ninth-century saint's life, recounting events of the 670s, tells that the missionary bishop Barbatus, when coming to

2 Greg. *Reg.*, XIV.12; cf. Paul *HL*, IV. 27 and 6, wrongly stating that Agilulf was converted.

restore Catholicism to Benevento, found its inhabitants worshipping a snake.[3]

The dearth of information for much of the seventh century leaves us in the dark as to the progressive Longobard conversion to Catholicism. After Grimoald, the kings were generally Catholic: stability of the faith at this highest level was vital in the overall conversion sequence. The late seventh century also saw the formal peace treaty between *Langobardia* and Byzantium (680) and the end of the Three Chapters schism (698); by these acts the political and religious conflicts between north and south and Longobard and Byzantine were largely cancelled out, as reflected in the subsequent periodic alliances between the sides.

From the late eighth century stems the *Historia Longobardorum*. Paul the Deacon's heroes are all pious Christians, both Longobard (particularly Liutprand) and non-Longobard (notably St Benedict and Pope Gregory). He plays down the pagan and Arian past and even modifies the tribe's legendary origins as set out in the *Origo gentis Langobardorum*. Yet Catholicism does not mean goodness, and Paul is decidedly cool towards Agilulf, Theodelinda and their dynasty, though partly this is due to their adoption of Byzantine court ceremony. Likewise the church-building kings Perctarit and Cunicpert, praised in the *Carmen de Synodo Ticinesi*, fail to merit Paul's favour. His 'de-paganizing' and his biases, in effect, bring his narrative into line with his own times, thereby distorting our picture of Longobard religious evolution.[4] Indeed, the prologues to Liutprand's laws show that, even in the 720s, the pagan past had been virtually erased: 'I, Liutprand, in the name of God the Almighty, most excellent king of the divinely chosen Catholic

[3] *Vita S. Barbati*, 1. Gregory's missions: Richards, *Consul of God*, 228–50.
[4] See discussion in Goffart, *The Narrators of Barbarian History*, 382–430.

nation of the Longobards. . .' Paul's *Historia Langobard-orum* offered a platform from which to back this claim, though the kingdom's fall in 774 did much to destroy his literary efforts.

Paul's cover-up job makes it hard to determine whether distinct Arian and Catholic Longobard factions existed, and whether a conflict between the two is represented in the seventh-century civil wars. A case can, in fact, be made for non-hostile toleration and even co-operation between the two faiths: the dethroning of the Catholic Adaloald in 626 came with the support of the Catholic bishops of the north; Rothari (who, even Paul the Deacon (*HL*, IV. 42) has to concede, was Arian) fails to reveal in his laws any hint of religious conflict or any attempt to Christianize his many pagan subjects; and Arian and Catholic Cathedrals coexisted in the capital of Pavia into the 690s – Paul even extends this duality to the rest of Longobard Italy. Only Authari's forceful verbal ban on Catholic baptisms betrays religious fervency. The Longobards, it can be argued, merely adapted to changing circumstances, using religion almost as a diplomatic tool, as shown first by their emerging as 'Catholic allies' to Justinian whilst in Pannonia, then in Alboin's anti-Byzantine switch to Arianism in 568, and later in Authari's and Agilulf's marriage to a Catholic. It is only from the later seventh century that kings begin to express a proper religious fervour through church and monastery building and missionary activities.[5]

Some of these religious vicissitudes may be evident in the archaeology, particularly in terms of burial rites. The pagan Longobard period in Italy (*c.*568–680) is marked

[5] On the question of paganism and Arianism see Wickham, *Early Medieval Italy*, 34–8, challenging G. P. Bognetti, *L'età longobarda*, iii (Milan, 1966), 71 ff. A sign of late pagan survival on Longobard soil comes in a mid eighth-century inscription from Filattiera, in eastern Liguria, recording the efforts of one Leodgar in 'destroying the idols'. See also the detailed study in Luiselli, *Storia Culturare*.

by burial with grave-goods: in the case of males, these items are heavily militaristic early on but become progressively less so over time, except amongst the elite; for women the wealth and variety of jewellery was emblematic of status. Burial in full dress, with weapons or personal fittings, implies a belief in an afterlife and a need to exhibit one's social trappings in the next world. The provision of food in pots points to the need for a packed lunch for the long journey. As noted, we have little knowledge of how this afterlife was visualized, but it cannot have been far removed from this world save for the company of Germanic gods.

Interaction with the largely Catholic Italian population may be observed in the adoption of elements of Mediterranean dress and in the burial of 'natives' in Longobard cemeteries. Longobard open-mindedness will have led to the progressive intake of Catholicism, although it is difficult to calculate its pace: artefactually, we may see crosses added to brooches or buckles, the use of gold-sheet crosses laid on the head or chest of the deceased (pl. 28), and the building of chapels in Longobard cemeteries – as probably occurs at Castel Trosino around the mid-seventh century. Changes undoubtedly commenced early on, and the impression is one of gradual Christianization and an adoption of elements of the religion before complete conversion. It is striking, however, that the provision of grave-goods diminishes rapidly after 650, indicating a more sudden change in rite. This need not be solely down to Christianity: economic factors may have also played a part, with the living less willing to part with metals that were becoming scarce. Rothari, noticeably, issued a law regarding the inheritance of both tools and weapons (law 225), but also heavily condemned the act of grave-robbing (*crapworfin*), meting out a fine of 900 *solidi* to violators of freemen's tombs (law 15). Rare instances of late seventh-century equipped graves are known, notably a tomb recently excavated near Magnano in Riviera in Friuli (containing silver-inlaid spurs, belt fittings, plus a seal ring incorporating a *solidus* of Constantine IV, of 668–80), but the vast majority of Longobard tombs by AD 675 lacked grave-goods and are indistinguishable from native tombs.

Longobard Builders and Buildings

The first century and a half of Longobard rule in Italy are all but invisible in terms of architectural remains. The sunken timber buildings found in Brescia, and the half stone-built houses in such towns as Brescia and Verona, or forts as Castelseprio and Invillino, give us an important indication of domestic architecture, but on an insufficient scale to allow worthwhile analysis: all we can say is that the Longobards lived in houses similar to those built by other German peoples such as the Saxons. Furthermore, the fact that these structures appear on previously Roman sites could even imply that they belonged, not to the Longobards, but to the non-German, native population.[6] The total number of ordinary houses so far identified is paltry, but we can be certain that the Longobards did not live in hovels: as work in Britain has shown, the Anglo-Saxons were skilled craftsmen and carpenters, fully capable of erecting a range of solid structures, and were not relegated – as was once long contested – to muddy, grubby, sunken pit-houses. For Britain, however, the evidence does point to a serious decay and abandonment of old Roman structures, in advance of the Saxon take-over: this contrasts strongly, of course, with Italy where Ostrogoths, Byzantines and

[6] Note, for example, the seventh-century timber houses found over the Roman forum in Luni: B. Ward-Perkins, 'Two Byzantine Houses at Luni', *Papers of the British School at Rome*, xlix (1981), 91–8. On domestic architecture see G. Pavan, 'Architettura del periodo longobardo' in *I Longobardi* (exh. cat., 1990), 236–9.

Longobards sought to maintain the urban fabric. Certain structures had long gone, such as the public fora, baths, temples, theatres, gymnasia and aqueducts, but these no longer counted as essentials; however, roads, defences, houses, cemeteries and, most importantly, churches, continued to be tended, and these all formed the backdrop to a revised form of urban life.[7]

This maintenance work was deemed a public duty, and the law-makers clearly assumed that money would be forthcoming and that workmen could be procured. Further, repairs on public structures such as town defences and churches imply a high skill factor, since the key targets for maintenance will have been towers, battlements and church roofs, all of which require scaffolding, the provision of cut stone, mortar, tiles and so on. To some degree materials could be culled from neighbouring ruins, but more often than not new timber would need to be cut and new tiles fired. The Longobard law codes barely mention the existence of builders: apart from Rothari's laws 144 and 145, mentioned above, a single issue under Liutprand refers vaguely to *magistri*, who are restricted to a maximum of three years away from home. Fortunately, however, the *Memoratorio de mercedes commacinorum* (see chapter 5) deals solely with the builders' guild. As well as providing a set of fixed prices for the various tasks of the building trade, it suggests that there was a recognized federation of craftsmen, trained to a degree of specialization and perhaps able to offer guarantees on their work – odd-jobbers no doubt abounded, but a legalized guild offered some security to would-be church-builders. Such guilds are attested in other fields such as marble-working, iron-working, document-writing, ship-building and salt-trading, indicating the survival of trained corps of professionals – again

[7] See in particular Ward-Perkins, *From Classical Antiquity to the Middle Ages.*

at the disposal of aristocrats. For the ordinary town-dweller or farmer 'do-it-yourself' work would have been customary: a capitulary of Charlemagne of 789, for instance, asks that on Sundays peasants should desist from doing work like tending vines, ploughing fields, cutting stone or building houses. In the countryside certainly, building in timber had always been prevalent and continued well into the Middle Ages – in towns, too, the bulk of the inhabitants will have built and lived in timber houses.[8]

Accordingly, surviving documentation relates primarily to the elite or, at least, to structures paid for by the elite. Some *magistri* were proud enough to sign their products, including Gennarius *magester marmorarius* at Savigliano in 755, the *pictor* Auripert at Lucca in 763 and Ursus and his trainees, who signed the ciborium in S. Giorgio di Valpolicella. Building specialists are noticeably often referred to in southern documents as *transpadani* (i.e. 'northerners') and were clearly freemen, equipped with staff and a range of tools and machinery. How far they could pick and choose their work is unclear, as we do not know how many members there were in the guilds. Liutprand's controls on prices and movements suggest a level of royal supervision, and in the eighth century it was certainly the royal families and the nobility who made most use of the *magistri*. From the ninth century references to these free artisans and guilds become increasingly rare, and in their place we see the rise of specialists, dependent on individual landowners – whether royal, noble or monastic – and distributed across farms and villages.

Despite documentary references to houses, mints and palaces, only religious structures survive from the late Longobard era. Almost without exception, however, these structures have been swamped by successive

---

[8] Wickham, *Early Medieval Italy*, 88–9; Galetti, 'La casa contadina nell'Italia padana' in Francovich (ed.), *Archeologia e storia del medioevo italiano*, 97–111.

Carolingian, Romanesque or more recent rebuildings or elaborations, and only careful architectural scrutiny and excavation can reveal the early medieval phases. Without excavation, only the dedication to such favoured saints as S. Salvatore, S. Michele or S. Giorgio suggests a Longobard foundation. In many other cases, the Longobard structure may be no more than a reworking of an early Christian edifice: large numbers of these late-Roman foundations appear to have been continuously maintained, backing the hypothesis of a fairly healthy native Christian population. In these instances the Longobard phase is often marked solely by the presence of fragments of stone-carved church fittings, only broadly assignable to the eighth century. The dates attributed to carvings or wall paintings do not of course date the church itself: decorative elements may relate to any phase of a church's existence. Debate has raged over the dating of the fine frescos within the small church of S. Maria Foris Portas at Castelseprio, for example, which have been assigned to various dates between the sixth and the tenth century and have been argued by some to be indicative of Byzantine, and by others of Frankish, workmanship; excavations within and around the church at least confirm its construction in the Longobard era. In Brescia, excavations in 1958–60 of the partially preserved church of S. Salvatore argued for a triple-apsed plan for the first monastic church built by Duke Desiderius from *c*.753; re-excavation now points to the possibility of an earlier T-plan church, dating to the late seventh century, followed in the mid-eighth century by an aisled church with single nave; the larger triple-apsed building may be a Carolingian modification (fig. 13).[9] These examples

[9] M. Carver, 'S. Maria Foris Portas at Castel Seprio'; Brogiolo, 'Trasformazioni urbanistiche nella Brescia longobarda', in G. Menis (ed.), *I Longobardi. Italia Longobarda* (1991), 108–13. On church architecture: A. Peroni, 'L'arte nell'età longobarda' in *Magistra Barbaritas*, 255–82; Pavan, 'Architettura del periodo longobardo' in *I Longobardi* (exh. cat., 1990), 236–98.

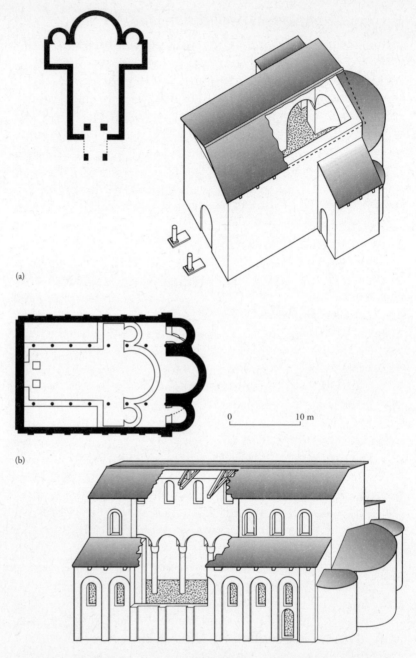

(a)

(b)

0   10 m

*Figure 13 Plans and reconstructions of the (a) late seventh-
and (b) mid-eighth-century phases of the church of
S. Salvatore, Brescia (Brogiolo 1993, figs 70, 71).*

serve to show that archaeological and art historical data are not foolproof, and that the reconstruction of a structural sequence must be attempted with caution.

As a result, it is not yet possible to identify a distinctly Longobard style of architecture nor an architectural sequence: churches of Longobard date may be single naved, aisled, triple-apsed, with or without crypts and even circular, in plan. Nor can we envisage a simple progression from plainer to more complicated forms. Architects were able to draw upon both early Christian and Byzantine models, and there were plenty of extant buildings to imitate. The conquest of the Byzantine zones in the eighth century, notably Ravenna in 751, will have offered further useful examples, though undoubtedly these buildings could have been seen well before the annexation. With no monumental architectural tradition behind the Longobards, inevitably we must argue for a native Italian input, although there is no clear indication that the *magistri commacini* were not Longobard. Rarely are the Longobard churches large affairs: given that many palaeochristian basilicas were still maintained, there was no pressing need for huge places of worship; instead, new structures often served the personal needs of royal or ducal families, whether as private chapels or monasteries or, more blatantly, as statements of authority. Such is the context claimed for the late seventh-century complex identified beneath S. Salvatore at Brescia.

At least fifty monasteries are known to have been active in the Longobard era, but our fragmentary documentation probably hides a much larger number of private foundations, in particular small urban establishments (fig. 14). Archaeological research of these monasteries is limited, often because of continuous redevelopment, and again we are dependent on stray architectural finds for chronological guidance. Structurally it is argued that the monasteries were small, clustered affairs before the eighth century, when more organic plans incorporating

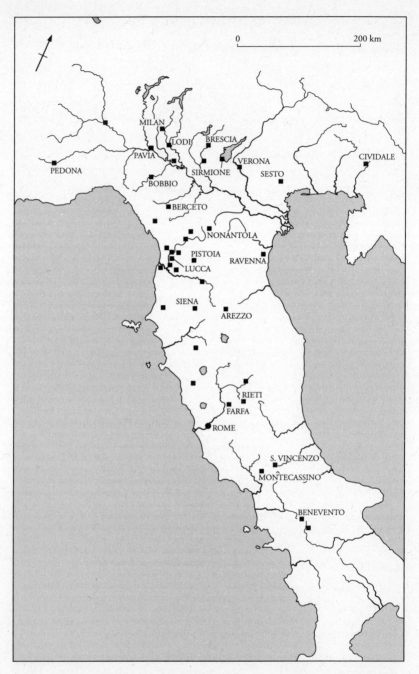

Figure 14 Map of recorded monasteries in Longobard Italy (after Wataghin Cantino 1989).

cloisters and precinct walls took hold. Pre-Longobard sites such as Farfa, Montecassino and S. Vincenzo al Volturno appear to have reutilized ruinous Roman structures, probably villas, in their primary plans, with more identifiably 'monastic' layouts emerging in the late eighth and ninth centuries. The key Longobard monasteries were well-endowed royal foundations, presented with fiscal lands as a starting point and subsequently endowed through private donations. These could occur in both rural and urban contexts, sometimes on royal or ducal estates and sometimes as attachments to palace complexes (as at Brescia, Pavia and Cividale).[10]

Many of these monastic foundations appear, on the basis of the documentary sources, to be active from the reign of Liutprand (712–44). The earliest documented seat is that of Bobbio, located 40 miles south of Pavia, near the modern border between Lombardy and Liguria. This was founded in 614 by the Irish missionary St Columbanus, previously active in Frankish Gaul (where he had established monasteries at Annegray, Luxeuil and Fontaine) and keen to extend his calming influence over other troubled waters. Agilulf, no doubt with the strong support of Queen Theodelinda, provided lands at Bobbio and, according to Paul the Deacon (*HL* IV, 41), encouraged various dukes to make donations to the establishment. Although Columbanus himself died in 615, his new monastic community, largely made up of Irish expatriates and living by austere rules, soon established itself as a scholarly centre with a renowned scriptorium and library. Unlike Gaul, however, where Columbanus's foundations prompted a wave of religious fervour amongst the Frankish elite, Bobbio did not spawn fledgling monasteries: more prominent royal

---

[10] G. Wataghin Cantino, 'Monasteri di età longobarda: spunti per una ricerca', *XXXVI Corso di cultura sull'arte ravennate e bizantina* (Ravenne, 1989), 73–100; C. Lawrence, *Medieval Monasticism*, (London, 1984), 36–75.

sanction was required for monasticism really to take
hold. When Liutprand founded Berceto, in the Apuan
Alps south-east of Bobbio, in 718, new factors seem to be
at play: not just the king's religious zeal and desire to
christianize fully the mountainous zones of Liguria, but
also political strategy, the demonstration of royal wealth
and authority, and an aim to cash in on ever-increasing
pilgrim traffic from Britain and Gaul to Rome. Strategic
siting of monasteries along important road, river and
lake routes, sometimes within fortresses, is an element
often overlooked in assessing the role of these complexes,
but it is essential when considering them in the context
of the localization of power from the eighth century onwards.

Detailed documentation in the form of charters and
chronicles exists for some of the major monasteries such
as Farfa and S. Vincenzo, though it relates chiefly to the
post-Longobard period. Good documentation is often
available for smaller establishments, including S. Maria
at Sesto al Reghena in Friuli, founded by Benedictine
monks between 730 and 735. In Sesto's case we can note
the donation of 762 drafted in the abbey at Nonantola,
in Tuscany, which records the gift of the whole property
(comprising lands, farms and houses) of the brothers
Erfo, Marco and Anto, sons of Duke Peter of Friuli, to
the Friulian monasteries of Sesto and Salto; a document
of 775 records that Charlemagne gave Sesto his protection and confirmed its possessions; royal and ducal donations extend into the tenth century and also report the
monastery's fortification in the 960s. Documents for
Sesto extend well into the fifteenth century. Surprisingly,
the resource of monastic archives is largely untapped, but
research, in particular on the archives of Farfa, in central
Italy, has already demonstrated the wide-ranging information that can be retrieved regarding the history of both
monastery and territory. The combination of archival
and archaeological work offers even greater potential, as

borne out in the S. Vincenzo project, which has allowed the first coherent analysis of an early medieval and medieval Italian landscape.[11]

Longobard Art and Sculpture

Many churches and monasteries in Italy display, or incorporate in their walls, fragments of carving from stone or marble chancel screens, altar fronts, pulpits or ciboria, which may offer the sole indication of an early medieval, perhaps Longobard, phase of embellishment. These reliefs are generally decorated with interwoven bands or vines framing bunches of grapes, leaves or flowers, often with doves in attendance; on more elaborate reliefs, the interlace work creates a border for depictions of such Christian symbols as peacocks, deer or lambs and, occasionally, of less obviously Christian elements such as fantastic beasts, griffins, sea monsters or dragons (pl. 36). Far less common are carvings depicting human figures, particularly secular ones; representations of Christ and the Virgin do occur, for example on the Altar of Ratchis at Cividale (see pls 19 and 22).

Inevitably there are problems with dating such pieces and, too often, they are simply assigned to a documented building phase. Attribution is more secure only with pieces bearing inscriptions: tombstones, dedications, sarcophagi or church fittings, such as the splendid Altar of Ratchis, dated to *c*.745, or the font and cover attributed to bishop Callistus, but in fact executed under the patriarch Siguald in *c*.770. When secure dates can be assigned, we then have temporal settings for the associated

---

[11] M. Torcellan, 'Lo scavo presso la chiesa di S. Maria in Sylvis di Sesto al Reghena. Relazione preliminare', *Archeologia Medievale*, xv (1988), 313–34; R. Hodges & J. Mitchell (eds), *San Vincenzo al Volturno. The Archaeology, Art and Territory of an Early Medieval Monastery*, British Archaeological Reports, Internat. Ser. 252, (Oxford, 1985).

Plate 36 Beautifully executed figurative screen panels of the first half of the eighth century, from the royal monastery of S. Michele alla Pusterla, Pavia. (Musei Civici di Pavia, Castello Visconteo.)

designs and can attempt to tie in uninscribed pieces. However, many of the basic designs had a long currency, running well into the Carolingian period and merging with early Romanesque elements from the late tenth century. Nevertheless, it is clear that such works were being carved from the reign of Liutprand onwards, and thus before the appearance of similar artwork in Byzantine and other non-Longobard areas of Italy. This need not imply that the ideas and forms were all originally Longobard; in fact, many of the designs have their roots in early Christian and Byzantine art. But there is a clear Germanic input in the use of the interlace and of the fantastic animals, so evident in much of Longobard metal-work, which suggests a healthy merging of artistic skills. The Germanic elements may not be all Longobard, either, for similar designs can be viewed in the illuminations of British and Irish manuscripts of the seventh century where they probably were Anglo-Saxon, rather than Celtic, features. In this respect, we must recall the Irish involvement in the foundation of Bobbio in Italy and of monasteries in Francia, and also the documented pilgrim traffic from Britain to Rome via *Langobardia*.[12]

The dating and derivation of more adventurous art forms, notably figured frescos or stucco work, such as can be seen in the famous Tempietto, the small church of S. Maria in Valle at Cividale (pl. 37), are open to even greater art-historical debate. The problem is that the majority of surviving art works cannot readily be fixed within the true Longobard period: even in the case of the Tempietto, dating wavers between the mid-eighth century and the early ninth century, and thus between Longobard-Byzantine and Carolingian.[13] Scholars do, at least, agree on a major revival of the arts under Liutprand from the second decade of the eighth century, and, thus, well before a similar revival of classical art forms in Rome. Longobard art continued to flourish and was maintained well into the second half of the century, and even after the fall of the Longobard kingdom, it survived both in the north and in the new southern states. The 'revival' probably hides a low-key continuation of these arts throughout the seventh century – churches such as S. Maria Antiqua in the Rome Forum certainly provide evidence for the persistence of high quality work, while figured murals (non-religious in design) are recorded by

[12] Peroni, 'L'arte nell'età longobarda' in *Magistra Barbaritas*, 229–97; A. Romanini, 'Scultura nella "Langobardia maior": questioni storiografiche', *Arte Medievale*, v (1991); M. Righetti Tosti Croce, 'La scultura' in *I Longobardi* (exh. cat., 1990), 300–24. A large body of the relevant material is collated in the series Corpus della Scultura Altomedievale.

[13] S. Tavano, *Il Tempietto longobardo di Cividale* (Udine, 1990).

Plate 37 The impressive figurative stucco decoration in the Tempietto, Cividale.

Paul the Deacon for Queen Theodelinda's palace at Monza *c*.600 (*HL*, IV. 22).

After 774 new Frankish patrons may have emerged, but we should not doubt that it was still largely Italo-Longobard artists and architects who were responsible for those buildings and their ornamentation that constitute the so-called 'Carolingian renaissance' in north Italy. Frankish sovereignty simply encouraged the growth and execution of ideas, and, indeed, after 800 the region of *Langobardia* became the point of diffusion for a distinct architectural style known as the Lombard First Romanesque, a mixture of Roman and Byzantine styles, combined with Frankish influences. Brickwork and vaulting were the main components of the new style, which was applied to churches and monasteries and spread westwards into Spain to create a Lombardo-Catalan style.[14] The importance of the Italian contribution is shown by the term *Lombardus*, which swiftly become synonymous with mason. North Italy was not unique, however: much of the peninsula enjoyed an architectural revival, most notably Rome, where a vast array of churches and hostels were built, repaired or embellished. Even if the Saracen incursions and the break-up of unified Frankish rule subsequently disrupted economic and artistic output, the architectural revival, once begun, was maintained, making churches our key structural guides in understanding the character and prosperity of Italian medieval cities.

[14] K. J. Conant, *Carolingian and Romanesque Architecture, 800–1200* (London, 1979), 107–11 – which, however, regards the works produced as 'ordinarily cogent and practical: often competent rather than inspired'.

Longobard Heritage: Benevento and Beyond

The Byzantine reconquest of Italy had marked, albeit fleetingly, a political unity of the peninsula that was to be lost for over thirteen centuries following the appearance of the Longobards in 568–9. The northern Longobard kingdom centred on Pavia had, with time, promised to recreate this unity, but papal pleas and Carolingian desires destroyed such hopes entirely. Unlike the Vandals in Africa or the Ostrogoths in Italy, the Longobards did not lose their name or identity as a result of their defeat. In the south, as will be discussed below, the Duchy of Benevento, self-elevated into a principality, received numerous Longobard refugees, reinforcing it in its task of opposing further Carolingian annexations. For a time its independence was strong, but, as elsewhere in Italy, internal pressures destroyed its cohesion and it was forced to split into small rival units. Yet, while its enemies remained weak, the Longobard name survived. The disunity of this state exemplifies the disunity of all the peninsula in the tenth century.

Charlemagne retained the name *Langobardia* and allowed many of the Longobard officials to continue in their administrative seats so long as their allegiance was evident, although where rebellion flared, as in the delicate border district of Friuli in 776, Carolingian functionaries rapidly moved in as replacements. Nevertheless, within a generation Longobard dukes had become Frankish counts. But both Carolingian and papal rule failed to provide stability in northern and central Italy respectively. In the north, Carolingian rule was for the most part ephemeral; there was no major influx of Franks, Germans or Bavarians, and few of the Frankish monarchs of Italy bothered to spend time in the peninsula. Only Louis II (844–75) consciously attempted to revive fortunes, with energetic legislative measures designed to counteract the evident signs of administrative and social decay – primarily, abuse of power, oppression, robbery, decrepit public buildings and amenities. Louis II was successful in many respects, but this success was all too dependent on his own energies. Interestingly, Louis II counteracted the growing power of the Frankish counts by selecting the bishops, who were also town-based, from amongst the Longobard aristocratic families. This power play developed after the death of the heirless Louis in 875, as rival counts and kings tore apart his carefully maintained bureaucratic framework. Hungarian and Arab incursions worsened the situation, and state authority fragmented, being forced to give progressively greater powers to the bishops. These events did not provoke an attempt to revive an independent *Langobardia*: although bishops and counts alike sought a united kingdom, for the most part they supported different German or French/Burgundian Frankish claimants; even the Italian claimants derived from Frankish stock. In time emperors or kings had little real say in the affairs of the Italian cities, which were moving increasingly towards the system of semi-autonomous communes.

To the south, the Church State, although nominally independent, was all too reliant on the goodwill of its saviour, Charlemagne, and duly fostered closer political, religious and economic ties. For the actual city of Rome the benefits are apparent on a variety of levels: after 775 we see a spate of projects designed to enhance the position of the pope, such as church embellishment and repairs, foundation of farm estates in the surrounding countryside, improved provision of the corn dole, repair to the city wall and certain aqueducts; there was also an intensification of pilgrim traffic to Rome's multifarious shrines. Everything points to an economic upturn, prompted by the removal of the Longobard threat – and presumably bolstered by grants and gifts from the Frankish court – combined with Rome's inclusion in the wider Carolingian orbit. However, with Charlemagne's death and the subsequent division of his Empire, Frankish power-politics resumed, to the detriment of the fringe regions of imperial power. Accordingly, c.830 Rome's renaissance was already wilting, and resistance against raiding Saracens (who sacked the Vatican in 846) was almost nonexistent. As in the north, centralized control progressively declined as the popes lost out to upwardly mobile noble families both within and outside the city; this fragmentation would increase as nobility vied for power.

The Fate of the Beneventan Principality

Further south, the Longobard duchy of Benevento had, by good fortune, avoided the fate of its northern fellows. Pope Hadrian urged Charlemagne to annex that territory, too, no doubt in the hope that the King would transfer its ownership to Rome. Charlemagne, however, held back: greater threats to his dominion lay far to the north in Saxony and in former Pannonia, leaving him no time to dawdle in Italy. Indeed Charlemagne's subsequent visits to Italy were fleeting, only sufficient to counter major civil and military strife between Rome and Benevento, and to gain his crowning as Emperor from Pope Leo III in 800. For the most part left to their own devices, the Beneventans achieved a tidy stability tucked in between various powers – Frankish, papal, Neapolitan and Byzantine. Fluctuations in these powers and in

Beneventan internal politics later tested Longobard strength to the full, but, with some difficulty, the independent territory persisted for almost three hundred years – in effect for longer than the old *Regnum Langobardorum*. As with its precursor, however, by the time of Benevento's fall in 1077 its character had become almost wholly transformed (fig. 15).

When Arechis elevated the Duchy into a principality, he clearly realized that his was the new Longobard domain and Benevento the new Longobard capital; indeed, the historian Erchempert later described the city as '*Ticinum gemellum*' – Pavia's twin (pl. 38). Diplomatic and trading connections with Byzantium put Benevento in a delicate position, and Arechis was fortunate that

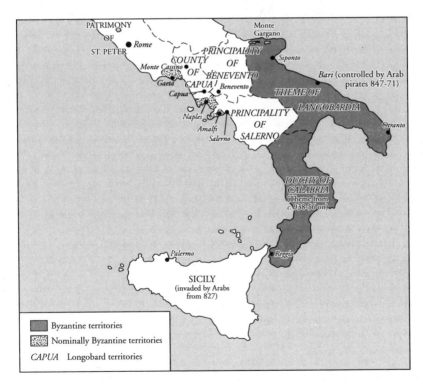

Figure 15 The southern states in AD 1000.

*Plate 38 Benevento: a tower along the course of the town
wall, repaired and extended in the eighth century.*

Hadrian's pleas to Charlemagne fell on deaf ears. However, royal visits in 786/7 to Montecassino and Capua,
both on Beneventan soil, were enough to compel Prince
Arechis to shelter in Salerno and to dispatch hostages,
among them his son Grimoald; Charlemagne's withdrawal allowed Arechis to reclaim his seat, but the death
that year first of Arechis' elder son and then of Arechis
himself left the Principality exposed. In line with policy
elsewhere in Italy, Charlemagne installed Grimoald as a
vassal duke-prince, subject to the Franks. Initially Grimoald III kept on the right side of the King and even
fought off, with Frankish support, a Byzantine attempt to
install the Hellenized Longobard Adalchis on his throne.
But, buoyed by this military success, Grimoald dropped
Charlemagne's name from his coins and charters in 791
and, in skirmishes with Charlemagne's sons, made Longobard independence plain (pl. 39).[1]

[1] Goffart, *The Narrators of Barbarian History*, 345–7.

Plate 39 Beneventan solidus *of Prince Grimoald III
(788–806). (Fitzwilliam Museum, Cambridge.)*

Grimoald died heirless in 806, although his replacement Grimoald IV was probably a relation. The new prince
lacked his predecessor's military skills, being forced in
812 to pay 25,000 *solidi* to Charlemagne, and from 814
Louis the Pious imposed an annual tribute of 7,000
solidi. In 817 Grimoald IV was murdered, and his successor Sico strove to restore Beneventan pride by attacking
Naples, but achieved minimal gain. He was succeeded by
his son Sicard, who was murdered during another con-
spiracy amongst the nobility in 839, which also caused
the eruption of a bloody civil war that split the Principality: Sicard's brother Siconulf established himself as
prince in Salerno and, for ten years, fought off Radelchis
of Benevento. The division of territory was formalized in
849 when Louis II forced a peace on the two sides, but
Siconulf's death shortly afterwards, followed by civil war
around Salerno and combined with Arab advances in
Apulia, caused Frankish interventions in the south to
continue. In fact, between 866 and 871 Louis II occupied
Benevento and utilized it as his southern base, minting
his own coin in association with Prince Adelchis. Adelchis got his own back by taking the Emperor prisoner
and expelling him, badly affecting Louis' political standing. Hostility towards Louis had even provoked an

alliance between Spoletans, Beneventans, Salernitans and Neapolitans, and when he returned in 872–3 these states countered his every move. The Longobards then allied themselves with the Byzantines instead, though this choice shortly backfired as land was ceded and lost: Salerno became a client state, and in 891 Benevento again was occupied by an enemy. By 900 the Byzantines held all of Apulia and created here their military *theme* (province) of *Langobardia* headed by the key ports of Trani and Bari. To the west and south the Byzantines now held almost all of Lucania and Calabria, although all three provinces suffered from attacks launched from Arab Sicily.[2]

Benevento and Salerno were territorially weakened; however, Benevento's union with the Principality of Capua from 900 to 981 at least gave the former some maritime capabilities to counter its eastern losses, and in Salerno the establishment of a long dynasty under Waifer in the 860s provided the state a degree of political stability. Uprisings in the Langobardia theme led to some Beneventan reprisals against Byzantium, which were largely ineffective; indeed, it is likely that the urban revolts in the theme were not calls for help to fellow Longobards but, rather, local responses to over-efficient Byzantine administrators. Pandulf I (943–81) of Capua-Benevento for a time headed the German emperor Otto's army in the south, but he was captured by the Byzantines and taken off to Constantinople in 969. When restored, he gained control over Salerno and thereby, nominally, held a large part of southern Italy. However, his control was so superficial that at his death the apparent unity disintegrated and the various states resumed their struggles against each other, as well as against the Arabs, the Byzantines and the German emperors. The situation

---

[2] Wickham, *Early Medieval Italy*, 60–3, 153–5; Grierson & Blackburn, *Medieval European Coinage*. 66–9, 72–3.

changed only in the eleventh century, with the increasing prominence in southern Italy of Norman mercenaries, who fought for Longobards, Germans, Apulian rebels and popes alike, bringing destruction and disruption. Not unlike the Longobard mercenaries and freebooters of the 570s–590s, who switched sides for personal gain, these Normans took full advantage of the confused situation and the military weakness of the southern powers. They first settled in Campania and Apulia, formally, as subordinates to Germans or to Longobards, but soon proved themselves physically impossible to dislodge or control. After 1050 they transferred their attention to corporate gain and rapidly conquered all of southern Italy, Muslim Sicily and even ventured into Greece and the Balkans. By 1077 an independent Benevento had ceased to exist, and Salerno followed suit, falling to Robert Guiscard and being made capital of the Norman duchy of Apulia.[3] The merging of these Norman conquests into a powerful military kingdom brought a much-needed cohesion back to southern Italy and soon prompted economic revitalization. But, of course, in sweeping away the disparate southern states, the Normans also swept away the last remnants of the Longobard political name, bringing to a close nearly five hundred years of history.

State and Society in Longobard Southern Italy

Within the principality of Benevento, towns and lands were supervised by *gastalds* or counts: since the prince himself had formerly been the sole duke, the *gastalds*

---

[3] H. Hoffmann, 'Die Anfänge der Normannen in Sud Italien', *Quellen und Forschungen aus italienischen Archiven und Bibliotheken*, xlix (1969), 95–144; G. Tabacco, *The Struggle for Power in Medieval Italy. Structures of Political Rule* (Cambridge, 1989), 176–81; E. Burman, *Emperor to Emperon. Italy before the Renaissance* (London, 1991), 132–9.

must have been dependent appointments from the start – thus in contrast with the pattern discussed for the northern kingdom, where *gastalds* had come to be appointed by the King to curb ducal excesses. *Gastald* control of major border fortresses, such as Acerenza and Capua, was, however, intensified by the growing territorial insecurity of the ninth century, and inevitably these nobles came to seek independence or, in some cases, even the throne. In their desire to secure allegiance, the princes were forced to cede more and more rights to these counts, leading to increasing decentralization of the state. Civil war and the formation of the breakaway states of Capua and Salerno show the Beneventan edifice crumbling already by the mid-ninth century. Fragmentation continued even within these reduced areas, as for example in Capua, where the sons and grandsons of Landulf I all built their own independent castles. Whilst princes could not always secure dynasties, for the most part they tried to secure territorial control by giving *gastaldates* out to family members. As in the case of Capua, however, loyalty was not easily gained, and private power progressively ate away at public power.[4]

It is difficult to discern the rest of the cast behind these leading actors: at Benevento (and, in imitation of this, at Salerno and Capua), the court comprised an elaborate array of officals, drawn from the ranks of the urban nobility, with titles borrowed from Pavian and Byzantine court ceremony. But many of these posts appear to have fallen redundant by AD 900, signifying a loss in resources and a rise of military over civil offices. Academic posts at the courts also disappear around this date. Longobard society was by then heavily feudal in character, dominated by a series of petty counts or lords, all more or less autonomous, housing local peasant populations within

---

[4] Wickham, *Early Medieval Italy*, 159–62, notes that 'eleventh century documents for Molise reveal a completely private world of counts freely making cessions to monasteries of what seems to have been public land'.

their castles. An important element in these Longobard states was the dominance of the countryside, and a relative absence of large urban centres. In the Beneventan and Capuan principalities rural castle-towns dominated small landed territories and were governed by single noble families. In contrast, on the Campanian coast the cities of Naples, Salerno and Gaeta were virtually islands with very little control over their hinterlands. In Byzantine Apulia, the theme of *Langobardia* consisted of numerous semi-autonomous cities and villages in which local families were granted offices and titles, and which were controlled by taxation and by the chief Byzantine officials, the catepans or *strategoi*. These officers oversaw rather than stifled local society, and although rebellions did occur, apparently, they were not attempts to remove Byzantine rule. As in seventh- and eighth-century Byzantine northern Italy, the impact of actual Greek culture was fairly low, and Longobard law and nomenclature remained to the fore in Apulia. This may suggest that the Longobard percentage of the population was high, perhaps reflecting a settlement of displaced northerners, but we have no evidence to prove this. Certainly by the year 1000 the Apulians were fairly cosmopolitan: the Norman chronicler William of Apulia, for instance, tells of the meeting on Monte Gargano between Melo, an exiled rebel from Bari, and a group of Norman knights, fresh from crusading exploits. Melo is described as a freeborn citizen, Longobard by birth, dressed in Greek fashion but with a turban on his head. Interestingly, he presents himself mainly as a man of Bari, highlighting the emergence of urban identities and loyalties in the Byzantine south, to be set in line with the development of the north Italian communes. Prosperity and patronage are reflected in *Langobardia* by the construction of substantial cathedrals and monasteries in towns such as Bari, Trani and Otranto in the early eleventh century. For Bari we also know of the huge tenth-century palace of the

catapan, identified beneath the Norman church of
S. Nicola, which incorporates sculptured material
derived from the governor's complex. Increased trading
potential is documented in most Apulian ports by the
appearance of merchants' quarters, and in the countryside by the foundation of new farms and villages to
produce grain, wine and olive oil for export; urban
growth is further revealed by the need to build new,
enlarged, circuit walls from the late tenth century.[5]

It is difficult to transfer this image of prosperity to the
Longobard principalities in the west, where there was
little scope for increased agricultural development
around the various private castles. But a distinction can
be made for castles within monastic lands. Detailed
documentary investigation combined with archaeological field-work in Molise has helped reveal the complex
pattern of landowning by the Benedictine monastery of
S. Vincenzo in the Volturno valley and beyond. This
monastery's landed wealth grew from ducal, princely and
royal gifts: in the eighth century over 500 sq. km were
given by the Beneventan duke, consisting mainly of
mountainous zones; grants and donations on variable
scales continued into the eleventh and twelfth centuries,
allowing for recovery of the site after its destruction by
Arabs in 881. After 940 rights were awarded to build and
exercise authority over castles and their tenants: such
foundations often involved clearance of woodland to
establish new arable zones, and rents were sometimes
staggered to give communities time to settle in. This
process of land colonization clearly helped in the economic rise of S. Vincenzo, which peaked in the late
eleventh century. Excavations have begun to reveal the
huge monastic structures of the day as well as the under-
lying eighth- and ninth-century complex (fig. 16); interestingly, traces of a late Roman villa were utilized in the

[5] Burman, *Emperor to Emperor*, 102–3, 119–25.

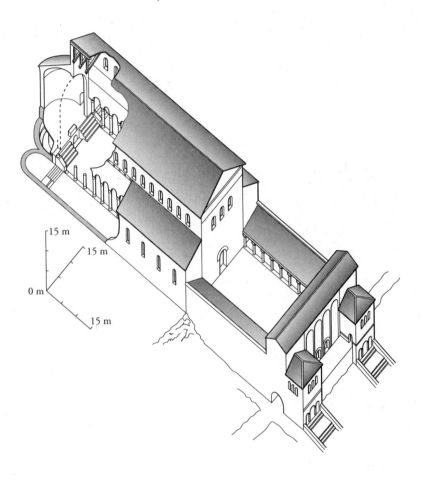

15 m

15 m

0 m

15 m

Figure 16 Proposed architectural reconstruction of the plan of the abbey church of S. Vincenzo Maggiore, S. Vincenzo al Volturno, c.840 (Sheila Gibson; British School at Rome Archaeological Archive, 1993).

fabric of the early monastery, as happened in the monasteries at Farfa and Montecassino. The excavations have also yielded fascinating information on the internal production of pottery, glass and metal-work, indicating that S. Vincenzo acted as more than just a religious focus (pl. 40): as a large, centralized land-owning body it also acted as a magnet for industrial activity, providing a market for dependent communities and, undoubtedly, for centres beyond. Field survey in the Volturno and Biferno valleys has meanwhile reinforced the view that Roman farms and villages were generally abandoned in the fourth to sixth centuries and has shown an emergence of fortified hilltop sites from the ninth century, but there are minimal traces yet of settlement activity between

Plate 40 Monastic 'doodles' on a tile in the refectory of the ninth-century abbey of S. Vincenzo al Volturno in Molise. (John Mitchell; British School at Rome.)

these dates. While excavations at S. Vincenzo verify an eighth-century foundation to the monastery, the contemporary peasant population remains somewhat elusive.[6]

Churches and monasteries were being erected in both towns and countryside throughout the ninth and tenth centuries, and many of these still survive in one form or another, complete with fragments of contemporary figured frescos, comparable to designs produced at S. Vincenzo. In the princely capitals of Benevento, Salerno and Capua elements of the ninth-century court chapels are visible (pl. 41); gastaldate centres such as Venosa and Teano present churches that overlie early Christian antecedents and are in turn overlain by Norman rebuildings; isolated churches include S. Pietro in Basento near Noci, and the tiny square chapel at Seppannibale. They are all fairly small and built in rough stone, and reveal an amalgam of styles, often based on late antique models, but combining Frankish and particularly Byzantine forms in terms of ornamentation. Graffiti, paintings and repairs are known for various of the characteristic cave churches such as Olevano, Prata and Monte Gargano, and scratched inscriptions at the latter record visits by various Beneventan notables extending from the seventh century into the 860s when the site was sacked by the Arabs; subsequent repairs show that the sanctuary remained a point of major pilgrimage.[7]

In these regions, too, not enough systematic archaeological study has occurred to allow us to comprehend

[6] Hodges and Mitchell (eds), *San Vincenzo al Volturno*; articles by R. Hodges and C. Wickham in Francovich (ed.) *Archeologia e storia del medioevo italiano*; and R. Hodges (ed.), *San Vincenzo al Volturno. The 1980–86 Excavations, Part I*, Archaeological Monograph of the British School at Rome, vii (London, 1993).

[7] M. Rotili, 'La cultura artistica nel Ducato di Benevento' in M. Brozzi, C. Calderini & M. Rotili, *L'Italia dei Longobardi* (Milan, 1980), 75–85; C. D. Fonseca, 'Longobardia minore e Longobardi nell'Italia meridionale' in *Magistra Barbaritas*, 127–84.

*Plate 41 The palace church of S. Sofia at Benevento, built
between 760 and 780.*

properly the character of Longobard and native settlement, particularly after the seventh century, when cemetery data grow scarce. Place-names and linguistic
evidence broadly demonstrate zones of Longobard influence, but most artefactual data relate to the indigenous population, perhaps signifying fairly swift cultural
fusion. One zone of interest lies between Lecce and
Taranto in south-eastern Apulia, marked by the presence
of toponyms recording the *Limitone dei Greci* and the
Paretoni (the 'big Greek frontier' and the 'big walls')
documented first in the eleventh century. These *Paretoni*,
now surviving only in parts as massive banking up to
7 m wide and 3 m high, most probably formed the
Byzantine defensive line against the Beneventan Longobard expansion into the heel of Italy from the later
seventh century; place-names such as *Sculca* and *Vigilia*
appear to pinpoint opposing Longobard positions to this
border. Such a defence may have remained in use well

into the ninth century, but detailed investigation has yet
to take place to determine the *Limitone*'s form and longevity.[8] Likewise, almost nothing is known of the mechanics of Longobard border control elsewhere in the
Beneventan territory, except for the presence of individual documented forts.

Coinage and Economy

The remarkable economic strength of the Principality of
Benevento is attested in the region's monetary output.[9]
However, the character of Beneventan coinage before the
late seventh century is wholly obscure, suggestive of a
duchy trying to find its feet. From the time of Duke
Gisulf (689–706) this picture changes, with an adequate
production of pseudo-imperial coins being set in motion;
noticeably, this happens roughly at the same time that
the northern Longobards were issuing a regal coinage. In
Benevento, in fact, the Byzantine emperor's bust was
retained right until the demise of the *Regnum*, which
suggests that the Duchy was more broadly involved in
trade with both Byzantines and Arabs, and that it therefore required the 'international' – or at least Mediterranean – coinage of Byzantium. This is further borne out
by the minting of gold *solidi*, inferior to Byzantine issues,
but of reasonable quality nonetheless (pl. 39). Unbroken
production of both *solidi* and *tremisses* can be followed
to 774, though with progressive reductions in weight and
fineness, to be set in line with reductions in both Byzantine

---

[8] See G. Uggeri, 'Il confine longobardo-bizantino in Puglia', XXXVII
Corso di cultura sull'arte ravennate e bizantine (Ravenna, 1990), and articles
by S. De Vitis and A. Coscarella on the limited data for Longobard settlement and cemeteries, in the *XXXVII Corso di cultura sull'arte ravennate e
bizantina*, (Ravenna, 1990).
[9] E. Arslan, 'La monetazione' in *Magistra Barbaritas*, 430, 443; Grierson
& Blackburn, *Medieval European Coinage. I*, 66–73.

and north Italian Longobard coin. From 774 Arechis II introduced a distinct Beneventan coinage, bearing the cloaked figure of the prince holding an orb with cross. However, Grimoald III was the first to place his full name on the coins, initially alongside that of Charlemagne, but after 792, when in revolt against the Franks, on its own. Whilst he failed to obey the Carolingian command to shave his beard off, Grimoald did at least acknowledge the importance of Carolingian contacts by introducing the silver *denaro* – similar but not too close to Frankish types. Benevento came further into line with Francia under Grimoald IV (806–17), who ceased the minting of gold coin, even though in 814 Louis the Pious imposed the hefty annual tribute of 7,000 such *solidi*. The *solidus* was revived by Sico, who added the image of the Longobard patron saint S. Michele to the reverse. By then the gold content of the *solidus* had dropped to a mere 35 per cent, and it diminished still further in the 840s.

The breakaway principality of Salerno initially sought to match Benevento by minting its own low-grade *solidi*; by 850, however, both sides abandoned these and produced only silver *denari*. In Salerno's case, examples of *denari* are extremely rare and disappear by *c*.900, after which Byzantine and Arab coins were adopted, until an eleventh-century mini-revival of Salernitan issues. In Benevento the 'princely' *denari* fared little better, being interrupted between 866 and 871 by violent occupations of the city by Louis II (who minted his own *denari*) and by Byzantines, Spoletans and Salernitans in 891–7. Benevento regained its independence, but its coinage came to an end in the tenth century, likewise losing out to superior imperial denominations.

Yet, despite the evidence of the eighth- and ninth-century *solidi*, there is restricted physical evidence for Benevento's inclusion in a wide Mediterranean trading network. Certainly, the plan and name of S. Sofia in the capital points to Byzantium as a source and, as discussed below, artistic traces in books and church murals demonstrate eastern as well as western influences, but material artefacts such as ceramics are, as yet, lacking. Primarily, however, this is due to restricted urban excavation, and undoubtedly such data will be forthcoming in the near future.[10]

Beneventan and Late Longobard Culture

The late cultural flourish of the Longobard kingdom under the stimulus of Carolingian stability in the north is personified by Paul the Deacon, author of the much-quoted *Historia Langobardorum* (pl. 42). His rise is noteworthy: of Friulian origin (he shows pride in his descent from one of the prime duchies of the kingdom), he was early on chosen for a holy life, as suggested by his Christian name; an education at the court of Ratchis in Pavia in the 740s was probably followed by a decade's learning at the Benedictine abbey of Montecassino in the northern quarter of the Duchy of Benevento. Because of his scholarly renown, he was employed as tutor to King Desiderius' daughter Adalperga, and he duly accompanied her to Benevento where she married Duke Arechis. In these years Paul composed poetry and also the *Historia Romana*, a history of Italy up to the death of Justinian in 565, which was presented to Adalperga by the time she was already a mother of three. Paul was probably based for most of his time at Montecassino, and undoubtedly it was there that he began writing the unfinished *Historia Langobardorum*, which formed a direct continuation of his earlier book. The Carolingian conquest of 774 is nowhere directly mentioned in this narrative, although a

---

[10] But see D. Michaeilides & D. Wilkinson (eds), *Excavations at Otranto*, i and ii (Lecce, 1992), for an indication of the range of finds to be expected.

Plate 42 Paul the Deacon's Historia Langobardorum.
(Museo Archeologico Nazionale, Cividale.)

few hints are discernible. As said, it was argued by ninth-century *continuatores*, such as Andreas of Bergamo and Erchempert of Benevento, that Paul could not bring himself to write of the fall of his people's kingdom. And yet he does speak directly and impartially of this in his *Gesta* of the Bishops of Metz, composed whilst a member of Charlemagne's own academic court at Aachen between *c*.782 and 784. How far Paul was merely exercising diplomatic skills in his unemotional relaying of the Longobard fall cannot easily be determined, although we do know that his journey to Francia was, in part, to secure the pardon of his brother (and presumably of other Longobards), held hostage since rebellious uprisings in Friuli in 776. At the same time, of course, his presence amongst literary and religious notables such as Alcuin will have greatly furthered his scholarly standing.

Goffart has argued that Paul held great hopes that the Beneventan principality, as legitimate successor to the Longobard *regnum*, would live in harmony with the Carolingian kingdom in Italy and that his influence would help to create firm bonds of alliance between the princes Arechis and Grimoald III and Charlemagne, which would ultimately lead to the decisive removal of the Byzantines from the south. If this is the case, then the most likely reason for Paul's failure to complete the *Historia Langobardorum* would be the Beneventans' unexpected alliance with the – in Paul's eyes – hated Byzantines, and the armed conflict with the Carolingians – in effect, Paul could not admit to the collapse of his unspoken dream. Perhaps significantly the narrative ends with the reign of Liutprand, one of Paul's heroes, who had come into the confidence of the Franks and had helped in fighting off the Saracens, but with whose death the first stages of Franco–papal union commence.[11]

Erchempert of Benevento's *Ystoriola Longobardorum Beneventum degencium* marks the continuation of literary output at the Longobard princely court in the later ninth century. His text begins where Paul had left off and seeks to stress Beneventan resistance to the Franks,

---

[11] Goffart, *The Narrators of Barbarian History*, nb 424–31. Cf. D. Bullough, 'Ethnic history and the Carolingians' in T. Holdsworth & P. Wiseman (eds), *The Inheritance of Historiography*, A.D. 350–900 (Exeter, 1986), 96–100; Cilento, 'La storiografia nell'età barbarica' in *Magistra Barbaritas*, 330, 343.

Neapolitans, Byzantines and Arabs, whilst highlighting Longobard pride and martial strength. Arechis' court in the late eighth century had contained academics, artists and architects, probably largely refugees from Longobard Pavia; their presence gave impetus to the development of more home-grown talent such as Erchempert, the grammarian Ursus and the poet Hilderic. Furthermore, a series of extant ninth- and tenth-century illustrated codices can be shown to have been produced at Montecassino and Benevento and signify both a healthy scriptorial activity and, on a broader level, the vitality of the Longobard Church; like the cycles of fine frescos preserved within the monastic church of S. Vincenzo al Volturno and in S. Sofia at Benevento, these codices reveal artistic links with both the Carolingian and the Byzantine orbits, indicating how Benevento lay in the middle of a flow of Mediterranean and northern influences.[12] Indeed, Montecassino long remained to the artistic fore in southern Italy, despite the Arab sack of the monastery in 883. The new princely courts at Capua and Salerno attracted their own group of scholars in imitation of Benevento, but the persistence of internecine warfare in time greatly restricted academic output and quality. Historians are attested at each: the noble abbot John at Capua and an anonymous monk at Salerno – both probably contemporaries of Erchempert, suggestive of an active academic rivalry. Of these works, the *Chronicon Salernitanum* stands out for its wayward and crude Latin, its legendary tales and borrowed passages – far more a collection of local legends than an official court history. All these sources continue to speak of the Longobards, even if the splintering of the Benevento principality had removed any vestigial ethnic unity. But

---

[12] Cilento, 'La storiografia nell'età barbarica', 344–7; G. Cavallo, 'Libri e continuità della cultura antica in età barbarica' in *Magistra Barbaritas*, 633–8, 651–4; M. Rotili, 'La cultura artistica nel Ducato di Benevento' in Brozzi, Calderini & Rotili, *L'Italia dei Longobardi* (Milan, 1980), 76, 81–2.

the Longobards were by now far more 'Italian' in customs and language: tellingly, the *Chronicon* mentions a 'German tongue, long ago spoken by the Longobards'.

From Liutprand to the Lega Lombarda

Likewise, political decay failed to sweep away all traces of the Longobards in the north of Italy. Here something of the pride in the Longobard past is attested in the deeds and words of the Pavian Liutprand, bishop of Cremona (*c.*920–72). Liutprand served as deacon and ambassador at the courts of Hugo of Provence and of his successor Berengar II, and thence at the court of the emperor Otto I in Germany, travelling often as his envoy to Byzantium. On one such occasion the Byzantine emperor Nicephorus, angered, tried to insult Liutprand by calling him 'not a Roman but a Longobard'. The bishop countered this by pointing out how the story of Roman origins was one of fratricide, homicide, corruption and evil, and that the worst possible insult would, in fact, be to be called a Roman. Indeed, as a north Italian, Liutprand spoke proudly of the multiplicity of cultural and ethnic stocks to be found: Longobard, Saxon, Frank, Lotharingian, Bavarian, Suebian and Burgundian.[13]

What emerges in the tenth and eleventh centuries is a centring of interest in the north and a distrust of Rome and the south. These are all echoes of later medieval and even modern Italian politics, with the creation of the breakaway parties of the Lega Nord, among them the Lega Lombarda, each marked by militaristic badges of defiance (fig. 17). A Lombard League was in fact already in existence in twelfth-century Italy, and at its peak in 1170 comprised a confederacy of thirty-six leading cities

---

[13] Liutprand, *Relatio*, ch.12 in MGH, *SS Rer. German.*, ed J. Becker, (Hanover and Leipzig, 1915), 182–93.

Figure 17 Medieval and modern combined: the symbol of the Northern League

and towns, brought together to counter the oppressive rule of the Emperor Frederick Barbarossa of Germany. The constitution of this *societas Lombardiae* promised corporate military forces to face the imperial army, the upholding of civic rights and the lawful ending of disputes between cities. The cities' combined resources permitted some other notable feats, including the rebuilding and refortification of Milan and the foundation of the new town of Alessandria in 1168. Victories against the Emperor allowed a successful restoration of liberties in 1183, and the League was dissolved. But, once the potential of this union had been recognized, it was inevitable that the Lombard League would reform when faced with imperial threat, as was indeed the case again in the 1190s, 1220s and 1260s. The Lombard League was the most prominent of a series of provincial or regional units, based around established and quasi-independent urban centres. To a large degree, however, these urban leagues hark back to the Roman administrative organization of Italy and mark a resurgence of regional identity rather than of ethnic or other cultural roots: in effect, the emergence of the Lombard League had nothing to do with Longobard ethnicity. Indeed, the terms league and regional state are misnomers, since their internal cohesion was weak, and allegiance was primarily to one or more dominant city or noble family – such as the Visconti of Milan.[14] Thus it is probably fair to argue that by the eleventh and twelfth centuries the term Lombardia was merely a memorial to the lost Longobard state. Its people, its culture and its architecture could trace links back to the former Germanic nation, but – by the time of Frederick – Lombard and Longobard must be seen as totally different labels.

Despite its history of long-term warfare and urban conflict, the region of medieval Lombardy was a prosperous one, benefiting fully from extensive national and international trade, notably of exotic goods brought by the Venetians from the East. The Lombard cities were above all famous for cloth-making and, later, for steel and silk manufacture. The wealth generated from this industrial activity is reflected in the far-flung banking business set up by the provincials – London's Lombard Street is a reminder of such thirteenth-century Anglo-Italian relations – while we can also note how the term Lombard became synonymous with usurer. Traders and the nobility used their money in other ways, however, most strikingly of course in building work: often this took the form of tall, often unstable towers poking up above the rooftops and acting as status markers; but a more permanent venture lay in church and monastery building, and here investors could tap into a fairly

[14] W. F. Butler, *The Lombard Communes: A History of the Republics of North Italy* (London, 1906), 127–58; Tabacco, *The Struggle for Power in Medieval Italy*, 295–320.

vibrant architectural scene. Lombardy, with Milan again as its cultural heart, features many examples of buildings erected in what has been termed the Lombard style, characterized in particular by its use of rib-vaulting.[15] Although Milan itself lacks structures of the Lombard First Romanesque (*c.*800–1000) – whose roots certainly lie in the architecture of the eighth-century Longobard kingdom – there are a number of examples in the Mature style (*c.*1050–1250), prominent amongst these the church of S. Ambrogio (*c.*1080–1130), where Lombard kings and German emperors were crowned. Overall, the style was viewed as rather unadventurous; accordingly, it took no major hold in architecture beyond northern Italy, the Alpine regions of Upper Burgundy and Switzerland, and Croatia and Hungary – although it did also foster some changes in Catalan Spain. Something of the Lombard style certainly can be traced to the south, but in the far south, in Apulia as in Sicily, Norman influences mingled with Byzantine and Muslim elements to create a variety of regional styles, each reflecting their own political affiliations. Thus, even in the field of architecture Italy lacked unity.

Words and Traditions: Longobard Survivals

In the later Middle Ages, popular texts such as Paul the Deacon's Longobard history were revived, and various legendary episodes found their way into popular storytelling. One example comes in *The Decameron*, by Giovanni Boccaccio (1313–75), comprising one hundred moralistic, anecdotal, passionate and bawdy stories of varied origin, set against the backdrop of a central Italy ravaged by the Black Death. Its popularity extended beyond Italy as far as England, influencing authors like

[15] Conant, *Carolingian and Romanesque Architecture*, 107–11, 386–410.

Chaucer and Shakespeare. One story these British authors failed to follow up appears as Novel II in the Decameron's Third Day, namely the tale of Queen Theodelinda, wife of the Longobard king Agilulf, and her unwitting seduction by a lusty groom – presumably pure fiction, but a good tale even so.

The Longobard tradition perhaps survives strongest in Friuli: here we find a series of legends and folk-tales attached to certain sites and various famous Longobard names. These include the tale of Queen Romilda and her flight away from invading Slavs to the caves of San Giovanni d'Antro; Theodelinda's fortification of Venzone in a day and a night;[16] and the duel between Duke Rodgaud and Charlemagne's lieutenant Roland on the 'Ponte d'Orlando' near Cervignano. Likewise, popular tradition identifies the 'masks' cut out of the rock in the hypogeum in Via Monastero Maggiore in Cividale as portraits carved by prisoners held there in Longobard times.[17] Popularity of all things Longobard is further shown by the presence of the Museo Archeologico Nazionale and Museo Cristiano at Cividale, housing superb collections of Longobard burial goods and sculpture from Cividale and from across Friuli; by the naming of the Piazza Paolo Diacono which contains not only a sixteenth-century townhouse reputedly marking the historian's birthplace but also the refreshing Caffè Longobardo; and even by the recent publication of a cartoon-strip version of the *Historia Langobardorum* (see pl. 12).

The Friulian dialect, meanwhile, preserves a fairly high number of Longobard loan-words and these, combined with place-names, are an additional reminder of the old Germanic settlers. As a whole, over 400 Longobard loan-words have been identified so far in the Italian language

---

[16] The 1976 earthquake flattened the defences in much shorter time, and the *comune* are slowly piecing it all together again.
[17] Brozzi, *Il Ducato Longobardo del Friuli*, 125–31.

and its dialects; many modern Italian surnames too, such as Catemari, Cataldo, Greppi, Prandi and Zilli, derive from Longobard personal names. These may not be major elements, but they do at least signify a healthy Longobard integration with the native Italian population in the early medieval and full medieval eras.[18] However, these are the intangible elements of the Longobard past; we must look to archaeology to reveal more of this tribe, its state and its culture, in order to piece together more coherently the Italy that emerged from the debris of the Roman world.

[18] Brozzi, *Il Ducato Longobardo del Friuli*, 133–6; Arcamone, 'I Germani d'Italia', in *Magistra Barbaritas*, 399–404; *I Longobardi*, (exh. cat. 1990), 153–6.

Bibliography and Abbreviations

Primary Sources

Many of the primary sources listed below have been edited in the extensive series Monumenta Germaniae Historica (MGH), published in Germany chiefly at the end of the nineteenth century. Some have been translated into English, either in the Loeb Classical Library series or as Penguin Classics, but only a few of these are recent works. In the left-hand column are listed the abbreviations used throughout this book.

Agathias   Agathias: *Histories,* English translation by J. Frendo (New York and Berlin, 1975).

Anon. Rav.   *Ravennatis anonimi:Cosmographiae et Guidonis geographica*, ed. M. Pinder & G. Parthey (Berlin, 1860).

Cassiodorus   Cassiodorus: *Variae*, ed. T. Mommsen, *MGH, Auctores Antiquissimi*, xii (Hanover, 1894). Selected translation by S. Barnish, Translated Texts for Historians, xii (Liverpool, 1992).

Cassius Dio   Cassius Dio: *History of Rome*, translation by E. Cary, Loeb Classical Library (London and New York, 1927).

Einhard *V. Car.*   Einhard: *Vita Caroli* with Notker, the Monk of St. Gall, *De Carolo Magno*, translation by L. Thorpe, Penguin Classics (London, 1969).

Fredegar   Fredegar: *Chronicarum*, ed. J. M. Wallace-

Hadrill as *The Fourth Book of the Chronicle of Fredegar with its Continuationes* (London, 1960)

Greg. *Reg.*   Gregory the Great: *Registrum Epistolarum*, ed. P. Ewald & L. Hartmann, *MGH, Epistolae I & II* (Hanover, 1887–99).

Greg. *HF*   Gregory of Tours: *Historia Francorum*, ed. W. Arndt & B. Krusch, MGH, *Scriptores Rerum Merovingicarum*, i (Hanover, 1894). Available in translation by L. Thorpe, Penguin Classics (London, 1974).

Lib. Pont.   *Liber Pontificalis. Texte, introduction*, ed. L. Duchesne, 3 vols (Paris, 1888–92). Translations by R. Davies in *The Book of Pontiffs (Liber Pontificalis)*, Translated Texts for Historians, Latin Ser., v (Liverpool, 1989) and in *The Lives of the Eighth Century Popes (Liber Pontificalis)*, Translated Texts for Historians, xiii (Liverpool, 1992).

Marius Av.   Marius of Avenches: *Chronica*, ed. T. Mommsen, MGH, *Auctores Antiquissimi*, xi (Berlin, 1894), pp. 37–105.

Menander   Menander Protector: *Excerpta*, translation by R.C. Blockley as *The History of Menander the Guardsman: introductory essay, text, translation and historiographical notes*, ARCA Classical and Medieval Texts. Papers and Monographs, xvii (Liverpool, 1985).

Notker   Notker, the Monk of St Gall: *De Carolo Magno*, with Einhard, in translation by Thorpe (1969).

Origo   *Edictus Rothari: Origo gentis Langobardorum*, ed. G. Waitz, MGH, *Scriptores Rerum Langobardicarum et Italicarum, saec. VI–IX* (Hanover, 1878).

Paul *HL*   Paul the Deacon: *Historia Langobardorum*, ed. L. Bethmann & G. Waitz, MGH, *Scriptores Rerum Langobardicarum et Italicarum, saec. VI–IX* (Hanover, 1878). An English translation occurs only in F. W. Foulke as

	Paul the Deacon. History of the Langobards (Philadelphia, 1907; repr. 1974), which includes *Pauli continuatio tertia.*
Proc. *BG*	Procopius of Caesarea: *De Bello Gothico*, translated by H. B. Dewing, Loeb Classical Library (London and New York, 1919–28).
Ptolemy	Claudius P. Ptolemy: *Geographica*, edited by C. Nobbe, (Leipzig, 1843; repr. 1966).
Strabo	Strabo: *Geographica*, translated by H. L. Jones, Loeb Classical Library (London and New York, 1944).
Strat.	Maurice: *Strategicon*, translation edited by G. T. Dennis (Vienna, 1981).
Tacitus	P. Cornelius Tacitus: *Germania*, translation by H. Mattingly, Penguin Classics (published with the *Agricola*) (London, 1970).
Velleius	Velleius Paterculus: *Res gestae divi Augustae*, translated by F. W. Shipley, Loeb Classical Library (London and New York, 1924).
Vita Sev.	Eugippius: *Vita Severini*, English translation by L. Bieler & L. Krislan, in the 'Fathers of the Church' series, v, (Washington, 1965).

Secondary Sources

General Works

Collins, R.: *Early Medieval Europe* (London, 1991).

Holmes, G. (ed.): *The Oxford Illustrated History of Medieval Europe* (Oxford, 1988).

Kiszely, I.: *The Anthropology of the Lombards*, British Archaeological Reports, Internat. Ser. no. 61, 2 vols (Oxford, 1979).

La civiltà dei Longobardi in Europa, Proceedings of the conference held at the Accademia Nazionale dei Lincei, Rome–Cividale 1971 (Rome, 1974).

Melucco Vaccaro, A.: *I Longobardi in Italia. Materiali e problemi* (Milan, 1982).

Menghin, W.: *Die Langobarden. Archäologie und Geschichte* (Stuttgart, 1985).

Menghin, W., Springer, T. & Wamers, E. (eds): *Germanen, Hunnen und Awaren. Schätze der Völkerwanderungszeit. Die Archäologie des 5. und 6. Jahrhunderts an der mittleren Donau und der östlich-merowingische Reihengräberkreis* (Nürnberg, 1987).

Tagliaferri, A. (ed.): *Problemi della civiltà e dell'economia longobarda. Scritti in memoria di G. P. Bognetti* (Milan, 1964).

Wallace Hadrill, J. M.: *The Barbarian West* (London, 1966).

Longobards on the Elbe and in Bohemia

Böhme, H.: 'Archäologische Zeugnisse zur Geschichte der Markomannenkriege, 166–180 n.Chr.', *Jahrbuch der römisch-germanischen Zentralmuseums Mainz*, xxii (1975), pp. 153–217.

Cunliffe, B.: *Greeks, Romans and Barbarians. Spheres of Interaction* (London, 1988).

Pleinerova, I.: 'Germanische und slawische Komponenten in der altslawischen Siedlung Březno bei Louny', *Germania*, xiii (1965), pp. 121–38.

Schmidt, B.: 'Die Langobarden während der römischen Kaiserzeit und langobardisch-thuringisch Beziehungen im 5. und 6. Jahrhundert', in *La Civiltà dei Longobardi in Europa* 1974, pp. 29– 40.

Svoboda, B.: 'Zur Frage der Langobarden in Böhmen', in Tagliaferri (ed.) 1964, pp. 55–64.

Todd, M.: *The Northern Barbarians, 100 BC – AD 300* (London, 1985).

——: *The Early Germans* (Oxford, 1991).

Wegewitz, W.: 'Stand der Langobardenforschung im Gebiet der Niederelbe', in Tagliaferri (ed.) 1964, pp. 19–54.

——: *Das langobardische Brandgräberfeld von Putensen, Kreis Harburg*, Die Urnenfriedhofe in Niedersachsen, x, ed. C. Schuchhard (Hildesheim, 1972).

——: *Rund um den Kiekeberg. Vorgeschichte einer Landschaft an der Niederelbe*, Hammaburg, viii, Vor- und

Frühgeschichte aus dem niederelbischen Raum (Neumunster, 1988).

Werner, J.: 'Zur Entstehung des Reihengräberzivilisation', *Archaeologia Geographica*, i (1950), pp. 23–32.

Zeman, J.: 'Böhmen im 5. und 6. Jahrhundert', in Menghin, Springer & Wamers (eds) 1987, pp. 515–27.

Longobards on the Danube

Adler, H.: 'Zur Ausplunderung langobardische Gräberfelder in Österreich', *Mitteilungen der anthropologischen Gesellschaft, Wien*, c (1970), 138–47.

Adler, H.: 'Maria Ponsee', *Fundberichte aus Österreich*, ix (1966–70), pp. 26–30, 147–8, 211–12.

——: 'Das langobardische Gräberfeld von Aspersdorf', *Fundberichte aus Österreich*, xvi, (1977), pp. 7–70.

——: 'Die Langobarden in Niederösterreich', in Windl (ed.) 1977, pp. 73–87.

Alföldy, G.: *Noricum* (London and Boston, 1974).

Barkóczi, L.: 'A 6th century cemetery from Keszthely-Fenékpuszta' *Acta archaeologica academiae scientiarum Hungaricae*, xx (1968), pp. 275–311.

Bertolini, O.: 'La data dell'ingresso dei Longobardi in Italia', *Scritti scelti di storia medievale*, (Livorno, 1968), pp. 21–61.

Bóna, I.: 'Die pannonischen Grundlagen der langobardischen Kultur im Licht der neuesten Forschungen', in Tagliaferri (ed.) 1964, pp. 71–99.

——: *The Dawn of the Dark Ages: The Gepids and the Lombards in the Carpathian Basin* (Budapest, 1976).

——: 'Ungarns Völker im 5. und 6. Jahrhundert. Eine historisch-archäologische Zusammenschau', in Menghin, Springer & Wamers (eds) 1987, pp. 116–29.

Christie, N.: 'Invasion or invitation? The Longobard occupation of northern Italy, A.D. 568–569', *Romanobarbarica*, xi (1991), pp. 79–108.

——: 'The survival of Roman settlement along the Middle Danube: Pannonia from the 4th to the 10th century A.D.', *Oxford Journal of Archaeology*, xi/3 (1992), pp. 317–39.

Friesinger, H.: 'Die archäologischen Funde der ersten zwei

Drittel des 5. Jahrhunderts in Niederösterreich', in Windl (ed.) 1977, pp. 62–72.

—— and Adler, H.: *Die Zeit der Völkerwanderung in Niederösterreich*, (Vienna, 1979).

Gömöri, J.: 'Grabungen auf dem Forum von Scarabantia, 1979–82', *Acta archaeologica academiae scientiarum Hungaricae*, xxxviii (1986), pp. 343–96.

Grafenauer, B.: 'Die Ansiedlung der Slawen in den Ostalpen und die Kontinuitätsfragen', *Arheološki Vestnik, Acta Archaeologica*, xxi–xxii (1970–1), pp. 17–32.

Haberl, J. and Hawkes, C.: 'The last of Roman Noricum: St. Severin on the Danube', *Greeks, Celts and Romans*, ed. C. & S. Hawkes (London, 1973), pp. 97–156.

Kandler, M.: 'Archäologische Beobachtungen zur Baugeschichte des Legionslagers Carnuntum am Ausgang der Antike', in Wolfram & Daim (eds) 1980, pp. 83–92.

Kiss, A.: 'Funde aus dem 5–6Jh. im Gebiet von Brigetio', *Folia Archaeologica*, xxxii (1981), pp. 191–208.

Kollautz, A.: 'Awaren, Langobarden und Slawen in Noricum und Istrien', *Carinthia*, clv (1965), pp. 619–60.

Lengyel, A. & Radan, G. (eds): *The Archaeology of Roman Pannonia* (Lexington, KY, and Budapest, 1980).

Mócsy, A.: *Pannonia and Upper Moesia* (London and Boston, 1974).

Mor, C. G.: 'La marcia di re Albonio', in Tagliaferri (ed.) 1964, pp. 179–97.

Müller, R.: 'Die spätrömische Festung Valcum am Plattensee', in Menghin, Springer & Wamers (eds) 1987, pp. 270–4.

Neugebauer, C. and J-W.: 'KG Neudorf (MG Neudorf bei Staatz, VB Mistelbach)', *Fundberichte aus Österreich*, xxiv–xxv (1985–6), pp. 331–3.

Salamon, Á. and Erdélyi, J.: *Das völkerwanderungszeitliche Gräberfeld von Környe*, Studia Archaeologica, (Budapest, 1971).

Schmidt, B.: 'Das Königreich der Thuringer und seine Provinzen', in Menghin, Springer & Wamers (eds) 1987, pp. 471–8.

Tejral, J.: 'Probleme der Völkerwanderungszeit nordlich der mittleren Donau', in Menghin, Springer & Wamers (eds) 1987, pp. 351–60.

Thomas, E.: 'Die Romanität Pannoniens im 5. und 6. Jahrhundert', in Menghin, Springer & Wamers (eds) 1987, 284–94.

Ulbert, T.: 'Zur Siedlungskontinuität im sudöstlichen Alpenraum, vom 2. bis 6. Jahrhundert n.Chr.', *Von der Spätantike zum frühen Mittelalter*, Vorträge und Forschungen, xxv, ed. J. Werner & E. Ewig (Munich, 1979), pp. 141–57.

Valic, A.: 'Gradisce nad Pivko pri Naklem', *Arheološki Vestnik, Acta Archaeologica*, xix (1968), pp. 485–508.

Váňa, Z.: *The World of the Ancient Slavs* (London, 1983).

Werner, J.: *Die Langobarden in Pannonien. Beiträge zur Kenntnis der langobardischen Bodenfunde vor 568*, Abhandlungen der Bayerische Akademie der Wissenschaften, philosophisch-historische Klasse, new ser., part 55 (Munich, 1962).

Windl, H. (ed.): *Germanen, Awaren, Slawen in Niederösterreich. Das erste Jahrtausend nach Christus*, Ausstellung des Niederösterreichen Landesmuseums (Vienna, 1977).

Wolfram, H.: *History of the Goths* (Berkeley and London, 1988).

—— and Daim, F. (eds): *Die Völker an der mittleren und unteren Donau im 5. und 6. Jahrhundert*, Conference publication of the Kommission für Frühmittelalterforschung, vol. 4 = Österreichische Akademie der Wissenschaften philosophisch-historische Klasse Denkschriften, vol. 145 (Vienna, 1980).

Wozniak, F.: 'Byzantine diplomacy and the Lombardic-Gepid wars', *Balkan Studies* xx (1979), pp. 139–58.

Longobards in Italy

Aberg, N.: *Die Goten und Langobarden in Italien* (Uppsala, 1923).

Arcamone, M.: 'I Germani d'Italia: lingue e "documenti" linguistici', *Magistra Barbaritas* 1984, pp. 381–409.

Bertolini, O.: 'Ordinamenti militari e strutture sociali dei Longobardi in Italia', *XV Settimana di studio del Centro Italiano di Studi sull'Alto Medioevo* (Spoleto, 1968), pp. 429–607.

Bognetti, G. P.: *L'età longobarda*, iii (Milan, 1966).

Brown, T. S.: *Gentlemen and Officers. Imperial Administration and Aristocratic Power in Byzantine Italy*, A.D. *554–800* (London, 1984).

Brozzi, M.: *Il Ducato Longobardo del Friuli*, Publicazioni della Deputazione di Storia Patria per il Friuli, vi (Udine, 1981).

Brozzi, M., Calderini, C. & Rotili, M.: *L'Italia dei Longobardi* (Milan, 1980).

Ceglia, V. and Genito, B.: 'La necropoli altomedievale di Vicenne a Campochiaro', in *Samnium. Archeologia del Molise* 1991.

Corsi, P.: 'Costante II in Italia', *Quaderni Medievali*, iii (1977), pp. 32–72; v (1978), pp. 57–107; vii (1979), pp. 75–109.

Delogu, P.: 'Il regno longobardo', *Storia d'Italia, I: Longobardi e Bizantini*, ed. P. Delogu, A. Guillou & G. Ortalli (Turin, 1980), pp. 3–216.

Falkenhausen, V. von: 'I barbari in Italia nella storiografia bizantina', in *Magistra Barbaritas* 1984, pp. 301–16.

Francovich, R. (ed.): *Archeologia e storia del medioevo italiano*, Studi nuova Italia scientifica archeologia, iii (Rome, 1987).

Goffart, W.: *Barbarians and Romans*, A.D. *418–584. The Techniques of Accommodation* (Princeton, 1980).

Hartmann, L. M.: *Geschichte Italiens in Mittelalter. II, i: Römer und Langobarden bis zur Teilung Italiens* (Gotha, 1900); *II, ii: Die Loslösung Italiens vom Orient* (Gotha, 1903).

Hessen, O. von: 'I Longobardi in Pannonia e Italia', in Francovich (ed.) 1987, pp. 23–8.

Hodgkin, T.: *Italy and her Invaders*, 8 vol (Oxford, 1892–9).

Johnson, S.: *Late Roman Fortifications* (London, 1983).

I Longobardi (exh. cat. ed. G. C. Menis, Milan, 1990).

I Longobardi e la Lombardia. Saggi (exh. cat., Milan, 1978).

Magistra Barbaritas. I Barbari in Italia (Milan, 1984).

Mastrelli, C.: 'La toponomastica lombarda di origine longobarda', in *I Longobardi e la Lombardia* 1978, pp. 35– 49.

Menis, G. C. (ed.): *I Longobardi. Italia Longobarda* (Marseilles, 1991).

Pauli, L.: *The Alps. Archaeology and Early History* (London, 1984).

Pavan, G.: 'Architettura del periodo longobardo', *I Longobardi* 1990, pp. 236–98.

Pertusi, A.: 'Ordinamenti militari, guerre in Occidente e teorie di guerra dei Bizantini, saec. VI–X', XV *Settimana di studio del Centro Italiano di Studi sull'Alto Medioevo* (Spoleto, 1968), pp. 631–700.

Potter, T. W.: *Roman Italy* (London, 1987).

Richards, J.: *Consul of God: The Life and Times of Gregory the Great* (London, 1980).

Schneider, F.: *Die Entstehung von Burg und Landgemeinde in Italien* (Berlin, 1924).

Tabacco, G.: *The Struggle for Power in Medieval Italy. Structures of Political Rule* (Cambridge, 1989).

Wickham, C.: *Early Medieval Italy. Central Power and Local Society, 400–1000* (London, 1981).

The Archaeology of Longobard Italy

Bierbrauer, V.: *Die ostgotischen Grab- und Schatzfunde in Italien*, Biblioteca Studi Medievali, vii (Spoleto, 1975).

——: 'Aspetti archeologici dei Goti, Alamanni e Longobardi', in *Magistra Barbaritas* 1984, pp. 445–508.

——: *Invillino-Ibligo in Friaul. I: Die römische Siedlung und das spätantik-frühmittelalterliche Castrum*, Münchner Beiträge zur Vor- und Frühgeschichte, xxxiii (Munich, 1987): *II: Die spätantiken und frühmittelalterlichen Kirchen*, Münchner Beiträge . . ., xxxiv (Munich, 1988).

Bosio, L.: 'Le fortificazioni tardoantiche del territorio di Aquileia', *Il territorio di Aquileia nell'antichità*, Antichità Altoadriatiche, xv (1979), pp. 515–36.

Brogiolo, G. P.: 'La campagna dalla tarda antichità al 900 ca. d.C.', *Archeologia Medievale*, x (1983), pp. 73–88.

——: 'Le città tra tarda antichità e medioevo', in *Archeologia urbana in Lombardia* (Modena, 1985), pp. 48–55.

——: 'Trasformazioni urbanistiche nella Brescia longobarda. Dalle capanne in legno al monastero regio di San Salvatore', in Menis (ed.) 1991, pp. 101–19.

——: *Brescia altomedievale. Urbanistica ed edilizia dal IV al IX secolo*, Documenti di Archeologia, ii (Mantua, 1993)

—— and Castelletti, L.: *Archeologia a Monte Barro. I. II grande edificio e le torri* (Lecco, 1991).

—— and Lusuardi Siena, S.: 'Nuove indagini a Castelseprio', *Atti del VI congresso internazionale di studi sull'alto medioevo* (Spoleto, 1980), pp. 475–99.

Brozzi, M.: *La popolazione romana nel Friuli longobardo, VI–VIII sec.*, Pubblicazioni della Deputazione di Storia Patria per il Friuli, xix (Udine, 1989).

Bullough, D.: 'Urban change in early medieval Italy: the example of Pavia', *Papers of the British School at Rome*, xxxiv (1966), pp. 82–131.

Calderini, C.: 'Il palazzo di Liutprando a Corteolona', *Contributi dell'Istituto di Archeologia*, v (1975), pp. 172–203.

Carver, M.: 'S. Maria Foris Portas at Castel Seprio: A Famous Church in a New Context', *World Archaeology*, xviii/3 (1987), pp. 313–29.

—— Massa S. and Brogiolo, G. P.: 'Sequenza insediativa romana e altomedievale alla Pieve di Manerba (BS)', *Archeologia Medievale*, xix (1982), pp. 237–98.

Ceglia, V.: 'Lo scavo della necropoli di Vicenne', *Conoscenze. Rivista Annuale della Soprintendenza Archeologica del Molise*, iv (1988), pp. 31–48.

Christie, N.: 'The Archaeology of Byzantine Italy: A Synthesis of Recent Research', *Journal of Mediterranean Archaeology*, ii/2 (1989), pp. 249–93.

——: 'The Alps as a frontier, A.D. 168–774', *Journal of Roman Archaeology*, vi (1991), pp. 410–30.

——: 'Longobard Weaponry and Warfare, A.D. 1–800', *Journal of Roman Military Equipment Studies*, ii (1991), pp. 1–26.

Dabrowska, M., Leciejewicz, Tabaczyńska, E. and Tabaczyński, S.: 'Castelseprio: scavi diagnostici, 1962–63', *Sibrium*, xiv (1978–9), pp. 1–128.

Dreossi, F.: 'Farra d'Isonzo (Gorizia). Scavi eseguiti in località Monte Fortin', *Atti della Accademia Nazionale dei Lincei. Notizie degli scavi di antichità*, iv/3–4 (1943), pp. 189–98.

Galetti, P.: 'La casa contadina nell'Italia padana dei secoli VIII–X' in Francovich (ed.) 1987, pp. 97–111.

Haseloff, G.: 'Die Funde aus dem Sarkophag der Königin Theodelinda in Monza', *Germania*, xxx (1952), pp. 368–77.

Hessen, O. von: *Die langobardische Keramik aus Italien* (Wiesbaden, 1968).

——: 'Die langobardischen Funde aus dem Gräberfeld von Testona (Moncalieri-Piedmont)', *Memorie dell'Accademia delle Scienze di Torino. Classe di scienze morali, storiche e filologiche*, iv (1971), pp. iv–120.

Hudson, P.: 'La dinamica dell'insediamento urbano nell'area del cortile del tribunale di Verona. L'età medievale', *Archeologia Medievale*, xii (1985), pp. 281–302.

Hyde, J.: 'Medieval descriptions of cities', *Bulletin of the John Rylands Library*, xlviii (1966), pp. 308–40.

Jørgensen, L.: 'A.D. 568: A Chronological Analysis of Lombard Graves in Italy', *Chronological Studies of Anglo-Saxon England, Lombard Italy and Vendel Period Sweden*, ed. L. Jørgensen, *Arkaeologiske Skrifter*, v (Copenhagen, 1992), pp. 94–122.

La Rocca Hudson, C.: ' "Dark Ages" a Verona. Edilizia privata, aree aperte e strutture pubbliche in una città dell'Italia settentrionale', *Archeologia Medievale*, xiii (1986), pp. 31–78.

—— and Hudson, P.: 'Riflessi della migrazione longobarda sull'insediamento rurale e urbano in Italia settentrionale', in Francovich (ed.) 1987, pp. 29–47.

Lusuardi Siena, S.: 'Insediamenti goti e longobardi in Italia settentrionale', *XXXVI Corso di cultura sull'arte ravennate e bizantina: Ravenna e l'Italia fra Goti e Longobardi* (Ravenna, 1989), pp. 191–226.

Maccabruni, C.: *Pavia: la tradizione dell'antico nella città medievale* (Pavia, 1991).

Mengarelli, R.: 'La necropoli barbarica di Castel Trosino, presso Ascoli Piceno', *Monumenti antichi della Reale Accademia dei Lincei*, xii (1902), pp. 145–380.

Mutinelli, C.: 'Das langobardische Gräberfeld von S. Stefano in "Pertica" in Cividale', *Jahrbuch der römisch-germanischen Zentralmuseums Mainz*, viii (1961), pp. 139–56.

Panazza, G. and Brogiolo, G. P.: *Ricerche su Brescia altomedievale. I. Gli studi fino al 1978. Lo scavo di via Alberto Mario* (Brescia, 1988).

Pasqui, P. and Paribeni, R.: 'La necropoli barbarica di Nocera

Umbra', *Monumenti Antichi della Reale Accademia dei Lincei*, xxv (1916), pp. 137–362.

Roffia, E. (ed.): *La necropoli longobarda di Trezzo sull'Adda*, Ricerche di archeologia altomedievale e medievale 12–13, (Florence, 1986).

Rotili, M.: 'Necropoli di tradizione germanica', *Archeologia Medievale*, x (1983), pp. 143–74.

Samnium. Archeologia del Molise (exh. cat., ed. by Capini, S. and Di Niro, A.: Rome, 1991).

Schmiedt, G.: 'Le fortificazioni altomedievali in Italia viste dall'aereo', *XV Settimana di studio del Centro Italiano di Studi sull'Alto Medioevo* (Spoleto, 1968), pp. 859–927.

Scotti, F. (ed.): *Longobardi a Romans d'Isonzo. Itinerario attraverso le tombe altomedievali* (Trieste, 1989).

Staffa, A.: 'Scavi nel centro storico di Pescara', *Archeologia Medievale*, xviii (1991), pp. 201–367.

Ward-Perkins, B.: 'L'archeologia della città', in Francovich (ed.) 1987, pp. 67–80.

——: *From Classical Antiquity to the Middle Ages. Urban Public Building in Northern and Central Italy*, A.D. 300–850 (Oxford, 1984).

Wickham, C.: 'Settlement Problems in Early Medieval Italy: Lucca Territory', *Archeologia Medievale*, v (1978), pp. 495–503.

Culture and Society

Arslan, E.: 'La monetazione', in *Magistra Barbaritas* 1984, pp. 425–44.

Baruzzi, M.: 'I reperti in ferro dello scavo di Villa Clelia (Imola). Note sull'attrezzatura agricola nell'altomedioevo', in Francovich (ed.) 1987, pp. 151–70.

Cavanna, A.: 'Diritto e società nei regni ostrogoto e longobardo', in *Magistra Barbaritas* 1984, pp. 351–79.

Cilento, N.: 'La storiografia nell'età barbarica. Fonti occidentali sui barbari in Italia', in *Magistra Barbaritas* 1984, pp. 317–50.

Conant, K. J.: *Carolingian and Romanesque Architecture, 800–1200* (London, 1979).

Fisher Drew, K.: *The Lombard Laws* (Philadelphia, PA, 1973).

Goffart, W.: *The Narrators of Barbarian History*, A.D. *550–800* (Princeton, 1988).

Grierson, P. and Blackburn, M.: *Medieval European Coinage. I. The Early Middle Ages, 5th–10th centuries* (Cambridge, 1986).

Hodges, R. (ed.): *San Vincenzo al Volturno. The 1980–86. Excavations, Part I*, Archaeological Monograph of the British School at Rome, vii (London, 1993).

—— and Mitchell, J. (eds): *San Vincenzo al Volturno. The Archaeology, Art and Territory of an Early Medieval Monastery*, British Archaeological Reports, Internat. Ser. 252 (Oxford, 1985).

Luiselli, B.: *Storia culturale dei rapporti tra mondo romano e mondo germanico*, Biblioteca di Helikon, i (Rome, 1992).

Peroni, A.: 'L'arte nell'età longobarda', in *Magistra Barbaritas* 1984, pp. 229–97.

Roffia, E. (ed.): *La necropoli longobarda di Trezzo sull'Adda*, Ricerche di archeologia altomedievale e medievale 12–13 (Florence, 1986).

Roth, H.: *Die Ornamentik der Langobarden in Italien. Eine Untersuchung zur Stilentwicklung anhand der Grabfunde*, Antiquitas, 3rd ser., xv (Munich, 1973).

Tavano, S.: *Il Tempietto longobardo di Cividale* (Udine, 1990).

Torcellan, M.: 'Lo scavo presso la chiesa di S. Maria in Sylvis di Sesto al Reghena. Relazione preliminare', *Archeologia Medievale*, xv (1988), pp. 313–34.

Venzone, P.: *L'Architettura religiosa dell'alto medioevo nell'Italia settentrionale* (Milan, 1942).

Wataghin Cantino, G.: 'Monasteri di età longobarda: spunti per una ricerca', *XXXVI Corso di cultura sull'arte ravennate e bizantina: Ravenna e l'Italia fra Goti e Longobardi* (Ravenna, 1989), pp. 73–100.

Werner, J. and Fuchs, S.: *Die langobardischen Fibeln aus Italien* (Berlin, 1950).

Benevento and Later

Belli D'Elia, P.: 'Il santuario di S. Michele Arcangelo tra VII e IX secolo e alcuni esempi di architettura altomedievale nella Puglia longobarda', *XXXVII Corso di cultura sull'arte ravennate e bizantina: L'Italia meridionale fra Goti e Longobardi* (Ravenna, 1990), pp. 93–107.

Belting, H.: 'Studien zum beneventischen Hof im 8. Jahrhundert', *Dumbarton Oaks Papers*, xvi (1962), pp. 141–93.

Bullough, D.: 'The Counties of the *Regnum Italiae* in the Carolingian Period, 774–888', *Papers of the British School at Rome*, xxiii (1955), pp. 48–168.

Burman, E.: *Emperor to Emperor. Italy before the Renaissance* (London, 1991).

Butler, W. F.: *The Lombard Communes. A History of the Republics of North Italy* (London, 1906).

Cilento, N.: *Italia meridionale longobarda* (Milan, 1971).

Delogu, P.: *Mito di una città meridionale. Salerno, secoli VII–XI* (Naples, 1977).

Fonseca, C. D.: 'Longobardia minore e Longobardi nell'Italia meridionale', in *Magistra Barbaritas* 1984, pp. 127–84.

Kreutz, B.: *Before the Normans. Southern Italy in the Ninth and Tenth Centuries* (Philadelphia, 1991).

Peduto, P.: 'Archeologia medievale in Campania', *La Voce della Campania: Cultura materiale, arti e territorio in Campania*, vii/10 (1979), pp. 247–62.

Rotili, M.: 'I monumenti della Longobardia meridionale', in *La civiltà dei Longobardi in Europe* 1974, pp. 203–39.

——: *La necropoli longobarda di Benevento*, Ricerche e documenti, iii, (Naples, 1977).

——: 'Schede di archeologia longobarda in Italia. Campania', *Studi Medievali*, 3rd ser. xxiii (1982), pp. 1023–31.

——: 'Il territorio beneventano fra Goti e Longobardi: l'evidenza monumentale', *XXXVII Corso di cultura sull'arte ravennate e bizantina: L'Italia meridionale fra Goti e Longobardi* (Ravenna, 1990), pp. 417–52.

Uggeri, G.: 'Il confine longobardo-bizantino in Puglia', *XXXVII Corso di cultura sull'arte ravennate e bizantina: L'Italia meridionale fra Goti e Longobardi* (Ravenna, 1990), pp. 479–510.

Index

Note: A page number in *italic* denotes an illustration.